Career in Hotel Management

Career in Hotel Management

Surinder Kumar Rai

RANDOM PUBLICATIONS
NEW DELHI (INDIA)

Career in Hotel Management

ISBN 978-93-5111-334-8

Published in 2014 in India by

RANDOM PUBLICATIONS

4376-A/4B, Gali Murari Lal, Ansari Road
New Delhi-110 002
Phone : +91-11-43580356, +91-11-23289044
e-mail: randomexports@gmail.com, sales@randompublications.com, info@randompublications.com

Type Setting by : Keystoneprintads, Delhi-110051
Printed at : Thomson Press (India) Ltd

Preface

Hotel management can include Hotel & Restaurant management, Cruise Ship Hotel management, Hospital Administration and Catering, Hotel and Tourism Associations, Airline Catering and Cabin Services, Club management, Forest Lodges, Guest Houses amongst others.

The ongoing liberalization of trade and opening up of economy has lead to revolutionary growth in hotel sector. Moreover the recent measures taken in promotion of tourism and rapid industrial growth have further given a boost the hoteliering because hotel industry is a closely linked one to the tourism industry. With increasing growth in this sector career opportunities are also growing day by day. Now the field is not limited within the country but has already extended to internationally operated chains of hotels.

A hotel manager or hotelier is a person who handles the everyday function and management of a hotel. Larger hotels often have management teams, instead of individual managers, where each member of the group begins to specialize on a certain area of interest.

Hotel managers oversee the running of hotels. They are responsible for food and refreshments, accommodation and amenities, entertainment and conference facilities. Large hotels may have individual managers responsible for each department such as housekeeping, maintenance, and food and beverages who have to report to the hotel's general manager. Duties include analysing financial data and targets, managing staff, dealing with customer complaints and ensuring compliance with regulations such as licensing laws. You may also be required to "muck in" when short staffed.

This book gives an elaborate account of some vital topics pertaining to the theme. This will prove vade mecum for aspirants and working hospitality equally.

I thank all associates of my group who have helped in the preparation of the book. My individual thanks go to "Random Publications" who have in print the book.

— ***Surinder Kumar Rai***

Contents

1

Introduction

Career management is defined by Ball (1997) as:

1. Making career choices and decisions – the traditional focus of careers interventions. The changed nature of work means that individuals may now have to revisit this process more frequently than in the past.
2. Managing the organisational career – concerns the career management tasks of individuals within the workplace, such as decision-making, life-stage transitions, dealing with stress etc.
3. Managing 'boundaryless' careers – refers to skills needed by workers whose employment is beyond the boundaries of a single organisation, a workstyle common among, for example, artists and designers.
4. Taking control of one's personal development – as employers take less responsibility, employees need to take control of their own development in order to maintain and enhance their employability.

Now that the job-for-life covenant between employer and employee has been superseded by an insecure and uncertain job market, career management has become a necessary survival skill rather than being an activity pursued by Ivy League alumni or people born with a silver spoon in the mouth. Job security is now based on knowledge, skills and added-value rather than length of service or loyalty to an employer. Career management is nothing more than a small investment of time, money and energy to protect the major source of revenue—one's job.

A 'hotel' or 'inn' is defined by the British law as 'the place where a bonafide traveller can receive food and shelter provided he is in a position to pay for it and is in a fit condition to be received'. Hence a hotel must provide food and lodging to a traveller on payment and has, in turn, the right to refuse if the traveller is drunk, disorderly, unkempt or is not in a position to pay for the services. Early travellers were warriors, traders or people in search of knowledge.

This was before the advent of hotels. Thus, warriors and conquerors pitched their tents for accommodation, while traders and people travelling for knowledge placed a high value on hospitality and sometimes traded their merchandise for lodging. Inn-keeping can be said to be the first commercial enterprise, and hospitality one of the first services for which money was exchanged.

Inns of biblical times offered only a cot or a bench in a corner. Guests stayed in large communal rooms with no sanitation and privacy. The rates were, of course, reasonable. The company was rough. Travellers shared the same quarters with their horses and animals.

In the third century AD, the Roman Empire developed an extensive network of brick-paved roads throughout Europe and Asia Minor, and a chain of roadside lodges was constructed along the major thoroughfare from Spain to Turkey. Till the industrial revolution of the 1700s, no significant improvement was made in the inns and taverns, and they were not very suitable for aristocrats. To accommodate wealthy travellers, luxurious structures were constructed with private rooms, individual sanitation and the comforts of a European castle.

These elegant new establishments adopted the French word for mansion - 'Hotel'. Not surprisingly, their rates, too, were beyond the reach of an ordinary person. In America early inns were modelled after European taverns, with sleeping quarters shared by two or more guests. Herman Melville, in his novel 'Moby Dick' had mentioned a seaman who checked into a room in a nineteenth century inn and woke up the next morning only to find out that he was sharing the bed with a cannibal. Hotels today are much more than just a place to sleep - many travellers view them as an integral part of a getaway experience. With the recent boom of boutique hotels, spiffed-up budget properties, and novelty accommodations, travellers can choose a hotel that is as much a selling point as the destination itself.

Early history of accommodation for travellers can be traced back to the Greek word 'xenia' which not only meant hospitality, but also the protection given to a traveller from discomforts. The city was bound to traditions of hospitality. In Sparta city, despite rigorous customs restricting visitors, goddess Athena was considered a 'protector of strangers' and hence her name, Xenia Athena. In this period travellers were mainly diplomats, philosophers, intellectuals and researchers. Guests were invited to stay with the nobleman. In ancient Olympia, buildings constructed with the aim of accommodating strangers are still visible. They were called 'Leonardo' and were built in fourth century BC. The concept of hospitality can also be traced back to ancient times. Mention of it is found in Iliad and The Odyssey by Homer.

Hotel keeping can also be traced back to many centuries and its evolution through the ages has been brought about by Britain's economical and industrial changes and developments. The next stage in the cycle of evolution of the hotel industry was the coming of the motor car. It enabled people to visit those parts of the country which could not be reached by railways. This gave birth to inland resorts and the hotel industry began to flourish. International air travel has helped create the modern stop-over hotel. With the increase in this form of travel, the number of hotels built close to airports has multiplied. Another trend in hotel keeping is the Motel, which is the twentieth century version of the old Coach Inn. People travelling the country by car, stopping overnight here and there; require not only refreshment for themselves, but also safe parking for their cars. Post houses, developed by the Trust houses Forte Group, are in fact the modern version of the old coaching inns. This is probably why Great Britain is considered as the 'motherland of hotel industry'.

The history of hotels is intimately connected to that of civilisations. Or rather, it is a part of that history. Facilities offering guests hospitality have been in evidence since early biblical times.

The Greeks developed thermal baths in villages designed for rest and recuperation. Later, the Romans built mansions to provide accommodation for travellers on government business. The Romans were the first to develop thermal baths in England, Switzerland and the Middle East. Later still, caravanserais appeared, providing a resting place for caravans along Middle Eastern routes. In the Middle Ages, monasteries and abbeys were the first establishments to offer refuge to travellers on a regular basis. Religious orders built inns, hospices and hospitals to cater for those on the move.

CAREER IN HOTEL MANAGEMENT

The ongoing liberalization of trade and opening up of economy has lead to revolutionary growth in hotel sector. Moreover the recent measures taken in promotion of tourism and rapid industrial growth have further given a boost the hoteliering because hotel industry is a closely linked one to the tourism industry. With increasing growth in this sector career opportunities are also growing day by day. Now the field is not limited within the country but has already extended to internationally operated chains of hotels.

The result is increase in the demand of well trained quality professional people who can manage the hotel business. Therefore the demand for Hotel Management as a professional course is growing in the country. The diversity of experience in hotel management is greater than in any other profession. Courses in Hotel Management often referred to as Hospitality Management, is offered in many renowned institutes. Hotel Management Course includes varied aspects of learning, both theoretical and practical.

There are several courses in Hotel Management like Diploma in Hotel Management (DHM), Bachelor of Hotel Management (BHM) and Post Graduate Diploma in Hotel Management (PGDHM). The minimum qualification required for a diploma and bachelor course in hotel management is 10+2 pass with English as a subject. A DHM/BHM course is of one and half to three year duration. Admission depends on the performance of the students in the written admission test, personal interview round and group discussion session. Besides these there are certificate courses in Hotel Management which are of six months to one year duration. Those with graduation can go for post graduate diploma courses the duration of which is one year.

Career Prospects

There are ample job avenues for Hotel Management graduates in various fields. They can join varieties of hotels and restaurants flourishing in the country. Students from reputed institutes of hotel management can join catering services of Railways, Airlines, Shipping companies, Banks and also in Defence sector.

There are many Clubs and hotel and tourism association who need the services of professional hotel managers. Besides industrial canteen and other institutional canteen of collages, schools, factories and company guest house also need the service of such people. A few proceed to pursue postgraduate studies in hotel management and opt for teaching jobs. Hospitals and other institutions also engage hotel management professionals. Moreover self employment opportunities are always available to Hotel Management graduates.

Institute Offering

Several institutes offer Hotel Management courses in the country. Some names are given below. State Institute of Hotel Management and Catering Technology, Tiruchirapalli; Delhi Institute of Hotel Management and Catering Technology, New Delhi; Government Institute of Hotel management and Catering, Dehra Dun and Almora; Maharashtra State Institutes of Hotel Management and Catering Technology, Pune and Nagpur; Institute of Hotel management Catering Technology and Applied Nutrition, Gangtok; Indian institute of Hotel Management, Aurangabad; Welcome Group Graduate School of Hotel Management, Manipal.

Remuneration

The emoluments vary between the different organizations which employ them. Minimum monthly emoluments are approximately Rs. 7500-Rs 10000 depending upon factors such as the category of employing hotel, institute from where the student graduated, city of location, etc. In public sector organization salary is lower than from industrial houses, private airlines, shipping companies etc. Self employment in this sector is always highly remunerative.

Career in Hospitality Sector can open doors in the industries like service apartments, hotels, restaurants, catering and canteen services, health care,

Ayurveda and spa centers, café's bars, discotheques, various clubs and many more. The employment graph of this industry is continuously rising. Fast developing technologies and the development in the field of science is also contributing to the sophisticated and the well-facilitated services of the hospitality industry.

So, it is time to decide what you will do with your life. What will you choose? Perhaps you might consider a career in the hospitality industry.

What is the hospitality industry? The hospitality industry is defined as the activity of providing lodging, food and beverage, and recreational services, which include but are not limited to hotels, motels, clubs, casinos, restaurants, recreation facilities, tourism, cruise lines, and theme parks. Wow, what a variety of options! A multi-billion dollar industry, hospitality is our country's third largest industry employing nearly 9.5 million people nationally. Your options are great, but what does this mean to you?

Check this out: the history of the hospitality industry dates all the way back to the Colonial Period when, in 1794, the first City Hotel opened in New York City. Things have changed quite a bit since then; the hospitality industry has experienced significant development over the years as it has faced World Wars, The Depression (ask your history teacher!),

and various social changes. The industry as we know it today began to take form in the early 1950s and 60s, leading the way for growth into the dynamic industry we know today. Career options in the hospitality industry have continued to grow along with the industry.

What career options are offered in the hospitality industry? Where do you start? What types of careers are available? These are the major questions to consider when pursing a career in the hospitality industry. The following descriptions outline the different levels of hospitality positions you might enter into.

Entry-Level: This is where you start; the experience and skill you will gain in these positions can prepare you for advancement in your career. Typically the tasks are related to your position and are a valuable component to the success of the hospitality entity.

Skilled-Level: This is the next step where you will develop specific skills and capabilities that can be transferred from one position to another (you are on your way).

Managerial-Level: This is when your experience, training and initiative are combined to create your ability to lead employees and manage business.

The following are specific career opportunities you can obtain in the hospitality industry:

Lodging:

- Hotel Manager
- Sales Manager
- Travel Journalist

- Front Office Manager
- Reservation Manager

Food & beverage:

- Restaurant Manager
- Kitchen Manager
- Banquet Manager
- Chef
- Bar/Club Manager

Recreational services:

- Campground Manager
- Tour Escort/Operator
- Meeting/Conference Planner
- Travel Consultant
- Recreation Specialist

As you can see you have many choices, but what qualities must you possess? The hospitality industry, like many other industries, seeks and requires a certain personality to be successful, you must:

- Like People
- Be a Hard Worker
- Have strong Communication Skills
- Be willing to Sacrifice
- Maintain a Professional Appearance
- Have "Common Sense" (be able to think on your feet to respond to guests' needs)

Although these qualities may seem simple, they are constantly put to the test due to the requests of people served by this very demanding industry. Regardless of where you work within hospitality, you will be required to exceed guest/customer expectations to ensure the experience they have at your facility is valuable, pleasant, and memorable.

Once you obtain a position and work hard, what can you expect to be paid (what is your worth)? We all expect to be well compensated for a job well done! Although the history of wages in the hospitality industry has been considered low, times have changed! Today, wages for the hospitality industry are very competitive as compared to those for other industries, and a wide range of salaries are available.

Several elements, beginning with capability/skill and performance, will impact your income; additionally, types of property, location, and position are factors that are also included. Employment outlook for the hospitality industry varies by occupation; however, wage and salary employment in hotels and other lodging places is expected to increase 13% from 2000-2010. This job growth is due to rising personal income, an increase in the number of two-income families, low-cost airfares, and a greater emphasis on leisure activities on in our society.

What type of education will you need to obtain a job in the hospitality industry? The industry is becoming increasingly complex with a greater emphasis being placed on specialized training. Demand is increasing for people with special skills obtained in colleges, junior colleges, technical institutes, vocational schools, and high schools. Programs range in length from a few months to several years.

Nearly 200 community and junior colleges offer 2-year degree programs in hotel and restaurant management. It is possible to obtain a 4-year college degree in the liberal arts or other fields and enter into a trainee or junior management track. However, a bachelor's and master's degree programs in hotel and restaurant management provides the strongest background for a career as a hotel manager, with nearly 150 colleges and universities offering programs. Graduates of these programs are highly sought by employers in this industry.

New graduates often go through on-the-job training programs before being given much responsibility. Eventually, they can advance to a top management position in a large chain operation. How do you find the right school/programme for you? First you need to ensure you are committed to achieving a higher education. Consult with your guidance counsellor, teachers, and parents.

Make sure you have prepared yourself for the academic testing that will be required for enrolment. Second, what are your financial options to pay for an education? Seek alternatives available such as scholarships, grants, loans, etc. Third, do your homework and research various types of institutions to find out which one is right for you. Ask what type of curriculum is offered, what type of experience is available, what type of placement support can you expect?

Lastly, remember your career decision must be YOUR choice. A career in the hospitality industry can be very rewarding and will take you along paths you may never had considered. The hospitality industry can be very exciting and glamorous, and it will afford you the opportunity to travel and work with thousands of people. Each day is different from the previous day. New challenges and increasing job opportunity is what makes the hospitality industry so great and why it has survived for so many years.

ORGANIZATIONAL EFFECTIVENESS

Organizational effectiveness is the concept of how effective an organization is in achieving the outcomes the organization intends to produce.

The idea of organizational effectiveness is especially important for non-profit organizations as most people who donate money to non-profit organizations and charities are interested in knowing whether the organization is effective in accomplishing its goals.

An organization's effectiveness is also dependent on an its communicative competence and ethics. The relationship between these three are simultaneous. Ethics is a foundation found within organizational effectiveness. An organization must exemplify respect, honesty, integrity and equity to allow communicative competence with the participating members. Along with ethics and communicative competence, members in that particular group can finally achieve their intended goals.

Foundations and other sources of grants and other types of funds are interested in organizational effectiveness of those people who seek funds from the foundations. Foundations always have more requests for funds or funding proposals and treat funding as an investment using the same care as a venture capitalist would in picking a company in which to invest.

Organizational effectiveness is an abstract concept and is basically impossible to measure. Instead of measuring organizational effectiveness, the organization determines proxy measures which will be used to represent effectiveness. Proxy measures used may include such things as number of people served, types and sizes of population segments served, and the demand within those segments for the services the organization supplies.

For instance, a non-profit organization which supplies meals to house bound people may collect statistics such as the number of meals cooked and served, the number of volunteers delivering meals, the turnover and retention rates of volunteers, the demographics of the people served, the turnover and retention of consumers, the number of requests for meals turned down due to lack of capacity (amount of food, capacity of meal preparation facilities, and number of delivery volunteers), and amount of wastage. Since the organization has as its goal the preparation of meals and the delivery of those meals to house bound people, it measures its organizational effectiveness by trying to determine what actual activities the people in the organization do in order to generate the outcomes the organization wants to create.

Activities such as fundraising or volunteer training are important because they provide the support needed for the organization to deliver its services but they are not the outcomes per se. These other activities are overhead activities which assist the organization in achieving its desired outcomes.

The term Organizational Effectiveness is often used interchangeably with Organization Development, especially when used as the name of a department or a part of the Human Resources function within an organization.

ORGANIZATIONAL COMMITMENT

In the study of organizational behaviour, organizational commitment is the employee's psychological attachment to the organization. It can be contrasted with other work-related attitudes, such as Job Satisfaction (an employee's feelings about their job) and Organizational Identification (the degree to which an employee experiences a 'sense of oneness' with their organization).

Organizational scientists have developed many definitions of organizational commitment, and numerous scales to measure them. Exemplary of this work is Meyer & Allen's model of commitment, which was developed to integrate numerous definitions of commitment that had proliferated in the research literature.

According to Meyer and Allen's (1991) three-component model of commitment, prior research indicated that there are three "mind sets" which can characterize an employee's commitment to the organization:

- Affective Commitment: AC is defined as the employee's emotional attachment to the organization. As a result, he or she strongly identifies with the goals of the organization and desires to remain a part of the organization. This employee commits to the organization because he/she "wants to". In developing this concept, Meyer and Allen drew largely on Mowday, Porter, and Steers's (1982) concept of commitment.
- Continuance Commitment: The individual commits to the organization because he/she perceives high costs of losing organizational membership (cf. Becker's 1960 "side bet theory"), including economic losses (such as pension accruals) and social costs (friendship ties with co-workers) that would have to be given up. The employee remains a member of the organization because he/she "has to".
- Normative Commitment: The individual commits to and remains with an organization because of feelings of obligation. For instance, the organization may have invested resources in training an employee who then feels an obligation to put forth effort on the job and stay with the organization to 'repay the debt.' It may also reflect an internalized norm, developed before the person joins the organization through family or other socialization processes, that one should be loyal to one's organization. The employee stays with the organization because he/she "ought to".

Note that according to Meyer and Allen, these components of commitment are not mutually exclusive: an employee can simultaneously be committed to the organization in an affective, normative, *and* continuance sense, at varying levels of intensity. This idea led Meyer and Herscovitch to argue that at any point in time, an employee has a "commitment profile" that reflects high or low levels of all three of these mind-sets, and that different profiles have different effects on workplace behaviour such as job performance, absenteeism, and the chance that they will quit.

Meyer and Allen developed the Affective Commitment Scale (ACS), the Normative Commitment Scale (NCS) and the Continuance Commitment Scale (CCS) to measure these components of commitment. Many researchers have used them to determine what impact an employee's level of commitment has on outcomes such as quitting behaviour, job performance, and absenteeism. However, some researchers have questioned how well these scales actually assess an employee's commitment.

In addition to methodological investigations of the validity and reliability of these scales, recent research has focused on determining the cross-cultural validity of Meyer and Allen's measures (do employees in other countries/ cultures experience commitment the same way as employees in the USA?), and on expanding the three-component model to other foci (such as commitment to one's occupation, department, organization change initiatives, and work team.

ORGANIZATION DEVELOPMENT

Organization development, according to Richard Beckhard, is defined as:

1. A planned effort...
2. Organization-wide...
3. Managed from the top...
4. To increase organization effectiveness and health...
5. Through planned interventions in the organization's 'processes', using behavioural science knowledge.

According to Warren Bennis, organization development (OD) is a complex strategy intended to change the beliefs, attitudes, values, and structure of organizations so that they can better adapt to new technologies, markets, and challenges.

Warner Burke emphasizes that OD is not just "anything done to better an organization"; it is a particular kind of change process designed to bring about a particular kind of end result. OD involves organizational reflection, system improvement, planning, and self-analysis.

The term "Organization Development" is often used interchangeably with Organizational effectiveness, especially when used as the name of a department or a part of the Human Resources function within an organization.

At the core of OD is the concept of an organization, defined as two or more people working together toward one or more shared goals. Development in this context is the notion that an organization may become more effective over time at achieving its goals.

"OD is a long range effort to improve organization's problem solving and renewal processes, particularly through more effective and collaborative management of organization culture-with specific emphasis on the culture of formal workteams-with the assistance of a change agent or catalyst and the use of the theory and technology of applied behavioral science including action research"

Kurt Lewin is widely recognized as the founding father of OD, although he died before the concept became current in the mid-1950s. From Lewin came the ideas of group dynamics, and action research which underpin the basic OD process as well as providing its collaborative consultant/client ethos. Institutionally, Lewin founded the Research Center for Group Dynamics at MIT, which moved to Michigan after his death. RCGD colleagues were among those who founded the National Training Laboratories (NTL), from which the T-group and group-based OD emerged. In the UK, working as close as was possible with Lewin and his colleagues, the Tavistock Institute of Human Relations was important in developing systems theories. Important too was the joint TIHR journal Human Relations, although nowadays the Journal of Applied Behavioral Sciences is seen as the leading OD journal.

OD is taught in many institutions worldwide, with no one legitimately able to claim to be the center of OD training. Leading institutions include the The Johns Hopkins University, Tavistock Institute of Human Relations, American University, Benedictine University that offers the only PhD programme in OD, Bowling Green State University, Case Western Reserve University, Claremont Graduate University, Fielding Graduate University, Pepperdine, Phillips Graduate Institute, the University of Southern California, Alliant International University, Sheffield Hallam University in England, the University of Monterrey in Monterrey, Mexico and Assumption University of Thailand.

CAREER IN HOTEL MANAGEMENT OVERSEE

Hotel managers oversee the running of hotels. They are responsible for food and refreshments, accommodation and amenities, entertainment and conference facilities. Large hotels may have individual managers responsible for each department such as housekeeping, maintenance, and food and beverages who have to report to the hotel's general manager. Duties include analysing financial data and targets, managing staff, dealing with customer complaints and ensuring compliance with regulations such as licensing laws. You may also be required to "muck in" when short staffed.

You must have a good head for business and enjoy working with people, being able to manage staff. You need good written and spoken communication skills with the ability to keep calm under pressure and solve problems quickly. You need to be well organised with plenty of energy and enthusiasm and be prepared to work long, unsociable hours. Training normally takes place on the job, gaining experience in different areas of the business.

You may start work at a lower level on the career ladder, working towards NVQs or other vocational qualifications or you can enter at management trainee level. Relevant NVQs include hospitality service at level 2, leading on to hospitality supervision at level 3 and management at level 4. A variety of degrees and HNC/Ds are relevant to hotel management, including hospitality management, international hospitality management, hotel and hospitality management, and hospitality and licensed retail management. Foundation degrees are also available in relevant subjects, such as hospitality business management.

However, academic qualifications are not always necessary and many people work their way up to management. Hotel chains often have their own structured management training schemes for graduates. Apprenticeships may be available for those under 24. In hotel chains, promotion may be into a strategic role such as corporate marketing or training. Experienced managers may open their own hotels.

Training is an integral part of ISO 9002 implementation in a hotel or any organization. A planned, systematic training process is required, as the skills needed for the development of a quality management system are still new to most service organizations. Sufficient time must be set aside for training in such areas as procedure writing and quality auditing.

Training and orientation should be conducted for new staff (including temporary staff) to provide them with the knowledge and skills necessary for the completion of tasks to specified standards. Training for management and existing staff should be initiated after needs analysis of the organization has been conducted. The organization should define the competence needed for each task that affects the quality of products.

Having well trained people to become members of the working group and to become involved in developing, implementing, using and maintaining the Quality System is vital to the success of the project. This emphasizes the importance of training to gain ISO 9002 certification. The term ISO and 9002 are explained at the beginning and a hotel case study is used at the end to demonstrate the practical method of implementing ISO 9002 standards.

Organization for Standardization

The International Organization for Standardization (ISO) is made up of national standards institutes from countries large and small, industrialized and developing, in all regions of the world. ISO develops voluntary technical standards that add value to all types of business operations.

These standards contribute to making the development, manufacturing and supply of products and services more efficient, safer and cleaner. "ISO is located in Switzerland and was established in 1947 to develop common international standards. Its members come from the standards bodies in over 135 countries".

The ISO technical committee was formed in 1979 to harmonize the increasing international activity in quality management and quality assurance standards.

Organizations Involved with ISO

There are three main types of other organizations that are involved with various aspects of ISO standards.

These are:

- Member bodies, the national organizations (or bureaus) of standards in 135 ISO member countries.
- Accreditation bodies, groups responsible for determining that registration groups meet the guidelines for the purpose of granting accreditation to the registrar to issue ISO certificates.
- Registrars, groups that inspect companies for proper adherence to ISO standards and issue ISO certificates to properly qualified companies. Registrars perform thorough registration audits prior to granting an ISO certificate and two surveillance audits each year that the certificates are effective.

Quality Assurance

ISO 9000 brings together the essential principles common to many different quality management and assurance standards into a single system. The intent of the standard is simply to help a company document and implement a basic quality system so that it has the capability to deliver the quality products and services that its customers request.

The ISO 9000 series covers the entire range of business processes from the moment the order is placed, through the entire production or service development process to the actual delivery of the product or service to the customer. It is important to note that ISO 9000 does not certify products or services or guarantee that quality goods or services will be produced. It simply certifies that a quality system is in place that should enable an organization to meet agreed-upon customer requirements and provide more consistent products or services. As part of the certification process, an organization implements a quality system based on one of three models relevant to the nature of its operation: ISO 9001, 9002 or 9003. Then a third party (an accredited quality system certification body) audits the company to certify that the system complies with the standard and that the quality system has been implemented. If the organization is found to be in compliance, a certificate is issued bearing the relevant standard.

Benefits

Among internal benefits of implementing the ISO 9002 standard are the following:

- Contributes to improvement through structure and discipline
- Improves efficiency through better documentation and communication

- Reduces rework
- Increases customer satisfaction and therefore reduces customer complaints
- Improves motivation and employee involvement through all levels of the process
- Improves the training process
- Improves positive management control

The eighth cycle of the ISO Survey of ISO 9000, conducted in 1998, revealed that the standards are growing in popularity in the Caribbean and the rest of the world. The Central and South Americas accounted for nearly 2% of the certificates issued worldwide. Fortyseven of these certificates were issued in Caribbean countries. Trinidad and Tobago accounted for approximately one third of these certified organizations. Jamaica came second with six organizations. Antigua and St Lucia received their first certificates in 1998. As has been experienced in the rest of the world, ISO certifications were more common in the manufacturing sectors compared to service sectors.

Up to October 1998 there were no hospitality service organizations achieving this certification in the Caribbean. Considering the importance of the tourism and hospitality industry to the Caribbean, as well as the large stock of hotel rooms in the Caribbean, this is disappointing. At the turn of the century the accommodation stock in the region had risen to around 250,000 rooms and is predicted to approach 400,000 rooms by the year 2020.

Training to Gain ISO 9002

The key to the success of the training process lies in the commitment of management to developing the process. Factors such as organization size, structure, requirements and culture have proven to be very important at the design stage. By involving the end users in the design, planning and implementation of training, it was easy to build the team spirit, a requirement for successful implementation of an ISO 9002 Quality Management System.

Suggested Foundation Training

For organizations that have not yet made a commitment to implementing a quality management system the following training programmes are suggested.

This will usually take a total of eight or nine days:

- ISO 9000 Quality Briefing. Examines the fundamental issues and the achievable and measurable benefits of the standard. (1 day)
- Executive Briefing. Provides a clear understanding of the economic benefits and critical success factors for implementing the standards to busy executives who will influence the decision to implement ISO 9000 within their organization. (half a day)

- ISO 9000 Appreciation and Interpretation. Lays the foundation for those individuals directly involved in implementing and maintaining the system. This course is also suitable to provide general quality awareness to all employees of a smaller organization. Maximum benefit will be gained when the employees are encouraged to participate in the setting up of the system. By extending "ownership" of the quality management system to as many people as possible, one can ensure that the system will work well on a day-to-day basis throughout the organization. (1 day)
- ISO 9000 Implementation. Provides sound, practical guidance on how to set about the task of designing and setting up a quality management system and see it through to a successful conclusion. (2 days)
- Documentation/Procedure Writing for ISO 9000. Provides practical guidance in the design, development and implementation of a workable documentation system. Participants will be able to write user-friendly documents, which are effective and suitable for the intended purpose. (1 day)
- Internal Quality Auditing. Provides practical instruction to all employees involved in this process. An additional day may be added for newly trained auditors to put theory into practice by conducting a live audit of the quality system. (2 days)
- Preparing for the Certification Audit. Ensures that the team has clearly understood the prerequisites for a successful assessment and provides guidance on the final preparation and fine-tuning of the quality system. The most common pitfalls – and how to avoid them – will be clearly identified, so that employees will be fully briefed and ready for assessment. (1 day)

The Training Process

ISO 9002:1994 (E) Clause 4.1.2.2 Resources states: "The supplier shall identify resource requirements and provide adequate resources, including the assignment of trained personnel for management, performance of work and verification activities including internal quality audits".

Clause 4.18 Training states: "The supplier shall establish and maintain documented procedures for identifying training needs and provide for the training of all personnel performing activities affecting quality. Personnel performing specific assigned tasks shall be qualified on the basis of appropriate education, training and/or experience, as required. Appropriate records of training shall be maintained".

All organizations implementing the Quality Management System standard (ISO 9002) must have an effective training process in place to satisfy these requirements. Quality and related training and education provide or enhance the knowledge and skills employees need to do their jobs effectively and efficiently. Job enrichment skills are gained and job rotation can occur, thereby enhancing employees' career opportunities.

A planned, systematic training process is instrumental in helping an organization achieve its quality objectives and improve its capabilities. Training can be seen as a four-step process. These four steps are represented in the training cycle, where the output of one stage provides the input for the following stage. Each stage must be monitored with the aim of closing the gap between required and existing competence. Training goals must be established, and later evaluated to determine the extent to which these goals were met. This evaluation process can lead to the identification of new goals, which should be addressed in the design of future training activities.

Definition of Training Needs

The first step in the training process towards ISO 9002 certification involves the conducting of a needs analysis of the organization. There are some useful signs, or symptoms, that may indicate the need for training.

These include:

- Dissatisfied customers
- High labour turnover, low morale
- Failure to attain targets on revenue, gross profit and net profit
- High accident, breakage, or wastage rates
- Conflict between departments, such as restaurant and kitchen, housekeeping and reception
- Absence of the skills required for procedure writing or quality auditing
- Absence of formal management review of the quality system.

The organization's strategic goals, quality objectives, training policy, quality management requirements, resource requirements and process design must also be considered when initiating training to ensure that the organization's needs are satisfied.

The following activities should also be carried out:

- Define and document the competence needed for each task that affects product or service quality (e.g. management verification activities such as internal quality audits). This is done through job analysis.
- Assess the competence of personnel to perform the task.
- Develop plans to close existing competence gaps.

The training policy stands as a symbol of management's commitment to this important activity. It provides guidance for the planning of training as well as a comprehensive guide on all elements of the training cycle. The training policy of Le Meridien Jamaica Pegasus is summarized below as an example.

- *Policy:* It is the policy of Le Meridien Jamaica Pegasus to provide training for new and existing employees, in order to continually improve the workforce skill, product performance and services.
- *Scope:* This covers all employees involved in delivering service to the hotel's clients.
- *Purpose:* To ensure that employees are equipped with the appropriate skills to perform their jobs.
- *Responsibility:* It shall be the responsibility of each departmental manager to ensure that employees have adequate training and experience for the jobs to which they are assigned. The training and quality assurance manager shall be responsible for administering and coordinating the hotel's training plan and activities.
- *Procedure:* Each employee who performs a service related to the customer, product or administration shall receive training in that area.

Competence requirements once set must be reviewed periodically to ensure that they remain relevant to the operation.

A variety of internal and external factors may be used to derive competence requirements:

- Organizational and technological change that impacts the company's product
- Data recorded at training programmes
- The organization's performance appraisal system
- Internal and external certification needed for the performance of specific tasks
- Requests from employees identifying opportunities for personal development
- Legislation, regulations, standards and directives

PLANNING FOR TRAINING

The training plan should be developed and documented at this stage. Included in the training plan are the objectives and expected outcomes of the training. All constraints should be determined and listed.

Typical constraints encountered in the hospitality industry include labour union requirements, human resource policy, financial considerations, timing and scheduling requirements (especially in a shift system), the availability, motivation and ability of the individuals to be trained. Factors such as the availability of in-house trainers to perform the training or the selection of reputable outside experts must be determined at this stage.

The training plan specification is important in establishing a clear understanding of the organization's needs, the training requirements and the training objectives.

Typical items to be considered in an organization's training plan are:

- The organization's objectives and requirements
- Specification for training needs
- Training objectives
- Selected trainees
- Training method and content outline
- Duration, dates and milestones
- Schedule of resources such as training materials and staff
- Financial requirements
- Criteria and methods for the evaluation of training outcomes, such as trainee's on the job performance and satisfaction level of customers

Implementation of Training

It is important that the organization provides the necessary training resources to ensure success of the training process. In addition, the organization must support the trainer and the trainee while monitoring the quality of the training delivered.

There will be resource and time constraints during the implementation of an ISO 9002 Quality System. These contraints have to be quantified and allowed for by reassigning work, working extra time, or scheduling extra employees.

Quality system training should address the following:

- Why a formal quality system is being introduced
- Why total participation in the quality system is necessary
- The quality policy of the company
- The documents making up the quality system – quality assurance manuals, procedures, work instructions – and their accessibility to workers.
- Use of forms and other records built into the quality system
- The role of internal auditors
- Corrective and preventive action
- Management review

Evaluation of Training

Evaluation aims to determine the effectiveness of the training process. The organizational and training objectives that were set must be examined to confirm that they have been met. The documents to be examined during the training evaluation are the training specification, training plan and records of the delivery of training.

Training results often cannot be fully analysed and validated until the trainee can be observed and tested on the job. A specified time period (after completion of training) should be agreed within which the evaluations will take place, in order to verify the level of competence achieved.

The evaluation process should include the collection of data and the preparation of an evaluation report analysing the data collected and making recommendations for improvement as required. All training must be documented in training records.

In quality management, reward systems recognize individuals as well as team contributions. A variety of tangible objects may be used to reward superior performance, including days off with pay, badges and medals. Awards functions may be held where recipients are lauded for their achievements. In the hospitality industry benchmarking tours of outstanding properties may be arranged.

The review of the training process should identify any further opportunities for improving the effectiveness of any stage of the training process. A commitment to continuous improvement lies at the heart of a quality management system, modelled from the ISO 9000 Standard.

QUALITY IN HOTELS

Ad hoc training and quality control have been common in hotels for centuries. Systematic training, as explained in the previous section, is a prerequisite to implementing a quality assurance management system. Ad hoc training is merely unplanned training and ad hoc quality control is mostly a post-process checking action.

These are not adequate to ensure quality standards to achieve ISO 9002 certification. A few hotels have, in the past, implemented steps to introduce "quality circles", essentially a Japanese concept with proven results in Japanese or similar cultures.

Dube et al. (2000) carried out an extensive review of the quality of lodging operations in the United States and noted that functional areas such as human resources, operations, corporate management and marketing receive more attention from management of hotels. They also noted that in the deluxe segment of hotels, the majority of best practices involved operations and human resources. Enz and Siguan (2000) examined thirteen champions in the lodging industry and analysed their best practices. The service-quality "champions" employed a variety of approaches, frequently in combination.

Some of the "champions", for example, worked on weaving key tenets into the fabric of the organization in an effort to disseminate service excellence standards and ingrain employees with them. Others focused on empowering employees to provide whatever service the employee deemed necessary to create guest satisfaction. Ritz-Carlton Hotels, for example, empowers all employees to spend up to US$2,000 to solve a guest problem, if needed. Although such initiatives are noted from hotels in different parts of the world to ensure quality service to guests, the popularity of ISO 9002 in the global hospitality industry has not been a phenomenal success. Up to late 1998, only 865 ISO 9002 certificates were issued to hotels and restaurants worldwide (ISO, 1998).

Hotel Operations

Maintaining standardization and required quality in the hospitality industry is very complex. A usual hotel has two main operations: rooms division (bell desk, guest services, reception, business centre, telephone switchboard, rooms, suites, laundry, public areas, etc.) and food and beverage operations (kitchen, restaurant, bars, night clubs, banquet and conference facilities, room service, minibars, kitchen stewarding, etc.).

The other departments (marketing, finance, human resources, engineering, security, computer systems, etc.) provide essential support services to rooms division and food and beverage operations. It is generally accepted that food and beverage operation is the most complex operation in a hotel. This is because it includes departments and sections where the quality of products and services is more visible, more difficult to maintain and can easily affect a hotel's image.

Apart from the quality of food and beverage products, longer operating hours, better quality linen, cutlery, crockery, glassware, design, wider choice of food and beverage items, better quality print of menu cards and beverage lists, more tasteful décor, better operating equipment, better tailored uniforms and better calibre of staff (in general) can be noticed in restaurants situated in five-star hotels in comparison with hotels of lower grades. The food and beverage service in five-star hotels has become more complex and challenging owing to the important fact that this class of clientele certainly pay much more money and in return expect a different and better service/product.

A survey carried out a few years ago revealed that waiting staff thought that expert serving techniques were the most important features of their work. The customers surveyed, on the other hand, indicated that what they valued most in a waiter was a smiling, agreeable, welcoming blend of social qualities. This does not mean that techniques are not important, since many guests appreciate a high level of practical skills and expect a fully professional service. However, the waiting staff who merchandise a "meal experience" must cultivate friendliness, good manners and the relevant social skills.

The quality of food and beverage service is a combination of predictions and characteristics on which an individual assesses whether the service will give satisfaction each time it is used, based on the guest's own set of values. A quality standard in food and beverage operations is a combination of characteristics accepted by the consensus of market segments as being appropriate to provide satisfaction for their particular purposes.

Therefore, it is important to base policy decisions with regard to quality standards of food and beverage service in a hotel or restaurant on identified and anticipated specific customer needs through research. Hospitality organizations seeking to ensure the continuous quality of their service processes should embark on quality assurance management systems. Only through a systematic process can a hotel achieve a globally accepted quality standard.

Quality Assurance

Terms such as five-star, deluxe, high standards, good service, and fair value for money mean totally different things to different people and are therefore meaningless until they are defined in clear, precise terms. Yet expensive hotel investments and crucial marketing decisions are often described with these phrases. Potential quality can be affected by technical and behavioural factors within organizations and from the environment. It is important to determine the variables that can be manipulated to control these factors, such as design of service process, selection, training, supervision, communication, peer relationships and rewards to ensure sustained quality assurance in hotels.

A Case Study

Le Meridien Jamaica Pegasus Hotel

In October 1998, the largest and premier business hotel in Jamaica, Le Meridien Jamaica Pegasus, became the first hotel in the Caribbean to achieve certification to ISO 9002 Quality Management Standards. This property, referred to as the Pegasus, has 350 rooms and at that time had 400 employees. A unique characteristic of the hotel is the exceptionally long years of service by many senior employees. In 1998 the average length of service to the Pegasus was sixteen years by the first line managers and nine years by the second line managers.

The hotel has four restaurants, two bars, a large ballroom, nine meeting rooms, a gym, two tennis courts, two swimming pools, a jogging track and a shopping arcade. The Pegasus opened in 1972 and has been managed by the same hotel company, Forte Plc. in the United Kingdom, for the last twenty-nine years. During this period, owing to changes within the managing company, the Pegasus underwent two name changes; in 1992 as "Forte Grand" and in 1997 as "Le Meridien". The second rebranding was more crucial, as to reach Le Meridien standards the hotel had to do considerable upgrading and staff training. In addition to the challenging rebranding process in 1997, the hotel was also faced with a financial problem triggered by an increase of four-star hotel rooms in Kingston by 42% and a decrease of tourist arrivals to Kingston.

The occupancy level was around 60% for a few years, but owing to the increase in room capacity in the city, a price war had started. This resulted in the average room rate falling from US$100 to around US$83. Giving in to union demands and agreeing to above-inflation salary increases in the past had resulted in payroll cost (as a percentage of revenue) increasing from 22% in 1995 to 32% in 1997. The bottom line impact of these challenges was that the profitability of the hotel gradually dropped from 22% in 1993 to an alarming 8% in 1997.

As a survival strategy the management was compelled to restructure the operations. While there is nothing new to the downsizing phenomenon, the incidence of organization downsizing has increased considerably in recent years. Commentators warn of the potentially damaging effects of downsizing and redundancy programmes on the survivors and the culture of downsized organizations.

The management decided to make 18% of the permanent staff redundant. A bold counterproposal of an unprecedented wage freeze was sent to the union who were demanding a 40% wage increase. The climate was not appropriate for introducing a quality management system that required high labour moral, motivation and commitment. However, the rebranding to Le Meridien and upgrading of the hotel had been committed with the owners. An official launching of "Le Meridien" (by the prime minister of Jamaica) for the end of 1997 had been confirmed.

In this context, the management decided to go ahead with the following during the 1997/1998 financial year:

- Redundancy of fifty-one employees
- Not changing the wage freeze stand in union negotiations
- Frequent frank dialogue with the employees with regards to the financial problems faced by the company and working together in "quality circles" to solve operational problems
- Internal marketing and public relations to convince the employees that quality assurance is the key to solving the financial problems
- Implementing the planned product upgrade
- Completion of the rebranding process by the end of 1997
- Introducing the ISO 9002 Quality Management system as a foundation for the future
- Reviewing the possibility of obtaining four-diamond grading by the

American Automobile Association (AAA) and the Green Globe Award within three years

Vision for the Future

The management decided to pay special attention to training and development of a quality culture at the Pegasus. The vision was that this culture would be the backbone of the future quality standards achievements. It was considered important for this backbone to be strengthened with strategic inputs and quality inputs of the desired standards. At the same time this backbone (quality culture) should be strong enough to hold the present (organizational culture) and the future (vision) together.

Quality Policy

The labour dispute at that time arose as a result of the union's refusal to accept a proposal for a moratorium by the management. In spite of the labour dispute, the management won the support of the employees for the quality vision and 300 employees signed a quality policy, which has been displayed in the lobby of the Pegasus for the last four years. The policy, which was developed with input from the 300 employees, states:

Le Meridien Jamaica Pegasus is committed to being the best up market business hotel in the Caribbean; by consistently delivering Le Meridien quality product and service standards, satisfying guest expectations, whilst building employee morale and achieving profit objectives. The agreed slogan is, "The Best Is Getting Better".

Quality Action

The following ten "commandments" related to the quality policy were developed with input from the 300 employees:

1. Make decisions based on findings from internal quality audits, guest surveys, employee surveys and Le Meridien quality audits.
2. Communicate the company policies and business objectives to all employees.
3. Employ skilled, committed and service oriented people with warm and friendly attitudes.
4. Train, develop, empower, reward and facilitate employees to achieve quality objectives.
5. Analyse productivity of the departments and take timely action to improve efficiency and profitability.
6. Satisfy shareholders by increasing the stock value.
7. Implement good public relations with all segments of the community.

8. Hold regular employee meetings to encourage innovative and creative thinking that will challenge conventional thoughts and practices.
9. Ensure that international standards with a European flavour, blended with the local culture, are implemented.
10. Implement ISO 9002 standards, receive and retain certification over the years.

The framed quality policy and quality actions are displayed in each department, section and office of the Pegasus.

Communication

Communication is the key to success in any process of change. For twelve months, quality and ISO 9002 became items on the agenda of many regular meetings, such as:

- Morning briefing (20 minutes – standing) – five times a week with all departmental managers
- Le Meridien/quality meeting (60 minutes) – once a week with departmental managers
- Purchasing/project meeting (40 minutes) – once a week with five executives
- All managers meeting (60 minutes) – once a month
- Managers and union delegates meeting (60 minutes) – once a month

The Le Meridien/quality meeting was a new meeting created to coordinate rebranding and implementing ISO 9002 during the 1997/1998 financial year.

Quality Analysis

Qualitative analysis of all corrective action forms (for every guest complaint) has to be done once a month as part of the ISO 9002 system. Corrective action forms are discussed at the morning briefings and with the use of a log, follow-up action is monitored by the general manager. The commitment from the general manager is essential for the system to work effectively and productively. Guest questionnaires, too, are analysed and distributed to all managers and departments once a month.

Foundation for the Future

The key hotel activities and external factors that had an impact on the hotel's performance from April 1997 to March 1998 are summarized below.

People

- A Le Meridien trainer from Paris trained thirty employees as on-the-job trainers and a series of training programmes for other employees was conducted by the trainers and management using Le Meridien manuals as guidelines.

- Twenty-three employees were trained as quality auditors to audit the quality of the operations of other departments.
- Good relationships were maintained with the union and employees in spite of prolonged wage negotiations and resulting industrial actions.
- Seven managers underwent brief training/exposure at Le Meridien New Orleans in the United States.
- Employees of the year were sent to Paris and London to join other employees of the year from seventy-three Le Meridien hotels on an award tour of exposure.
- The executive chef won an award "For Excellence in Food Preparation, Delivery and Presentation" during 1997, from the Jamaica Observer newspaper.

Product

- Le Meridien image, service and product standards were introduced and the hotel was rebranded as Le Meridien Jamaica Pegasus on October 9, 1997 with the prime minister of Jamaica as the guest of honour.
- Various projects were undertaken to implement the essential upgrading. These included complete refurbishment of two bedroom floors, installation of a new chiller, installation of a new fire alarm system, painting the building exterior, upgrading of tennis courts, upgrading of gardens and public areas, etc.
- Food and beverage concepts were changed. The coffee shop was upgraded and a section was air-conditioned, the gourmet restaurant concept was fine-tuned to blend with the historic significance of Port Royal and the wine club was transformed into a pizza cellar. All menus were changed.
- The ISO 9002 Quality Management system was introduced. The hotel developed a quality policy with input from most of its employees.
- The hotel continued to be the focal point of social activities in Kingston, often being chosen as the location for major banquets. The hotel continued organizing food festivals and other major events, including 101 holiday events during the last 38 days in 1997.
- The hotel won the Jamaica Observer newspaper's first ever "Table talk" food award for the "Food Event of the Year".
- The Le Meridien mystery guest programme, with a 1,000 point

checklist, was introduced by internally arranged monthly mystery guests.

Promotions

- Room reservations, banquet bookings, sales, public relations and advertising were combined and a new marketing department was created with the objective of being more aggressive in marketing.
- The start of the twenty-fifth year of operations of the hotel was celebrated with the governor general of Jamaica as the guest of honour.
- Management sales calls to local clients were accelerated.
- The hotel continued to be the focal point during the Jamaica Carnival. A "wet-feete" was held at the hotel as part of the carnival celebrations.
- A major wedding expo was held.
- Le Meridien promoted the hotel in its regional and worldwide publications, sales and advertising campaigns.
- The hotel continued to be in the limelight through planned public relations and publicity.
- Familiarization tours were arranged for Le Meridien vice president–sales, sales director, and reservation agents, to Washington, D.C., New York and London.
- Frequent participation in Le Meridien sales conferences and planned sales trips to North America, South America and Europe.
- Participation in Le Meridien sales promotion activities.

Profit

- Towards the end of the financial year, British Airways reduced the allotment of thirty-four rooms per day to six rooms per day as most crew members were provided accommodation in Montego Bay instead of Kingston.
- The number of rooms in Kingston was increased by 32% and the four-star category rooms were increased by 42% within a year. At the same period, the arrivals to Kingston were reduced by 2%. With the supply of rooms in Kingston greatly exceeding the demand, the hotel experienced revenue problems. The hotel undertook major restructuring and re-engineering, affecting fifty-one job positions (18% of the total permanent workforce), which were made redundant. The hotel spent J$11 million as redundancy payments, but was able to recover this within eight months from the savings on labour cost.

- For seven months, the hotel held its position of a wage freeze against the union demand for a 40% wage increase for year one and a 35% increase for year two, for line employees. After two "sit ins" and a strike, the matter was referred to the Industrial Disputes Tribunal and a 7.5% wage increase for year one and a 7.5% increase for year two were awarded. This is a "landmark" award in the Jamaican hotel industry as salary increases in hotels had been in the range of 30% to 60% for many years prior to this award. As a result of this award, a single-digit wage increase has become the norm in the Jamaican hotel industry today.

TOURISM & HOSPITALITY

India boasts of the world's highest mountains, miles of coastline with excellent beaches, tropical forests and wildlife, adventure tourism, desert safari, lagoon backwaters, ancient monuments and World Heritage Sites, forts and palaces, and of course, the Taj Mahal.

The Indian tourism and hospitality industry has thus emerged as one of the key sectors driving the country's growth. The tourism sector is thriving, owing to a huge surge in both business and leisure travel by foreign and domestic tourists.

According to the latest Tourism Satellite Accounting (TSA) research, released by the World Travel and Tourism Council (WTTC) and its strategic partner Accenture, India's travel and tourism industry is expected to generate approximately US$ 100 billion in 2008 and almost US$ 275.5 billion by 2018, growing at an average of 9.4 per cent over the next ten years.

Moreover, according to the TSA research, travel and tourism is expected to contribute 6.1 per cent to India's national gross domestic product (GDP) and provide almost 40 million jobs by 2018. Also, a country brand index (CBI) 2008 survey, conducted by FutureBrand—a leading global brand consultancy—in collaboration with public relations firm Weber Shandwick's Global Travel & Lifestyle Practice, has ranked India second in the value-for-money index.

The rapid growth of India's tourism industry has been instrumental in South Asia being the preferred tourist destination as noted by the UN World Tourism Organisation (UNWTO). Foreign tourist arrivals during the period January–October 2008 increased by 370,000 to 4.32 million as compared to 3.95 million during the corresponding period of 2007.

Number of foreigners visiting India as tourists in October 2008 was 453,000 as compared to 331,000 in September 2008. Consequently, foreign exchange earnings from tourism in India rose from US$ 8.293 billion during January to October 2007 to US$ 9.696 billion during January to October 2008. Earlier, in 2007, total number of foreign tourists visiting India was 5.08 million - an increase of 14.3 per cent over 2006.

OUTBOUND TOURISTS

A booming economy and increase in disposable income has led to a massive growth in the number of Indians travelling abroad. In 2007, 9.78 million Indians went abroad for tourism, an increase of 17.3 per cent over 2006. Indian outbound tourist flow is expected to increase at a compounded annual growth rate (CAGR) of 13.30 per cent during 2008–2012, according to a new report titled, "Indian Tourism Industry Analysis", by RNCOS, a leading market research and information analysis company.

Along with the rise in the number of Indians travelling abroad, both the total and per capita expenditure spent abroad has been increasing. For example, according to the European Travel Commission, average spend per trip of Indian outbound tourists has increased from US$ 611 in 2000 to US$ 822 in 2006. Similarly, Euromonitor International estimates the outgoing tourism expenditure from India to grow to US$ 21 million by 2011, representing a growth rate of over 25.7 per cent between 2006 and 2011.

MEDICAL TOURISM

"First World treatment' at Third World prices" is how industry sources define medical tourism in India. Although India is a recent entrant into medical tourism, it is fast catching up.

According to a study by McKinsey and the Confederation of Indian Industry (CII), medical tourism in India could become a US$ 2 billion industry by 2012 (from US$ 350 million in 2006). Credit Suisse estimates medical tourism to be growing at about 25–30 per cent annually. Indian hospitals are fast becoming the first choice for an increasing number of foreign tourists and as per a Credit Suisse estimate; nearly 180,000 medical tourists were treated in India in 2004.

The key selling points of the medical tourism industry are its cost effectiveness and its combination with the attractions of tourism. Many travel agents are now selling combined packages of treatment and vacation. India has some of the best hospitals and treatment centres that are equipped with infrastructure and technology, which are at par with those in the US, UK and Europe at a fraction of the costs –only a tenth and sometimes even a sixteenth of the cost in the West.

In fact, according to the World Travel and Trade Council, Indian tourism demand will continue to grow at a rapid pace. It estimates the demand to grow at an average of 8.8 per cent between 2004 and 2013, making India the world's third fastest growing tourist market. The boom in the Indian tourism industry has cascaded to the rural areas as well. India continues to attract tourists owing to its splendid historical architecture and rich culture along with beautiful beaches, rural tourism or what now is called 'responsible tourism' is also fast gaining popularity with travellers flocking to discover the best in rural arts and heritage.

HOSPITALITY INDUSTRY IN INDIA

Hospitality segment, just like many other segments in India is booming at an unprecedented pace. India faces a huge challenge of being "under roomed" while the economy is growing rapidly. This provides for a huge opportunity for hospitality industry. A lot of large real estate developers are also investing into this business to bridge the demand-supply gap and leverage the opportunity. A number of cities have blossomed with suburban "Silicon Valley" type Special Economic Zones (SEZs).

This is mostly driven due to strong growth in IT, BPO segments, increase in foreign travelers, emphasized focus on tourism by government, affordable airlines fares, etc. Several other factors such as Commonwealth Games in Delhi are fueling the need further. The middle class is becoming more prosperous and native Indian tourist travel is growing rapidly, particularly in places such as Goa, Kerala and Rajasthan.

Bangalore, Hyderabad, Chennai, Gurgaon, Pune and the suburbs of Mumbai are the areas attracting international investment and as expected, are the cities with the largest development pipelines. Combined, these cities account for 89 of the 161 projects in the pipeline and 16,734 guestrooms, which is 68% of the rooms in India's total pipeline. Of the 161 projects in India's pipeline, 100 will have 4 and 5 star designations. The other 61 are 1, 2 and 3 star developments. A number of them are new economy brands recently designed for the Indian market place. Taj's Ginger Hotels is one such brand, Lemon Tree and Red Fox are others in this category. Almost all the major hotel operators such as Starwoods, Hilton, and Intercontinental have significant growth plans for India and have multiple projects in works or in pipeline.

MEANING OF HOSPITALITY

For an in depth understanding of the term of hospitality, the starting point is the etymology of the word itself. The word hospitality derives from the Latin *hospes*, which is formed from *hostis*, which originally meant a 'stranger' and came to take on the meaning of the enemy or 'hostile stranger' (hostilis) + pets (polis, poles, potentia) to have power. Furthermore, the word *hostire* means equilize/compensate.

If you combined the above etymological analysis with the story of Telemachus and Nestor you can develop in your mind the Greek concept of sacred hospitality. First of all, Telemachus is a complete stranger for Nestor, however he was hosted and treated more than warmly. In the Homeric ages, hospitality was under the protection of Zeus, the chief deity of the Greek pantheon. For that reason Zeus was also attributed with the title 'Xenios Zeus' ('xenos' means stranger).

The semantic behind this was to highlight the fact that hospitality for Ancient Greeks was of the utmost importance. A stranger passing outside a

Greek house, could be invited inside the house by the family. The host washed the stranger's feet, offered him/her food and wine, and only after he/she was comfortable could be asked to tell his/her name. After having welcomed Telemachus, Nestor asks his unknown guest to introduce himself to find out that he was the son of Odysseus. By that time, the man in front of him was a complete stranger, a *hostis* as described in the etymological analysis of hospitality at the beginning. Nonetheless, Telemachus was equilized with his host.

Another meaning that is included in the etymology of hospitality. Note also that one of the Nestor's sons slept on a bed close by Telemachus to take care that he should not suffer any harm. This means that hospitality for Ancient Greeks include also the idea of protection. Lastly, Nestor put a chariot and horses at Telemachus' disposal so that he could travel the land route from Pylos to Sparta in two days, having as charioteer Nestor's son Pisistratus. The last element of hospitality as can be realized is guidance. Based on the story above and its current meaning, hospitality is about compensating/equalizing a stranger to the host, making him feel protected and taken care of, and at the end of his hosting, guiding him to his next destination.

HOSPITALITY SERVICE

The concept of Hospitality Services, also known as "accommodation sharing", "hospitality exchange" (short "hospex"), and "home stay networks", refers to centrally organized social networks of individuals who trade accommodation without monetary exchange. While this concept could also include house swapping or even time share plans, it has come to be associated mostly with travelers and tourists staying with one another free of charge. Since the 1990s, these services have increasingly moved away from using printed catalogs and the telephone, to connecting users via the internet. As of March, 2008 over 1,000,000 people are registered users of these internet networks.

SESQUICENTENNIAL HOSPITALITY AT RIZVI

Hospitality' is an annual tradition at Rizvi and this year it was conducted as part of the ongoing sesquicentennial celebration of the University of Mumbai. Rizvi college of Hotel Management is a premier institute, training students for a career in hotel industry. We at Rizvi firmly believe in the old age philosophy as propagated by Kautilya that -Degrees alone are not enough. During their three years course students need to walk that extra mile to enhance their practical knowledge. In order to achieve that a lot of responsibility is shouldered by the faculty, representatives from the industry and the students themselves. The college faculty is in constant touch with the hotels to understand the industry's specific needs and the same input is passed on to the students.

The students on their part do a lot of self-learning when sent for training in the hotels. It is with this compatible liaisoning that we stride forward to achieve our objective of grooming students, who then step into the world with confidence & self pride. Hospitality is an endeavour and a step in the direction of strengthening the students and combining academics with practical knowledge. It is a forum wherein students from Catering Colleges all over India get together to participate and compete, to bring to the fore their individual skills and talent in the core areas of Hospitality Industry namely, Front Office, Food Production, Food & Beverage Service and House Keeping.

HOTEL INDUSTRY OVERVIEW

Hotel Industry directly or indirectly provides Business to following industry:

- Hotel industry provides business to Travel Agency
- Hotel industry provides business to Tour Operators
- Hotel industry provides business to Transportation.

Points to know for Hotel Industry:

- Hotel industry Information
- Hotel industry News
- Hotel industry Trends
- Hotel industry Analysis
- Hotel industry Jobs
- Hotel industry Statistics
- Hotel industry Associations
- Hotel industry Overview
- Hotel industry Report
- Hotel industry History
- Hotel industry Careers
- Hotel industry Courses
- Hotel industry Experts
- Hotel industry Facts
- Hotel industry Marketing
- Hotel industry Problems
- Hotel industry Research
- Hotel industry Services
- Hotel industry Terms
- Hotel industry Profits

From the ancient time the place providing both safe food and safe accommodation to the customers is the meaning of Hotel or Hotel Industry. Food, Accommodation and Dress are the 3 most essential things which every one need. And Hotel Industry alone provide 2 basic things:- Food and Accommodation. There are just three front side of the Hotel Industry Earnings:- In providing Rooms, Banquets and Restaurants.

Types of Hotels in Hospitality Hotel Industry:

- Commercial Hotels
- Airport Hotels
- Conference Centers
- Economy Hotels
- Suite or All-Suite Hotels
- Residential Hotels
- Casino Hotels
- Resort Hotels

Earnings for Hospitality Hotel Industry:

- Hotel Industry get Revenue in providing Rooms
- Hotel Industry get Revenue in providing Banquet Halls
- Hotel Industry get Revenue in Restaraunts
- Additional Hotel Industry get revenue as
  - For telephone call services in hotels
  - For laundry services in hotels
  - For travel services in hotels
  - For internet services in hotels

Hotel Industry Management Course:

Hotel Industry plays a vital role in reducing the level of Unemployment, Even after Engineering, and Doctors, hotel industry proffession, comes with a great scope, hotel management teaches a lot to students, even the basic etiquites in hotel management course includes:-

- Online hotel management course helps in "How to deal with Customers to hotels?"
- Online hotel management course helps in "How to deal with emergency situations in hotels?"
- What is the Basic Telephone Manners? can be known in Online hotel management course.
- Helps in Personality Development.

In India, National Council of Hotel Management and Catering Technology (NCHMCT) is a semi Govt. Hotel industry Institute that has approx. 30 centres in all over India. Apart from this there are thousand of other colleges that teach us about Hotel Industry. And Hotel industry colleges and Hotel industry Institutes after completion of Hotel industry course provide the employment to their students in Brand Hotels.

Hotel industry training is also an very important part of this course, because Hotel industry studies are just the guides, but Hotel industry training makes one perfect, Hotel industry training also helps the students in selecting their area of interest as Food section in Hotel industry and Hotel industry Beverage Production, Food and Beverage Services, Hotel industry accommodation operation, Hotel industry front desk, Computers in Hotel industry, Nutrition in Hotel industry, Hotel Engineering, etc.

Hotel industry Course also includes making a Survey Report on any topic in Final year, which makes the students go for research studies. Hotel industry research courses helps in removing many disqualities of the candidates like shy, communication skills, English, lack of confidence, etc.

Department of Hotels that are available for guest 24 X 7:-

- Hotel industry kitchen department
- Hotel industry Food Production department
- Hotel industry Engineering department
- Hotel industry Front desk department
- Hotel industry Housekeeping department
- Hotel industry Food & Beverage Service department
- Hotel industry Gym/ Health Club/ Sports department
- Hotel industry Parking/ Shops department
- Hotel industry Parking/ Shops department

Hotel Industry Kitchen/ Food Production: Kitchen & food production is a department of hotel that responsible for food. Even hotels having Coffee Shop provides 24 hour services to the guest. Hotel Industry Engineering:- If any problems come in room, bulb fuse, A/C not working, then we have to contact Hotel Engineers, they are also available 24 hours.

Hotel Industry Front desk:- Front desk is 1st impression on guest, if guest like this section then only he will go for other option like restaurant, laundry, etc.

Front desk consists of young and energetic staff who is always (24 x 7) be there to help guest, they are also responsible for Business Centre, Internet Access. He is also responsible for making C-Form for Foreigner Clients, providing safety lockers to the guest. Taking Reservation by Telephone, E-Mails, and Fax from the guest. Also providing guest Money Exchange Services.

Hotel Industry Housekeeping:- Housekeeping are available 24 X 7 for guest, making their bedroom, bathroom, etc. Providing guest Laundry services, also do day to day room cleaning for guests.

Hotel Industry Food & Beverage Service:- They include providing guest the services whether in rooms, Restaurants or Banquets, or in Conference rooms.

Hotel Industry Travel Desk:- They are responsible for arranging day to day travels for the guest. They also do the ticket confirmation work, and also provides the information for sightseeing to the guests.

Gym/ Health Club/ Sports:- Medium and large hotels are providing Gyms, Swimming Pool, Health Club, Beauty Parlour, Saloon, games like Billiards, Pool, etc. facilities to their guests. Most of the Hotels are providing these facilities complimentary with the rooms.

Parking/ Shops:- Few Star hotels providing big parking space, shops in the restaurant itself for the guest conveyance, so that they can get the things in hotel itself.

Hotel Management:

- Food & Beverage Manager
- Restaurant Manager
- Assistant Restaurant Manager
- Conference & Banqueting Manager
- Conference & Banqueting Sales Manager
- Front Office Manager
- Restaurant Manager

To ensure service delivery at every point of sale in the Food and Beverage Department. He or she therefore supervises and co-ordinates the Food and Beverage Department.

Key Responsibilities:

- To ensure that the customer promise is delivered and that customers are satisfied within the framework of financial targets set.
- To ensure that guests receive high quality service
- To ensure that the applicable regulations are complied with
- To be responsible for his or her own results
- To optimise the supply chain and the use made of raw materials

Skills:

- Team management, leadership & team player
- A liking for organisational work
- Effective management: delivering profit centre profitability
- Sales ability
- Adaptability: coping with the diversity of customers and their needs
- Thoroughness

- Sensitivity to customers: good relationship skills
- Spirit of initiative
- Financial awareness

Qualifications:

- A-levels (professional) in service-related subjects
- Significant food and beverage experience (5 years)
- Experience of working in positions of high responsibility in the hotel or food and beverage sectors and managing teams of at least 20 staff.

Hotels are amongst the most visible and important aspects of a country's infrastructure. Hotel industry is a closely linked one to the tourism industry. A number of factors like promotion of tourism and rapid industrial progress have given a boost to hoteliering.

The recent liberalisation of trade and opening up of economy will further lead to revolutionary growth in this sector. With increasing globalisation, career opportunities in this field are not only limited within the country but there are chains of hotels which operate internationally providing scope of a career abroad. It is a glamorous profession which has a bright future. With the growth of hotel industry propelled by foreign and domestic tourism and business travel, the demand for well trained quality personnel too has grown impressively.

The diversity of experience in hotel management is greater than in any other profession. Hotel industry involves combination of various skills like management, food and beverage service, housekeeping, front office operation, sales and marketing, accounting.

Today, the rise in corporate activity (leading to greater number of business trips) as well as the wish to travel on holiday has made the hotel industry a very competitive one. One can enter this field by direct entry or through hotel management institutes. For direct entry the vacancies are generally advertised in the newspapers and the minimum prescribed qualification is graduation with 50% marks. They are trained by the hotels themselves. But qualified personnel's are always given a higher preference.

Minimum qualification required to go for a course in hotel management is 10+2. For certificate, diploma and bachelors courses 10+2 is sufficient. Duration of certificate courses is six months to one year. Bachelor and diploma courses are of duration one and half to three years. Those with graduation can go for post graduate diploma courses the duration of which is one year. Selection to most government recognised institutes is based on common entrance test.

Test consists of English, Reasoning, General Science and General Knowledge. The test is of two hour duration and is held around April every year. The test is followed by a group discussion and interview, in which a person's personality and confidence is seen. Private institutes also conduct tests of their own, the pattern of which is almost the same.

Some of the prominent schools that conduct courses in this area are: The Oberoi centre for Learning and Development, 1 Sham Nath Marg, New Delhi-110054; Indian Institute of Hotel Management, Rauza Bagh, Aurangabad-431001; Welcomgroup Graduate School of Hotel Administration, Valley View Hotel, Manipal- 576119, National Council for Hotel Management and Catering Technology, Pusa, New Delhi. Course areas include food processing, Food and beverages service, Accommodation operation or front office, hotel accountancy, Business communication, French language, hotel engineering, computer, nutrition and food service, Hotel laws, Principles of management, sales and marketing management, Human resource management.

They should have a good organizational background, excellent communication and interpersonal skills, strong commitment and self-discipline. One must be an extrovert, co-operative, polite and respectful to the guests, have patience to deal guest criticism even when you know you are right, willing to work hard even at odd hours and yet be cheerful.

Job Prospects

Lots of lucrative and interesting openings are there for hotel management graduates in various fields like:

- Hotel & Restaurant management
- Airline Catering and Cabin Services
- Club management
- Cruise Ship Hotel Management
- Hospital administration and catering
- Hotel and Tourism Associations
- Forest Lodges
- Guest Houses
- Institutional Management (supervising canteens in college, schools, in factories, company guest houses etc.)
- Catering departments of railways, banks, armed forces, shipping companies etc.
- Hotel and catering institutes
- Self employment

Career options

A hotel consists main departments such as Operations, Front office, House keeping, Food and Beverages, Accounting, Engineering/ Maintenance, Sales and Security. Each department has a number of positions that one can opt for.

General Operations

General Manager who is the main in charge, is the coordinator and administrator, responsible for staff management, financial control, provision of services, quality control and customer care. Depending on the size of the hotel, general managers could have assistant managers to supplement their work.

Front Office

It is the centre of all activities. Important functions of receiving the guests, making room reservations, handling correspondence and preparing bills and keeping accounts of the guest services are handled at the front office. The department is headed by Front office manager or Executive House-keeper who supervises and co-ordinates the work. Then there are Assistant Manager, Lobby executive, front office supervisor, information assistant, receptionist, bell captain, bell boy, doorman etc. to perform their assigned roles.

House Keeping

The work of keeping the hotel, the rooms, the bars, the restaurants etc. clean and making it presentable to the guests and ensuring facilities and comfort to them is handled by this department. Those handling this department are Chief executive house keeper, floor supervisor, room attendants, linen supervisors, Maids etc.

Food and Beverages Department

This department is the hub of the hotel industry and is responsible for all the food that is prepared and served in the hotel. The main functions performed by the department are- presentation, preparation and service of food and beverages involving kitchen, bar and baker.

Overall in charge of kitchen is known as Chef de Cuisine, the in charge of section is called Chef de Partis and the one who supervises and coordinates the work of Chef de partis is known as Sous-Chef. One who cooks food is known as Cook, the person in overall charge of dining hall is called Maitre de hotel, Captain in charge of part of dining hall is known as Chef de Range, one who serves food is Demi Chef de Range or Steward.

Then there is the restaurant hostess who makes the guests comfortable and deal with any complaints by the guests. Those serving drinks are bartenders.

Accounting Department

This department deals with both cash and credit transactions, i.e. all the financial transactions like purchase of materials, offering of services to the guests etc. This department also compiles information required for budgeting, pricing of food and services and so on. Professionals like cash, cost and works accountants are given higher positions in the department. Chief cashier, cash clerk/bill clerk are the positions handled in this department.

Sales & Marketing

This department keeps in touch with travel agents and tour operators as well as other potential corporate clients in order to sell hotel facilities. Advertising and Public Relations is also normally handled by this department.

FUTURE OF HOSPITALITY OPERATIONS

The mechanisation of housekeeping has happened - the traditional mop has gone for a toss and high-gloss flooring that requires crystallisation is the latest. Praveen K Singh brings to light the best housekeeping practices happening in India.

The Indian hotel kitchen has been experiencing an evolution of sorts, with incorporation of new technology, smaller space, etc. Praveen K Singh finds out the latest trends in kitchen design and foodservice equipment industry. The F&B curve is rising, making way for institutional consumerism. Sanjeev Bhar discusses the changes and challenges lined up for this sector.

The Indian hospitality industry's rapid growth is being derailed owing to high attrition and fickle loyalty of its most important resource - people. Neeti Mehra finds out how training can ensure peak performance as technology develops, guest demands increase and outsourcing of jobs swells. It has the power to transform the Indian hospitality industry that is driven by aggressive competition, demanding customers and thin profit margins. Sanjeev Bhar examines how it can take the industry to an even more progressive phase.

History repeats itself as Indian hoteliers make the same mistakes as their Western counterparts, writes Vivek Nayak. Marketing your hotel successfully on the Internet is easier than you think it is, says Milind Mody. Security in this service-oriented industry has come to occupy a significant position in orer to protect guests from crime risks and compromise their reputation and goodwill.

Vikram Kharvi investigates. "Design can be an art. Design can be aesthetics. Design is so simple, that's why it is so complicated". Preeti Kannan analyses the future trends in interiors and designs.

If we saved energy the way to did money, India would probably be among the power-rich countries in the world. Priya Krishnaswamy looks at how hotels can do their bit. As tourism in India takes centrestage, international hospitality brands making a beeline for the hotel and restaurant circuit are looking to franchising as their main strategy. Express Hospitality dwells into the evolution of the concept.

Spas, associated only with resort hotels earlier, are now becoming a fixture in city hotels as well. Bhavika Jhaveri finds out more about the therapeutic experience. Waste is an issue of increasing importance in the hospitality industry. Express Hospitality explores how environmental issues are driving the industry towards more sustainable management of solid and liquid waste.

TOURISM

Tourism is a growing industry in India. Hoteliering as well as tourism account for the major foreign earnings for our nation. The declining value of the rupee and a good image of India as an exotic tourist destination have boosted the tourism and hotel industry in India during the late nineties.

It is very surprising to note that small countries like Indonesia, Mauritius, Seyshells, Malaysia, Hong Kong and Thailand have been able to do very well on the tourism front. India is the ancient cultural cradle of the world. It has fascinating tourist destinations like the Taj Mahal, The Khajuraho temples, the marble mountains, The Gateway of India, the Red fort and the Qutub Minar, The Ajmer Palace, The Bharatpur, Bird Sanctuary, The city of Canals and many more. We Indians are also not aware of the beauty of our country.

Our ancient cities, palaces, lakes, temples, gardens, minarets, mosques, and lakes mountains delightful experiences for all the travelers as well as visitors. The foreign tourist longs for a tryst with India and loves to visit each and every corner of this vast country. Our tourism exchange earnings are less than $1.5 billion and account of 0.5 per cent of the total tourism traffic of the world. On the other hand, the tourism earnings of Singapore are $34 billion. The same figures are $6.5 billion for Malaysia. The facts do not point towards a healthy trend. We have not to depend merely upon the dollars – rupee parity but also, we have to generate enough of interest about the Indian subcontinent in the minds of the tourists so that they continue to come here and enjoy being here.

The problem of Kashmir has not been solved. Ten years before many tourists were kidnapped and a few of them were killed by the Kashmiri militants. Although the situation is under control, yet the army has to keep strict vigil over the sea.

Therefore, the inflow of tourists is less. The situation is much better now and many Indians and foreigners visited Kashmir. Central India, The North Eastern states, Calcutta, Mumbai, New Delhi, Khajuraho, and Goa are the most popular tourist destinations. Rajasthan is paradise for the foreigners and this state provides a wide range of cultural and ethnic diversities to the visitors. The foreign tourists are appalled at the state of Indian catering services, roads, guides services, hotels motels, and transportation services and above all, the degrading environment of the Indian subcontinent.

We would have to provide four star amenities to the tourists at the prices of three state standards. If we do not follow this norm, we would lose tourists to the United States of America, Seychells, Mauritius, Singapore, Thailand, Hongkong, and Japan. These countries offer entertainment, good quality rooms, and transportation, liquor, as well as food, at the most competitive prices. They follow international tourism norms in terms of catering, hospitality, and hygiene. We do not follow any norms and this leads to aversion on the part of the tourists from India. It is fortunate to note that hotel management and tourism have become serious subjects as well as vocations. The government as well as the private institutions has launched many courses in tourism as well as hotel management. The professionals in tourism and travel are required by tour operators as well as airlines.

The sea cruisers and airlines also need hospitality staff and chefs are required around the world. Hotel professionals are also in great demand. This would boost the hotel industry as well as the economy. The services of tourist guides, catering, roads, air travel, sanitation, transportation, and telecommunications would have to be operated on professional grounds. The international agency is doing well to promote and regulate air travel around the world. The Government of India is also doing its best. The participation of the private firms has also increased. However, a lot needs to be done in this crucial area. We can earn a lot through tourism as well as hotel industries. Our outlook and approach would have to be professionalized if we want to achieve concrete results in this fastest growing industry.

SCOPE OF HOSPITALITY INDUSTRY

In the milieu where change in inevitable, everyday brings forth new challenges. The hospitality industry too over the years has evolved ways and means to keep pace with the changing times and demand.

Hotel business is the oldest commercial endeavour, know to mankind. Hospitality is one of the Worlds fastest growing Industries. Today tourism is the single largest industry in the world employing over 150 million people globally.

One out of ten people in the world are employed by this industry. Today 4 million people in India are employed in Hotel, Catering and Tourism industry. The industry is growing at a healthy rate of 5% annually. In the year 2006 itself tourist arrival in India recorded 5.5 Lakhs. With the onset of globalisation the hospitality industry in India is witnessing a burgeoning growth with the demand for more rooms growing every year throwing open ample opportunities for employment.

The Demand for hotel rooms has doubled with special international events round the corner, like the 2010 Commonwealth Games as well as the 2011 World Cup Cricket. With foreign investment pouring in stock markets crossing the 20000 mark in early 2008, and with FOREX earning recorded at 3,400 Crores. There is one crucial need in the industry and that is the need for TRAINED MANPOWER. Gone are those days when only large 5 star hotels engaged trained staff, now even medium sized establishments desire trained staff to provide their guests with professional service.

It is estimated that within the next few years approximately 2 Lakhs Trained Hotel Management Professionals are required in India alone. It is but obvious that there are unlimited career opportunities in this field. Similar opportunities are available for students from Bhutan and Nepal in their own countries too.

HOSPITALITY: THE PROMISING FUTURE OF HOSPITALITY CAREERS

Hospitality careers are one of the fastest growing fields of work nowadays. It is not only popular in the US but even in different countries that you go to. This industry has an international scope which makes it a popular one. A lot of literature says that the future of hospitality careers is very promising. But how come do they say this? Well, there are a couple of factors why you can have a very promising future in this type of career. Here are some of them.

THE MARKET: TOURISTS AND LOCALS

The common misconception about careers in this category is that it only pertains to job positions that could be found in hotels and restaurants. It is true that there are a number of positions in hotels and restaurants that take the responsibility of being hospitable but there are also other industries that have this kind of role such as: car hiring trades, air-conditioning services, building industry, plumbing, airlines, casinos, entertainment organisations, IT companies, taxi operators, recruitment agencies, and retail services. All these and more are included in the category of hospitality.

As you can see, most of these are what you may call the "essentials" in the realm of tourism. And for sure, you know how important tourism is in whatever place or country you may be. Thus, you can expect that an industry like this could definitely bloom even in the coming years. However, it is not only tourists that these jobs serve. Even locals alike are served too.

For sure you make use of the services of taxi cabs, plumbers and most of all restaurants. This factor makes the whole industry more stable. Even if it's not the peak season of tourists, locals are still there to keep the industry alive and beating!

GLOBALIZATION

In relation to tourism, there is the factor of globalization. It is undeniable that globalization is hastily coming into being. More countries are getting connected with one another in terms of business relations and investments. This is a pretty good sign for the hospitality industry as they can expect more international visitors to be coming their way in need of hospitality and their services.

The Lucrative Compensation

Another factor why this career has a brilliant future ahead is because of the huge possibility of attaining a very lucrative pay. The basic salary already pays well. But there is that big chance of getting promoted, which gives you a higher projected income. Unlike in other fields where you've been working for 10 years and nothing have changed, in this industry, the more experience you've got, the more the chance you can get a higher position.

The Perks

Other than the high income you'll be getting, you also get to receive a lot of perks and benefits. For instance, tips are very rewarding with this kind of jobs.

Just think of the many customers you can serve and the high potential of meeting good tippers in just one day. The perks you get from companies are great too. There are a lot of bonuses and benefits. However, it highly depends on the company that you'll be working with.

Stressful Lifestyle

It is undeniable that times are pretty hard these days. This is why a lot of people resort to paying others to do things for them. This is somewhat an important factor in this industry. Since they've got the money, then they'll simply pay others to do it for them. It is that simple in the life of the rich and famous. So, why not take advantage of it?

The hotel industry is a mature industry marked by intense competition. Market share increases typically comes at a competitor's expense. Industry-wide, most growth occurs in the international, rather than the domestic, arena.

Common American hotel classifications are as follows:

- Commercial Hotels cater mainly to business clients and usually offer room service, coffee-shop, dining room, cocktail lounge, laundry and valet service as well as access to computers and fax services.
- Airport Hotels are located near airports and are a conveniently located to provide any level of service from just a clean room to room service and they may provide bus or limousine service to the air lines.
- Conference Centers are designed to specifically provide meeting space from groups; they provide all services and equipment necessary to handle conventions.
- Economy Hotels provide a limited service and are known for clean rooms at low prices meeting just the basic needs of travelers.
- Suite or All-Suite Hotels are hotels which offer spacious layout and design. Business people like the setting which provides space to work and entertain separate from the bedroom.
- Residential Hotels used to be very popular. The typical residential hotel offers long term accommodations.
- Casino Hotels are often quite luxurious. Their main purpose is in

support of the gambling operation. Casino hotels often offer top name entertainment and excellent restaurants.

- Resort Hotels are the planned destination of guests, usually vacationers. This is because resorts are located at the ocean or in the mountains away from inner cities. Resort hotels may offer any form of entertainment to keep their guests happy and busy.

While the practice of renting space to travelers stretches back to antiquity, what could be considered the modern concept of a hotel derives from 1794, when the City Hotel opened in New York City. While the practice of renting space was not new, the City Hotel was purported to be the first building devoted exclusively to hotel operations.

For it's time, the building was quite large and possessed 73 rooms. Similar operations soon appeared in such nearby cities as Baltimore, Boston and Philadelphia. Interestingly, New York City's first skyscraper was a hotel - the six story Adelphi Hotel. Hotels took a distinct step up in style and class when the Tremont House opened in Boston in 1829.

This hotel was considered by many to be the beginning of what was regarded as first class service. With 170 rooms, the Tremont House was a large facility. In addition, the hotel offered features which, for the time, were amazing.

Private single and double rooms were available, which offered not only privacy, but also security. In addition to water pitchers and a washing bowl, free soap was provided in each room. The Tremont House offered French cuisine and, reportedly, was the first hotel to have a Bellboy. In 1908, the Buffalo Statler opened, marking the beginning of the modern commercial hotel era.

Many services now considered standard were introduced by the Statler, including such amenities as a light switch next to the door, private bathe, ice water and a morning newspaper. The Statler set the standard of the day by being clean, comfortable and affordable. The Statler served as the pattern for hotel design and operation for many years.

In the 1920's, hotel building entered a boom phase and many famous hotels were opened, including the Waldorf Astoria, New York's Hotel Pennsylvania, and the Chicago Hilton and Towers, which was originally named the Stevens.

Motels began to replace roadside cabins as use of the automobile spread throughout society. Offering clean rooms with adjacent parking, motels enjoyed great popularity with the traveling public.

In the 1950's and 1960's, the practice of franchising appeared within the industry. Franchising enabled entrepreneurs to expand their operations without the use of substantial capital. For much of their history, hotels were owned and operated by individuals. However, as franchises and chains began to appear, individually owned hotels found themselves increasingly at a competitive disadvantage. By the 1960's, independent prospects began to improve as the result referral organizations such as Quality Courts, Best Western, Master Host and Best Eastern. From the 1980's forward, mergers and acquisitions became common within the industry, and brands become hotly traded commodities. Recently, use of management companies has entered the mainstream. As a result, many chains are more involved in management than in ownership. These chains realize a much more predictable and steady income stream than had normally been yielded by ownership.

2

Career in Hospitality, Travel and Tourism

Tourism industry has achieved a fast growth rate to emerge as the major driving force of the global economy. On the basis of growth rate, India has been ranked the second, with Montenegro and China on the first and third position respectively. Over the next ten years, India is all set to gain an annual growth rate of 8.8 per cent in the travel sales sector. This immense growth in travel and tourism industry has created plenty of job opportunities for hospitality and travel sales jobs in India.

CAREER SCOPES

A person willing to make a career in hospitality jobs should look for openings in the avenues such as Tourism Department, Travel Agencies, Hotels, Road and Airlines Transport, Tour Operators, Time Share Companies, Holiday Consultants and Banks.

ELIGIBILITY

To get admitted in hospitality and travel sales courses, one should be a higher secondary pass. One can also pursue the courses through correspondence courses. Candidates proficient in at least one foreign language are preferred.

EDUCATION

Institutes certified under the Ministry of Culture and Tourism and other professional institutes offer degree and diploma programs. Some of the reputed institutes are:

- National Council for Hotel Management, Catering Technology and Applied Nutrition, Delhi
- Institute of Hotel Management, Aurangabad
- International Institute of Hotel Management, Kolkata

REMUNERATION

Job in hospitality and travel sales offers attractive pay packets. Salary scales often vary within the industry. Naukri Hub offers information on hospitality and travel sales jobs in India. Habitat world is the part of Old World Hospitality Pvt. Ltd, a group business with interests in Hospitality, Entertainment and Exports. The Company operates Hotel Broadway, New Delhi and chain of restaurants in India under title of Chor Bizarre.

The service industry is one of the most flourishing industries in India today. Hospitality can be termed as the service given to people. The travel and tourism sectors, hotel industries etc. are in constant need of the people. The Hospitality Sector mainly focuses on the services that are provided to the customers.

However, candidates opting for the Career in Hospitality Sector have to go through a rigorous training programme to be able to sustain the ever growing demand of this industry. Many colleges and universities across the country offer courses in the hospitality sector. The career scope after the completion of these courses is very wide and promising.

CAREER AS TOUR OPERATOR

Holidays are meant for relaxation; to rejuvenate your energy and to spend quality time with your loved ones. To fulfill this task efficiently, it is imperative to have the best Tour Operator to be your travel planner, who has got the experience, infrastructure, commitment and who is a real professional to plan your holidays. A tour operator typically combines tour and travel components to create a holiday. Tour operators organize tours to the various tourist spots and manage the travel and stay of the tourists. Tour operators need people for selling the concept and then to accompany the groups to the destinations. They arrange modes of transportation, accommodation, lunch and dinner for their clients.

There is no need of specific course as such, to be a tour operator. With practical experiences in this field along with adequate capital, one can be a tour operator.

However, Degree/Diploma/Certificate courses in Travel and Tourism can give one a professional outlook and provide an edge over others. For some of these courses minimum qualification is 10+2 pass, while for others it is bachelor's degree. Besides, there are Tourism and Travel management courses which are more advantageous for tour operators.

Career Prospects

The best option available to tour operator, is to start their own tour/travel agency. Before starting his own venture he should have practical experience of running a tour operation. Besides, one should have adequate capital to start a tour company. However, one can also work with tour/travel companies. They can seek suitable employment opportunities in government tourism departments too.

Institutes Offering

Any course related to tourism and travel sector can gives you an insight into tour operations. Such courses are available in various colleges across India. Some important institutes which offer courses in travel and tourism are: The Government of India Tourist Offices; Indian Institute of Tourism and Travel Management (IITTM), New Delhi, Kolkata and Gwalior; Kurukshetra University, Haryana; Delhi University, Delhi; Annamalai University, Tamil Nadu; MS University, Baroda; National Institute of Tourism and Hospitality Management, Hydrabad; Tezpur University, Assam and Institute of Tourism and Future Management, Chandigarh.

Remuneration

Career of a tour operator is highly remunerative. A trainee tour operator working with a travel/tour company can easily earn Rs 8,000 – 15,000 per month. After 5-7 years of experiences one can set up his own tour operation. Income in self-employment venture depends upon the nature and size of the business.

CAREER AS TRAVEL AGENT

Planning a vacation or trip can be a difficult and time-consuming task. Therefore most of the travelers seek the assistance of travel agents. The role of a travel agent is to help travelers sort through vast sea of information to help them make the best possible travel arrangements. Travel agents offer advice on travel destinations and make arrangements for transportation, car rentals, hotel accommodations and tours for travellers. They also do bookings for most of the major cruise lines. They also promote travel packages of resorts and specialty travel groups by marketing them to their clients. They also advise their clients on the customs to be kept in mind, exchange rates and best deals at restaurants and tourist attractions they do it all.

Although no specific qualification is required to be a travel agent, a Degree/Diploma/Certificate courses in travel & tourism can offer leverage to an aspirant. A travel agent is to be well versed in everything from climatic conditions peculiar to that nation/city/region, clothing to be worn to currency exchange rates.

A travel agent should have general business skills, sales skills, empathy and the knowledge of a seasoned traveller. A background in geography, communication, world history and computers and foreign languages is an added bonus.

Career Prospects

Travel agents can work with travel agencies, tour groups, national and international airlines, hotels, transport and cargo companies and government tourism departments. Besides, many cruise liners and resorts also use travel agents to promote travel packages and lure customers to visit them. Once you learn the ropes and have a steady clientele, you can even open up your own tour and travel agency.

Institutes Offering

Although no specific courses for travel agents are offered, a degree in related field can be an added advantage. Institutes offering various courses in tour and travel are: Indian Institute of Tourism and Travel Management (IITTM), New Delhi, Kolkata and Gwalior; Kurukshetra University, Haryana; Delhi University, Delhi; MS University, Baroda; Institute of Tourism and Future Management, Chandigarh.

Indira Gandhi National Open University, New Delhi; Tezpur University, Assam; Andhra University, Andhra Pradesh; Madurai Kamaraj University, Tamil Nadu and Himachal Pradesh University, Himachal Pradesh.

Remuneration

Generally travel agents earn handsome amount. A fresher working in a travel agency can get monthly salary of Rs 8,000-12,000. With gaining of experience one can expect hike in pay packages. Those travel agents having their own travel agency have handsome earnings depending upon the size of their business.

CAREER AS TOUR GUIDE

One of the easiest modes of entertainment is traveling. Traveling has become very easy these days. The growth of travel and tourism industry has opened up many job opportunities.

Tour guide is a preferred job options for many and are in growing demand these days. Job of a travel/tourist guide is both remunerative and challenging. An efficient tourist guide can make any place look beautiful and captivating to the tourists.

For doing this he must uphold the cultural traditions and heritage of the place along with social customs and even local legends. A travel guide must have extensive knowledge of the tourist destinations particularly associated with art, architecture and culture.

Tour guide training courses are conducted by the Tourism Offices of Government of India, which is held in Delhi, Mumbai, Chennai and Kolkata. Only graduates from any stream are eligible.

After the completion of the course, the guide is certified and given a license. Besides, Indian Institute of Travel and Tourism Management (IITTM) also offers short-term courses for graduates. Tourist guide license is issued both at the state and central level by the Tourism Department after taking a test depending on their needs.

There are also Tourism and Travel Administration/ Management courses offered by several institutes.

Career Prospects

Opportunities for tour guides exist with public as well private sectors. Tour guides can find job opportunities in tourism departments and tourism directorates of the union and state governments.

They can also work in the private sector with travel agencies and tour operators. For these professionals good prospects also lie with airlines, hotels and transport. Tour guides can also work as travel journalists or travel writers. They can work as a freelancer too. Self employment is good option in this sector. Generally, after gaining experience and recognition in an established travel agency, agents start their own firms.

Institutes Offering

Tourism courses are becoming more and more popular day by day. To cope with the growing demands of tour guides, several institutes offering training courses for them. They are: The Government of India Tourist Offices; Indian Institute of Tourism and Travel Management (IITTM), New Delhi, Kolkata and Gwalior; Kurukshetra University, Haryana; Delhi University, Delhi; Vikarm University, Sri Venkateswara University, Annamalai University, Tamil Nadu; SNDT University, Mumbai; Meghalaya Tourism Department, Shillong and MS University, Baroda.

Remuneration

To put it in precise terms, a tourist guide's profession is endowed with immense potentials. Travel guiding is a field, where initial struggle does pay rich dividends. Earnings of tour guides vary depending on skill, abilities, professionalisms and customer satisfaction.

Regional tour guides may charges from Rs 400 and above for an eight hour day. They may earn between Rs. 30,000-40,000 and even more in the three to four months of the tourist peak season.

CAREER AS CHEF

The growth in hospitality industry has giving rise to a growing demand for professional chefs. As a chef, one not only gets the opportunity to spice up palatable dishes, but also make a fortune by way of it. It is the chef, who holds the recipe for the success of an eatery or a catering business. If one nurtures the desire to win a million hearts by serving people with good food, a career as a chef is the right answer.

A degree or a diploma certificate in Hotel Management and Catering Technology open up many interesting employment avenues. There are four - year degree or a three - year diploma courses available in hotel management. The minimum qualification to enter into these courses is 10+2 pass. These courses are offered by various hotel management institutes across the country. For the degree course, an entrance exam is conducted by the National Council of Hotel Management and Catering Technology (NCHMCT). Short duration certificate courses are also available in food processing and cookery science. Besides specialization degree in any of the three areas: cold kitchen, hot kitchen and Bakery & Confectionery may open up more job opportunities.

Career Prospects

Professional chefs may find jobs in hotels, restaurants, air catering, food processing companies, catering in confectioneries, cruise liner, corporate catering, etc. Departmental catering services of defence and railways departments are also open to them. They also can work in canteens operated by universities, colleges and private schools. Chefs also become a food writer or food journalist. A two-year post graduation degree from IHM institutions can offer you to join as faculty member in government or private institutions offering hotel management courses. And, of course, you can become an entrepreneur by setting up your own business. In addition to all you can find a job in abroad as Indian chefs are lately much in demand in countries like the USA, Australia and Canada.

Institutes Offering

Courses in hotel management and food processing are offered by several institutes in India.

Some most important among them are: Institute of Hotel Management, Catering Technology and Applied Nutrition, New Delhi, Ahmedabad and Goa; Indian Institute of Hotel Management, Aurangabad; The Welcome Group Graduate School of Hotel Administration, Manipal; The Oberoi Centre of Learning and Development, New Delhi; Government Institutes of Hotel Management and Catering, Dehradun and Almora; The Oriental School of Hotel Management, Mumbai, Delhi and Vadodara; National Council for Hotel Management and Catering Technology, New Delhi; Delhi Institute Of Hotel Management, New Delhi; State Institute Of Hotel Management And Catering Technology, Thuvakkudi and Amity School Of Hospitality, Noida.

Remuneration

Even though the pay scales may vary from place to place, the differences are not too many. A new entrant can earns about Rs. 10,000 - 15,000 per month. After gaining 5-7 years of experience one can easily earns Rs.50, 000 - 60,000 per month. As you reach the top and become the Executive chef, your salary can be anything between Rs. 1 lakh - 2 lakh per month.

CAREER AS AIR CABIN CREW

Air cabin crew is a comprehensive term comprising Flight supervisors, Pursuers, Air hostesses and Flight attendants. Their responsibility is to look after the welfare, comfort and safety of passengers traveling in the aircraft. Their main duties are to check passenger's tickets, assisting them in storing luggage, demonstrate safety measures like fastening seat belt, use of emergency equipment and show exit doors etc. They also check out that sufficient food and beverage, first aid kits and other emergency equipment are on the flight. On the flight they serve meals and drinks. They are trained to deal with emergencies and apply safety drill and help passengers. They also have to tackle special problems like ill health of passengers.

To be an Air Cabin Crew member the minimum education qualification should be 10+2 pass or intermediate or Graduate from a recognized University. The age limit of the candidates should be between 17 and 27 years. Besides, some physical attributes are also required for the course.

The minimum height of the aspirants should be157.5 centimeters and weight should be in proportion to height. Most airlines appoint only unmarried candidates. Candidates must have a normal eyesight of 6/6 uncorrected vision in each eye. Fluency in multiple languages may be an added advantage. The applicant should have pleasing personality and clear complexion. There are many short duration training courses for air cabin crew members.

Career Prospects

Air Cabin crew have multiple career options. They can seek job opportunities in public sector airlines like Indian Airlines and Air India. However, most of the Cabin crew members preferred private airlines operating on domestic as well as on international routes. Private airlines like Jet Airways, Kingfisher, Spice Jet, IndiGo, Sahara Airlines are the preferred place for cabin crews. With experience they become supervisors and assign and oversee the work of junior cabin crew members. Most airlines allow crew members to opt for other jobs within the airline depending on their suitability for the positions available. Some airlines as a routine assign administrative and other ground duties to senior in flight staff members.

Institutes Offering

As the job demands for cabin crew are increasing day by day, numerous training institutes in India are offering various courses for Cabin crew members. Some prominent institutes among them are: Indian Airlines Ltd. Central Training Establishment, Hyderabad; Delhi Flying Club Ltd, New Delhi; Sahara India Aviation Academy, New Delhi; Skyline Educational Institute, New Delhi; Flytech Aviation Academy, Secunderabad; Indian Aviation Academy, Mumbai; Kuoni Academy of Travel, Delhi; Air Hostess Academy, Delhi; Frankfinn Management Consultants, Delhi and Freebird Aviation & Management Services, Trivandrum.

Remuneration

It is true that the pay scales are attractive and the perks and allowances are alluring in the airlines sectors. To begin with the salary of an air cabin crew member is anything between Rs 20,000- 25,000 per month in the public sector airlines. In private airlines pay packages are even higher. The emoluments in private international airlines are even 3 times higher than what is paid in public sector. Besides attractive perks you get free air tickets for yourself and family on the routes covered by the airlines. With little bit of experiences one can easily get Rs 30,000 - 40,000 per month. Senior personnel may earn up to Rs 75,000 per month.

HOSPITALITY AMONG TOP CAREER CHOICES FOR YOUNGSTERS

A study conducted by Associated Chambers of Commerce and Industry of India (ASSOCHAM), shows that there has been a radical change in the preferences of today's youngsters. No more they are targeting at BPO jobs but are instead looking forward to hospitality, aviation and retail, which are newer and promising areas. According to the study, the change is due to lack of job security and erratic work conditions in BPOs and other sectors. The study cites, 'By now, confronting a high attrition rate of 25 to 30 per cent together with the projection of facing a 30 to 40 per cent staff shortage in the next two years, BPOs seem set for tough time as urban youth 'rove' to newer and promising areas such as aviation, hospitality and retail'.

Venugopal N Dhoot, president of ASSOCHAM, says, "A number of youngsters after passing class twelfth who were earlier seeking opportunities for jobs in BPOs and call centres, are now interested in joining other attractive areas of hospitality, retail, aviation, animation, journalism, designing and entertainment."

The study titled 'Urban youths new emerging choices for career making,' cites hospitality, aviation and retail sectors are experiencing shortage of up to 25 to 30 per cent of skilled personnel. Venugopal adds, "With this change in preference, there is likely to be some make up for the scarcity." He explains that the change is due to the definite pay package with incentives. Also, the working conditions and lifestyles seem to be much more reasonable and in harmony in the jobs in hospitality, aviation and retail, he said.

Hotel management refers to professional management techniques used in the hospitality sector. These can include hotel administration, accounts, marketing, housekeeping, front office or front of house, food and beverage management, catering and maintenance. Hospitality management is the academic study of the running of hotels, restaurants, and travel and tourism-related business.

Hospitality and Tourism Management (HTM) can be a business major in either a Bachelors of Science, or a Bachelors of Arts. Graduate students graduate with a Masters of Business Administration, a Masters or Science, or a Doctorate of Philosophy in Hospitality and Tourism Management. It is a focus that is studied by individuals that are intending to work in the

Hospitality Industry, examples of which are; Hotels, Resorts, Casinos, Restaurants, and Events.

Within the HTM concentration there is generally:

- Food Management and Operations (Examples: Food Science, Food Selection and Preparation, Food and Beverage Operations)
- Lodging Operations (Examples: Hotel Operations, Resort Management, Lodging Management, Financial Management and Cost Control for Hospitality Organizations)
- Global Tourism (Examples: Travel and Tourism Management, Tourism Analysis, Hospitality and Research Methods)
- Sustainable Tourism (Examples: Natural Destination Management, Responsible Tourism, Green Tourism and Eco-Tourism, Alternative and more Environmentally friendly ways of working within the whole Tourism industry)
- Tourist Attractions Management (Examples: Heritage Attractions, Arts and Cultural Attractions, Industrial Attractions, City Based Attractions, Retail Attractions, Natural Attractions)
- Entertainment Management (Examples: Theme Park Management, Theatre Management, Cinema Management, Museology, Live Music and Music Festival Management).
- Event Management (Examples: Hospitality Sales, Catering Management, Hospitality Marketing Management)

Several large corporations such as Marriott, Hyatt, Wyndham and Hilton Hotels have summer internships in training programs for students majoring in Hospitality and Tourism Management, to help students get valuable work experience. The Florida International University School of Hospitality & Tourism Management is the highest ranked hospitality and tourism programme in the southeast United States and one of the top six in the nation as reported by the latest study published in the Journal of Hospitality and Tourism Education. It is also the only Hospitality & Tourism Management School to offer an American degree through its campus in The People's Republic of China—The FIU Tianjin Centre.

The Purdue University College of Consumer and Family Sciences's Hospitality and Tourism Management programme has been ranked first in the nation by both industry recruiters and an evaluation conducted by Virginia Tech that applied the *U.S. News & World Report* methodology to the academic unit level. An evaluation conducted by "Caterer & Hotelkeeper" in August of 2006 described École hôtelière de Lausanne, Hotelschool The Hague and the School of Hotel Administration at Cornell University, as "[making] up the big three international centres of hotel education." Although all three schools may apply different styles to their programs, they all share a curriculum that utilizes practical and theoretical based learning that eventually leads to a management degree.

In September 2007, Taylor Nelson Sofres (TNS) Travel & Tourism (UK) the world's largest provider of custom research and analysis conducted a broad industry survey amongst a large sample of hiring managers from leading international hospitality organizations around the world. The primary purpose of this survey was to establish the relative 'ranking' of the various international hospitality management schools providing university level programs from which these employers are likely to recruit staff.

École hôtelière de Lausanne has been chosen as the world's best hotel school. Hospitality refers to the relationship process between a guest and a host, and it also refers to the act or practice of being hospitable, that is, the reception and entertainment of guests, visitors, or strangers, with liberality and goodwill. Hospitality frequently refers to the hospitality industry jobs for hotels, restaurants, casinos, catering, resorts, clubs and any other service position that deals with tourists. Hospitality is also known as the act of generously providing care and kindness to whoever is in need.

COMMERCIAL PILOT CAREER

Indian Aviation industry has two distinct branches: Commercial and Military. Commercial aviation includes Commercial aviation includes passenger airlines and cargo planes, international air services and charter operations. Military aviation includes the Indian Air Force and the aviation arms of the Navy and Army. A commercial pilot basically flies aircraft carrying passenger or cargo or both, unlike an air force pilot who flies fighter aircraft defending the country from enemy attack. The job of commercial pilot is the most glamorous and exciting job in aviation.

It is highly rated and one of the most adventurous career which requires intensive training. This is a highly specialized job which requires knowledge of air navigation, interpretation of meteorological reports, operations of sophisticated electronic and mechanical controls. They are the captains in charge, who are responsible for the safety of the crew and passengers or cargo.

To become a commercial pilot one has to first possess a Student Pilot License (SPL). The basic minimum eligibility for a SPL is that candidate should have passed his/her Higher Secondary Examination with at least 50% marks in Physics and Mathematics and should have over 17 years of age. He should register himself at a flying club which is recognized by Directorate General of Civil Aviation (DGCA).

Besides these qualifications certain other things are also required for this registration like a medical certificate, security clearance and a bank guarantee. After successful completion of SPL examination one can apply for Private Pilot License (PPL) which is the second step to be a commercial pilot. The training includes sixty hours of flying which comprises dual flight, solo flights and cross-country flying. A Commercial Pilot License may be obtained only after a PPL has been acquired. CPL training includes 250 hours of flying. With the CPL, a pilot can take up any professional assignment.

Career Prospects

Commercial Pilots have wide varieties of employment opportunities in government as well as private domestic and international airlines, cargo planes, charter planes and private planes.. They can be employed in public sector airlines like Indian Airlines and Air India. They also have the option of joining private domestic (Air Deccan, IndiGo, SpiceJet) and international airlines (Kingfisher, Jet Airways, Sahara). Even large corporate houses with their own aircraft require the services of pilots. As the government plans to widen the air services network, the demand for this profession would continue to grow. Nowadays even the corporate are entering this sector, further making this profession an exciting career option. With globalization jobs as commercial pilots are available in airline companies outside India like USA, UK, Australia and some European countries.

Institute Offering

Some of the flying clubs imparting training in flying from where SPL, PPL, and CPL, training can be completed are: Flying Training Institute, Calcutta; Government aviation Training Institute, Bhubaneswar; Karnal Aviation Club, Karnal, Haryana; Government Flying Club, Lucknow; School of Aviation Science and Technology, New Delhi; Mumbai Flying Club, Mumbai; Rajasthan State Flying School, Jaipur; Asiatic International Aviation Academy, Indore; New Flight Services (India) Ltd, Indore; Acumen School of Pilot Training, New Delhi; Anugrah Allied Aviation Services (p) Ltd., New Delhi; International School of Aviation (ISA), New Delhi.

Remuneration

Commercial Pilots get attractive remuneration and incentives. The starting monthly salary of a commercial pilot ranges from Rs. 40,000 to Rs. 150,000 per month, depending on the airline and one's experience. The earning includes special benefits in form of contributory provident fund, gratuity and medical facilities. They are also entitled to a range of benefits and allowances in addition to housing, medical and out- station allowances, as well as free or concessional air passages for their immediate family and dependants. Pay scales of commercial pilots in the public sector organizations depend on the grade level of the positions. Earning is even higher in private international airlines.

AIR HOSTESS AS CAREER

The most important aspects of air travel are to make the journey of the passenger as much as comfortable and safe. It is here the air hostess play a great role. They are people who welcome passengers aboard an aircraft. They help them in their seating arrangements and arranging their hand baggage in the proper manner. They ensure the safety-belt arrangements and demonstrate the use of emergency equipment. They make the necessary announcements inside the flight.

Air hostesses and flight stewards have to be on duty throughout the duration of the flight looking after passengers in general and taking special care of air-sick travelers, sick children and babies; and also the elderly people or very young who are traveling alone. They serve meals to passengers and to the crew.

Many young girls as well as boys opt for the career because of the exciting experience of flying, visiting different places, interacting with different kinds of people on board and for the very attractive pay package. Liberalization of air policies has increased the private operation of air services and this has created immense job opportunities in this field.

For admissions into the Air Hostess Training Courses the eligibility criteria may vary from institute to institute. However most of the parameters remain more or less the same in most of the institutes. Minimum academic qualification should be 10+2 pass or graduate or diploma holder in hotel management. Age of the candidates should be between 17 to 25 years.

There are also certain physical criteria for selection into this course like minimum height of 157.5 cm, weight proportionate to the height, normal eyesight and fair to clear complexion etc. Besides, air hostess should be proficient in languages like English, Hindi and Foreign languages, eligible for Indian Passport, unmarried and have pleasing personality. Admission is made through different stages of test. After initial screening, the candidate has to qualify written test and subsequent group discussions and interviews.

Career Prospects

After successful completion of Air Hostess Training Courses, there are large scale career opportunities waiting for the Air Hostess. They can find ample job avenues in public and private sector airlines.

With privatization, foreign collaboration and open sky policies round the corner the future is quite bright for aspiring Air Hostess.

Most airline offices are looking to increasing their fleet and there is a demand for Air Hostesses. They can find employment in public career like Indian Airlines and Air India. Besides better job option are also available in privately owned domestic and international airlines namely Sahara, Singapore airlines, Jet Airways, Kingfisher, IndiGo, Spice Jet, Air Deccan etc. An Air Hostess has every chance to be promoted to the post of Senior Flight Attendant and then Head Attendant.

Career as an Air Hostess would last for about eight to ten years, after that she could move on to the ground duties including the job of a Ground

Hostess, Check Hostess, training of airhostess or work in the management level. The span of their flying career as symbols of hospitality may tend to be contractual, but experienced cabin crew are successfully absorbed in alternative careers in travel and tourism, hotels and in mass media, to name a few prominent options.

Institutes Offering

Some of the renowned Air Hostess training institutes in India include Free Bird Aviation & Management Services, Trivandrum; Frankfinn Management Consultants(New Delhi, Thirunananthapuram, Kochi, Mumbai); Pacific Airways New Delhi; SISI-CMTES Hospitality and Aviation School, Secunderabad; Air Hostess Academy, New Delhi; Livewel Academy, Mumbai; Aptima Air Hostess Academy, New Delhi; Flyers Inc, New Delhi; Appliq Airways Academy Pvt. Ltd., Agra; Global Institute Of Flight Care & Management, New Delhi; Indian Aviation Academy, Mumbai; Sristy's School of Air Hostess, Hyderabad.

Remuneration

Air Hostess as a career is highly remunerative and prestigious. Although salaries of an Air Hostess depend upon the airlines she is getting into, the starting salary may Rs 25,000 to Rs 40,000 per month in domestic airlines. Air Hostess working with international airlines gets more salary as compared to the one in domestic airlines. The salary of a senior airhostess is about Rs 60,000 to Rs 80,000 in public sector airlines. This is even more in private international airlines which may go up to Rs 2 - 3 lakhs per month in Indian currency.

CAREERS IN TRAVEL & TOURISM

Tour and Travel industry within the service sector is one of the largest foreign exchange earners in the Indian economy. It provides millions of employment opportunities directly to the people associated in this sector. Indirect employment opportunities are also available in many associated services.

The vast travel and tourism industry includes Government tourism departments, Immigration and customs services, travel agencies, airlines, tour operators, hotels etc and many associated service industries such as airline catering or laundry services, Guides, Interpreters, Tourism promotion and sales etc. India is a vast country with diverse cultures and traditions.

Our country offers a great attraction for those who crave to know about the splendor and magnificence of one of the oldest civilizations of the world and for its scenic beauty. With the increasing globalization and opening of our economy to the world, travel and tourism in India is getting a great impetus. Technology, coupled with the growth of tourism globally, has had a large impact on transforming these jobs significantly. This forecasts a bright future for all those who choose to make a career of travel and tourism.

There are graduate level, postgraduate level, diploma and certification courses available to pursue in travel and tourism industry. Some of these courses are Masters in Tourism administration (MTA), Post Graduate Diploma in Tourism Management (PGDTM), Post Graduate Diploma in Tourism (PGDT), and Diploma in Destination Management etc. For courses at undergraduate level one must have passed 10+2 examination.

A graduate in any discipline can pursue post-graduate degree in tourism and travel. For admissions into these course candidates need to clear the entrance test, group discussions and interviews which are conducted by the Directorate and Department of Tourism.

Candidate proficient in any foreign language is generally preferred. Duration of these courses vary from one year to two years depending on the kind of course one prefers. Besides there are many short-term Certificate courses which are of less than a year's duration. The minimum eligibility for Certificate courses is 10+2 pass.

Career Prospects

Career opportunities in travel and tourism exist both in the public and private sector. As far as public sector is concerned, there are opportunities in the tourism department of the centre and the states as Tourism Officers, information assistants and Tourist guides etc. Another good prospectus for qualified tourism professionals are in the private sector with travel agencies, tour operators, airlines, hotels, transport and cargo companies etc. After a few years of experience, they can also start their own business by handling all travel requirements of their clients.

Institutes Offering

There are several universities/collages/institutes in India that offer various courses in travel and tourism. Some names are given below. Sri Krishnadevaraya University, Anantapur, (A.P.); Dravidian University, Kuppam,(A.P); National Institute of Tourism and Hospitality Management, Hydrabad; Tezpur University, Assam; Institute of Tourism and Future Management, Chandigarh; Indian Institute of Tourism and Travel Management, New Delhi; Skyline Business School, New Delhi; Sri Venkateshwra College, University of Delhi, New Delhi; YWCA of Delhi Women's Training Institute, New Delhi.

Remuneration

Jobs in the travel and tourism industry offer good remuneration. Pay scale differs at different level depending upon qualification, experience. Approximate salaries at different posts are given below. Counter Clerk Rs. 1,500-2,000, Assistant Rs. 2,000-2,500, Junior Executive Rs. 3,000-3,500, Regional Manager Rs. 3,800 -4,500 and General Manager Rs. 5,000-6,000. Regional tour guides may charges from Rs400 and above for an eight hour day. They may earn between 30,000-40,000 Rs or more in the three to four months of the tourist peak season.

FUTURE FOR AVIATION AND HOSPITALITY INDUSTRY

Industry leaders from Aviation and Hospitality sector came together to phase out the doubt of safe career in the aviation and services sector among the aspirants during a round table conference organised by AHA Air Hostess Academy today.

Mr.Anil Bhandari, MD - JHMInterstate Hotels India Ltd, Mr.Kamal Hingorani, VP – SpiceJet, Mr.John Powell, Regional Manager - North & East India - Qantas Airways, Mr.Pran Dasan, Regional Manager - South Asia & Pakistan-Kuwait Airways addressed the students on this occasion. Ms.Sapna Gupta, Founder and Director, AHA Air Hostess Academy and Mr.Rajan Mehra, Business Head, Strategic Alliance Department, AHA was also present during the session.

During the discussion all speakers were unanimous on the point that current downturn is a temporary phenomenon and these Industries will eventually bounce back - and in a much bigger way! India's potential in both Aviation and Hospitality has not been met. Further in comparison to even its much smaller neighbours like Thailand and Singapore and Sri Lanka, India has a lesser frequency of flights and in the hospitality sector the total number of Hotel rooms is minuscule compared to its neighbours.

For instance Bangkok alone has more Hotel rooms than all combined in India. More than 500 aspirants from all branches of AHA Air Hostess Academy in Delhi NCR were part of this discussion. Talking on the future prospects in the aviation and hospitality industry and this initiative of bringing industry leaders on a single platform Ms.Sapna Gupta, Founder & Director - Air Hostess Academy said, "The current dark phase is most likely to be over by early next year and once again, we should see a robust growth in Aviation and Hospitality sector! We have ample opportunities to be explored and all concerned parties including Government of India are working extremely hard at the moment in this direction."

Lots of lucrative and interesting openings are there for hotel management graduates in various fields like:

- Hotel & Restaurant management
- Airline Catering and Cabin Services
- Club management
- Cruise Ship Hotel Management
- Hospital administration and catering
- Hotel and Tourism Associations

- Forest Lodges
- Guest Houses
- Institutional Management (supervising canteens in college, schools, in factories, company guest houses etc.)
- Catering departments of railways, banks, armed forces, shipping companies etc.
- Hotel and catering institutes
- Self employment

A hotel consists main departments such as Operations, Front office, House keeping, Food and Beverages, Accounting, Engineering/ Maintenance, Sales and Security. Each department has a number of positions that one can opt for.

ENGINEERING/ MAINTENANCE DEPARTMENT

Qualified engineers are appointed for the maintenance of the building and various machines involved in the premises. They are assisted by necessary staff in the electrical and mechanical departments. Mechanical Engineers, Electrical Engineer, Plumbers, carpenters etc are employed by this department.

Then there is the Security department which provides security to the guest and their belongings and employs security Officers/ guards for this purpose. Retires Army personnel are preferred by this department.

SOME OF THE BEST HOSPITALITY INSTITUTES IN INDIA

FHRAI INSTITUTE OF HOSPITALITY MANAGEMENT

The FHRAI Institute of Hospitality Management offers 4-year programmes in both International Hospitality Administration and International Culinary Administration, certified by Ecole hoteliere de Lausanne (EHL), Switzerland. It also facilitates students to get them a BA degree in tourism from the Indira Gandhi National Open University and offers a one-year diploma in hotel operations and a 3-year BSc in Hospitality and Catering Management from the Sikkim Manipal University.

All applicants must have passed their 10+2 or equivalent and must have a good knowledge of English. The fees for the International Programme (IP) in Hospitality Administration are Rs 1.8 lakh per year and the fees for the IP in Culinary Administration are Rs 2 lakh per year.

Hostel fees are Rs 50,000 per year and are optional. The 3-year BSc in Hospitality and Catering Management costs Rs 3.5 lakh in total. The FHRAI offers scholarships on the basis of need and merit. Most banks are open to providing student loans too.

Entrance to the FHRAI IHM is based on a written test, group discussion and personal interview, all of which are conducted on the same day. Students have been placed and interned in places like the Oberoi, the Hyatt Regency, the Marriot, the Trident Hilton, the ITC Sheraton, the Imperial Grand and many other places.

Address:
FHRAI Institute of Hospitality Management,
Plot No. 45, Knowledge Park III,
Greater Noida- 201 306
Phone: 0120 2323626-30
Fax: 0120 2323631
E-mail: director@fhraiinstitute.com, info@fhraiinstitute.com

INSTITUTE OF HOSPITALITY MANAGEMENT, GOA

Admissions to the IHM in Goa for the BSc in Hospitality & Hotel Administration are done on the basis of the All-India Joint Entrance Exam conducted in April. It is three-year course and costs a total of Rs 1.4 lakh.

Other courses include a one and a half year year Crafts Course in Food Production and Patisserie which costs Rs 27,000 and a 24-week Crafts Course in Food & Beverage Service costing Rs 13,000. Admissions to the these courses are based on merit.

The institute also has a 3-month short term course in Food Production and Patisserie (conducted thrice a year) for which no qualifications are required and there is no age limit. A working knowledge of English is necessary and the course costs Rs 12,500.

It also offers a number of 6-day/3-weekend career and certificate courses in skills ranging from house keeping to fruit carving. These course cost between Rs 1,700 and Rs 2,500. They also offer weekend courses in Thai cooking, basic bakery etc for less than a Rs 1,000.

Address:
Institute Of Hotel Management,
Catering Technology & Applied Nutrition,
Alto Porvorim, Bardez, Goa - 403 521.
Phone: + 91 832 2417252/ 2417379/ 2411142
Fax: + 91 832 2417209
E-mail: ihmgoa@sancharnet.in

ARMY INSTITUTE OF HOTEL MANAGEMENT AND CATERING TECHNOLOGY

The AIHMCT runs a 4-year Bachelor in Hotel Management course, charging Rs 36,500 per annum plus Rs 15,000 on admission. Admissions are based on the candidates' performance in the written admission test and personal interview in the ratio 60:40.

The AIHMCT is one of the best catering institutes in the country, however, admissions are reserved for the children of ex-servicemen.

Address:
Army Institute of Hotel Management & Catering Technology,
Nagareshwara Nagenahalli, Kothanur Post,
Bangalore 560 077.
Phone: 91 080 64543206/ 64543207
E-mail: principal@aihmctbangalore.com

MS RAMAIAH COLLEGE OF HOTEL MANAGEMENT

The MSRCHM is part of the Gokula Education Foundation. It is affiliated with the Bangalore University and has been offering a 5-year BHM course since 1995. Anyone who has completed their class XII is eligible. Annual fees are Rs 95,000 but scholarships are automatically granted based on the Class XII marks (Rs 20,000 pa for those scoring above 70 per cent and Rs 10,000 pa for those scoring above 60 per cent).

It also has short duration courses in basic communication, advance communication, lifestyle etiquette and lifestyle hosting. It also offers foundation courses in housekeeping, front office, food production, food and beverage service. It has 1-year apprentice programmes in various specialisations. Students have been placed with such companies as ITC, Taj, Royal Orchid etc.

Address:
MSRCHM, MSR Nagar, Msrit Post, Mathikere,
Bangalore 560067
Phone: 91 80 3601829
Fax: 91 80 3601815
E-mail: Principal@msrchm.edu

SAPTHAGIRI COLLEGE OF HOTEL MANAGEMENT

The Sapthagiri College of Hotel Management, established in 1989, offers a three-year BHM course as well as a three-year BSc in Hospitality. The fees are approximately Rs 35,000 per year. Admissions are based on the candidates' performance in the Class XII exams.

Address:
Saptagiri College of Hotel Management, Kavoor,
Mangalore 575015
Phone: (0824) - 481672
E-mail: Somayaji@saptagiri.com

COLLEGES OFFERING HOSPITALITY SECTOR COURSES

The National Council for Hotel Management and Catering Technology, which is an autonomous body under the Ministry of Tourism, Government of India, regulates academics for hospitality and hotel administration. The All India Council of Technical Education (AICTE) also approves the Hotel

Management Institutes. You can pursue different courses depending on your interest and qualification. Some of these courses are- Diploma in Bakery and Confectionery, Diploma in House Keeping, Diploma in Front Office, Diploma in Food and Beverage Service, Diploma in Food Production, Certificate Course in Hotel and Catering Management, Craftsmanship Course in Food and Beverage Service, Craftsmanship Course in Food Production, Post Graduate Diploma in Dietetics and Hospital Food Service, Post Graduate Diploma in Accommodation Operation and Management, M.Sc. in Hospitality Administration etc.

Depending on one's qualification one can find jobs in the hospitality sector as Management Trainee, Customer Relations Executive, Marketing/Sales Executive, Kitchen Management/ House Keeping Management, Catering Officer or Chefs in Hotels, Flight Kitchens, Cruises, Fast Food Chains and allied industry. You can also find jobs as cabin crew in National and International Airlines, as Executives in Tourism Development Corporations and Resort properties or as faculty in Hotel Management Institutes or Food Craft institutes. Moreover the option of being a self-employed entrepreneur also remains open.

INSTITUTES IN INDIA

HOTEL MANAGEMENT

Certificate/ Craft Courses

Certificate Course in Bakery & Confectionery
Certificate Course in Cookery
Certificate Course in Flight Catering Operation
Certificate Course in Food & Beverages
Certificate Course in Food Craft Management
Certificate Course in Food Production
Certificate Course in Food Production & Patisserie
Certificate Course in Front office
Certificate Course in Hospitality Facilities and Housekeeping Operations
Certificate Course in Hotel Catering Management
Certificate Course in Hotel Operations & Management
Certificate Course in House keeping
Certificate Course in Restaurant & Counter Service
Craft Course in Bakery & Confectionery (CCBC)
Craft Course in Food Production (CCFP)
Craft Course in House Keeping (CCHK)

PG Diploma Courses

Dual PG Diploma in Hotel & Business Administration
PG Diploma in Accommodation Operation

PG Diploma in Bakery Science & Management
PG Diploma in Food & Beverage Division Management
PG Diploma in Hospitality Marketing & Sales
PG Diploma in Hotel/ Hospitality Management (PGDHM)
PG Diploma in Room Division Management
PG Diploma in Tourism & Hoteliering Management
PG Diploma in Tourism and Hotel Management
PGP in Hospitality & Tourism

Diploma Courses

Advance Diploma in Culinary Arts & Patisserie Studies
Advance Diploma in Hospitality and Hotel Administration
Advanced Diploma in International Hotel & Business Administration (ADIHBA)
Diploma in Accommodation Operation
Diploma in Bakery and Confectionery (DBC)
Diploma in Catering Technology
Diploma in Cookery
Diploma in Cruise Galley Operations
Diploma in Culinary Arts & Patisserie
Diploma in Food & beverage Service
Diploma in Food Production (DFP)
Diploma in Front office/ Reception Operation
Diploma in Hospitality Management
Diploma in Hotel & Tourism Management
Diploma in Hotel Management
Diploma in Hotel Management & Catering Technology
Diploma in Hotel Management, Catering & Food Science
Diploma in Hotel Operation, Catering & Applied Nutrition
Diploma in International Tourism
Diploma in Office Management & House Keeping
Diploma in Room Division Management (DRDM)
Diploma in Travel Tourism & Airlines Management
Dual Diploma in International Hotel Management (DIHM)
Galley Assistant Familiarization Programme
Integrated Diploma in Hotel Management & Catering Technology
International Diploma in Hotel Management
Preparatory Course As Costa Cruise Chef

Bachelor Courses

B.A in International Hospitality Management
Bachelors Degree in Catering Technology & Culinary Arts
Bachelor's Degree in Hotel Management & Catering Technology (BHMCT)

Bachelor of Hotel & Tourism Management
Bachelor of Hotel Management (BHM)
BSc in Catering Technology & Hotel Management
BSc Nutrition, Food Service Management, Dietetics

Master Courses

Master of Hotel & Tourism Management
Master of Hospitality Management (MHM)
MBA in Hospitality & Tourism

HOTEL MANAGEMENT COURSES

The boom in the tourism industry has resulted in the immense growth of hotel industry in India. The hotel industry promises a bright future for anyone who wishes to take up a career in this segment. The students opting for hotel management career courses must have an affinity towards socializing and understanding the needs of the people.

As hotels fall under the service industry, the motive of hotel management courses in India is to prepare the students to face the challenges of this competitive world. As far as tourism industry in India is concerned, it is attracting tourists from across the world and this definitely calls for quality hospitality.

Hotel management is one of the most interesting career options in the contemporary job market. Career training from a recognized and reputed hotel management institute is just an icing on the cake. In India there are many hotel management institutes and colleges which provide hospitality or hotel management courses. These hotel management courses make one aware of the operating-sections of the hotel industry like front office, general operations, sales and marketing, food and beverage, service keeping and catering.

3

Career in General Managers in Hotel Industry

INTRODUCTION

General manager is a descriptive term for certain executives in a business operation. It is also a formal title held by some business executives, most commonly in the hospitality industry.

GENERIC USAGE

A manager may be responsible for one functional area, but the general manager is responsible for all areas. Sometimes, most commonly, the term *general manager* refers to any executive who has overall responsibility for managing both the revenue and cost elements of a company's income statement.

This is often referred to as profit and loss responsibility. This means that a general manager usually oversees most or all of the firm's marketing and sales functions as well as the day-to-day operations of the business. Frequently, the general manager is responsible for effective planning, delegating, coordinating, staffing, organizing, and decision making to attain desirable profit making results for an organization.

In many cases, the general manager of a business is given a different formal title or titles. Most corporate managers holding the titles of chief executive officer (CEO) or president, for example, are the general managers of their respective businesses. More rarely, the chief financial officer (CFO), chief operating officer (COO), or chief marketing officer (CMO) will act as the general manager of the business. Depending on the company, individuals with the title managing director, regional vice president, country manager, product manager, branch manager, or segment manager may also have general management responsibilities.

In consumer products companies, general managers are often given the title brand manager or category manager. In professional services firms, the general manager may hold titles such as managing partner, senior partner, or managing director. In non-profit enterprises, the general manager is often given the title executive director.

INDUSTRY-SPECIFIC USAGES

Hotels

In hotels, the General Manager is the executive manager responsible for the overall operation of a hotel establishment. The General Manager holds ultimate authority over the hotel operation and usually reports directly to a corporate office or hotel owner. Common duties of a General Manager include hiring and management of a management team, overall management of hotel staff, budgeting and financial management, creating and enforcing business objectives and goals, managing projects and renovations, management of emergencies and other major issues involving guests, employees, or the facility, public relations with the media, local governments, and other businesses, and many additional duties.

The extent of duties of a hotel General Manager vary significantly depending on the size of the hotel and company; for example, General Managers of smaller hotels may have additional duties such as accounting, human resources, payroll, purchasing, and other duties that would usually be handled by other managers or departments in a larger hotel.

Sports Teams

In most professional sports, the general manager is a team executive responsible for acquiring the rights to player personnel, negotiating their contracts, and reassigning or dismissing players no longer desired on the team. The general manager may also have responsibility for hiring the head coach of the team.

For many years in U.S. professional sports, coaches often served as general managers for their teams as well, deciding which players would be kept on the team and which ones dismissed, and even negotiating the terms of their contracts in cooperation with the ownership of the team. In fact, many sports teams in the early years of U.S. professional sports were coached by the owner of the team, so in some cases the same individual served as owner, general manager and head coach.

As the amount of money involved in professional sports increased, many prominent players began to hire agents to negotiate contracts on their behalf. The intensified contract negotiations that resulted, as well as the overall increased need for professional business management, drove many sports teams to separate the positions of coach and general manager. Some coaches, for example Andy Reid, Mike Holmgren and Mike Shanahan however, still insist on being allowed to fill both positions as a condition of employment.

In some sports leagues salary caps have been adopted to maintain a competitive balance and in these leagues it is one of the functions of the general manager to ensure all player contracts are in accordance with these caps, as well as consistent with the desires of the ownership and its ability to pay.

General managers are usually responsible for the selection of players in player drafts and work with the coaching staff and scouts to build a strong team. In sports with developmental or minor leagues, the general manager is usually the team executive with the overall responsibility for "sending down" and "calling up" players to and from these leagues, although the head coach may also have significant input into these decisions.

Some of the most successful sports general managers have been former players and coaches, while others have backgrounds in ownership and business management.

The term is not commonly used in Europe, especially in soccer, where the position of manager or coach is used instead to refer to the managing/ coaching position. The position of director of football might be the most similar position on many European football clubs.

A CONCEPTUAL FRAMEWORK OF THE HOTEL GENERAL MANAGER'S JOB

The purpose of this chapter is to offer a comprehensive review of the prominent research themes relating to hotel general managers. The review aims to consolidate work in the area, drawing primarily from hospitality literature. The rationale for undertaking this task lies in three directions. First, the notion of a 'hotel general manager' carries a number of preconceived perceptions surrounding the nature of the profession and the people who undertake it.

Typical perceptions of general managers include; people who work long hours, have a high degree of mobility, are highly sociable, and are committed to their jobs and to the hotel industry. Whether these popular notions are myths or realities can be addressed by research exploring the characteristics of this profession.

Given that within the hospitality industry a hotel general manager is viewed as a target job, and as general managers arguably hold the key executive position in the hotel industry, it is important to ascertain what is known about the people and the occupation. Second, there have been a number of authors who have reviewed and commented upon the current state of hospitality research and have criticised hospitality research for its lack of theoretical foundation. Although it is beyond the scope of this chapter to comment on these authors' views, this review aims to explore to what extent research concerning general managers draws from a range of theoretical backgrounds.

The review demonstrates that in the area of hotel general managers, some of the research themes draw upon established theoretical foundations. For example, the established managerial theory, career theory, and personality psychology. The third justification for the review is that any brief investigation into the literature exploring hotel general managers reveals a wealth of information exploring a diversity of research themes and issues. Building on the work of Guerrier and Lockwood, who reviewed research regarding managers in hospitality, this chapter offers an updated attempt at classifying and summarising the current themes. The aim here is to show the current state of research regarding hotel general managers.

Although they should not be regarded as mutually exclusive, six main categories for discussion are identified, these are; issues relating to managerial work, hotel managers' careers, the personality characteristics of hotel managers, functional responsibility, skills and competencies, women hotel managers, and emerging themes. The issues concerning managerial work and hotel managers' careers draws from wider hospitality literature, and is not confined solely to that concerning general managers. Taking a developmental approach, each of the categories is explored in turn. Finally, tentative suggestions for future research are made.

It is important to note at this stage that although the paper offers a comprehensive review, the huge volume of literature available inevitably means there will be some omissions. Therefore, this review consolidates only the themes of greatest prominence to date.

MANAGERIAL EFFECTIVENESS

Drawing from theoretical foundations of managerial research in addition to the studies that examine managerial effectiveness as part of wider research and Stone, managerial effectiveness and what makes a successful manager has also been a widely studied area of research in its own right. At a macrolevel much of the research offers a review of work and contributes also to new studies, with the dominant approach exploring leadership styles as part of managerial effectiveness. Worsfold examined the relationship between leadership and managerial effectiveness in the hospitality industry. The author reviewed existing leadership research on hotel managers, followed by a description of leadership styles of effective hotel managers from a major hotel company.

Achorn cited the research by the Sheraton hotel group who interviewed 3500 managers in order to identify specific behaviours and attributes that mark the difference between success and failure in the hotel manager's job. The results indicated that managers with good communication skills, a good education, and who are prepared to be adaptable and keep pace with change are most likely to be successful.

Ley assessed the contribution of time spent in leadership roles or time spent in entrepreneurial roles as a means of effectiveness of hotel general managers. In this research on hotel managers from seven hotels with 140 bedrooms each in the USA, Ley concluded that when the leadership and entrepreneurial activities of the managers are examined, it appears that highly effective managers spend less time on leadership and more time on entrepreneurial roles than their less successful colleagues.

Furthermore, the successful managers spent more time *per se* on the job than less successful managers. Fawcett defined three viewpoints on how to make more of managers. The views are those of the employer, the graduate and the educationalist. The author argued that some consensus needs to be developed which examines the convergent and divergent needs of these three groups in order to begin to determine how to 'make more' of managers. Mullins and Davies asked the question what makes for an effective hotel manager? The authors reviewed recent research, and conclude that although there are a variety of factors which make for effective hotel management, the central requirement is competence at dealing with people.

Moving away from a focus on leadership, an alternative viewpoint drawing from psychological theory is introduced. Peacock examines the issue of what makes a successful hospitality manager from the perspective of managers' subjective measures of success. The survey sampled 200 hospitality managers who were asked how they determine whether they have done a good job. From the responses, seven classifications were devised.

The largest category comprised those managers who defined success in financial terms, followed by those who defined success in terms of the customers. The third largest group defined success in operational terms, followed by internal factors, staff terms, and the smallest group took their performance measure from their superiors. In addition, the type of establishment effects the manager's perception of success, and with regard to the type of manager, gender differences are also found in the perception of success. Peacock suggested that personal definitions of success could also effect career patterns.

He stated that:

- The manager who concentrates primarily on pleasing the boss, rather than self or the customer, is more likely to move up the corporate ladder. The gender differences in success perspectives could help to explain the extremely low proportion of senior female hospitality manager..

The use of psychology as an aid for hotel managers' decision making was examined by Gore. The survey reveals that hotel managers' decision making could be made more effective from an adoption of the training methods of Russo and Shoemaker.

A useful training programme could be devised in this way by making managers more aware of the common decision traps, how people fail to learn from experience, improving feedback on decisions made, and by facilitating ways of deciding. Managerial effectiveness would benefit from improved decision making. A behavioural approach is provided by Eder and Umbreit, who identified three dimensions of managerial effectiveness. These are: short-term profit indicators, tangible results such as sales growth and budget compliance, and intangible factors such as employee morale, guest complaints and market share changes. The study highlighted the problems of linking hotel manager behaviour to results, and argues that intangibles appear to be the strongest links to key managerial behaviours, for example, changes in employee turnover rates may suggest a way to analyse how well the manager is motivating and communicating with employees.

Curiously, given the predominance of research into empowerment, none of the studies refer to empowerment as a tool of management effectiveness. The focus is on leadership styles and psychological measures. The boundaries of the different research fields do not overlap.

Finally, related to managerial effectiveness, measurement techniques for evaluating managerial effectiveness are constantly under review and are being tried in the hospitality industry. Umbreit argued for the development of a valid performance criteria as a key to effective management of human resources.

He argued that the behaviourally anchored scale, which is a scaling format for evaluating job performance, fits the needs of the hospitality industry. This technique focuses on actual behaviours not personality traits. The subjective judgement of BARS is noted by Ilgen and Feldman, and Bernardin and Beatty urge the inclusion of objective data. It appears that a mixture of both objective and subjective data would be the best way of assessing managerial effectiveness in the hospitality industry. As a test, Umbreit and Eder attempt to link hotel manager behaviour with outcome measures of effectiveness.

Miscellaneous Research

At the micro level, there are a number of other miscellaneous issues that have been examined with regard to managerial work in the hospitality industry. Although they are not extensive subjects. For example, Worsfold examined management selection in the hospitality industry. He argued for more care to be taken in management selection if companies are to cut large costs associated with manager wastage, and looks at ways of improving management selection. Ross examined work attitudes and management values in the hospitality industry.

Here an attempt is made to assess the values and attitudes of recent hospitality graduates that influence them towards work in the hospitality industry in Australia. Management needs, such as achievement, autonomy, affiliation and dominance, are regarded as important by many of the respondents. The subject of manager's work motivation has been addressed by a number of authors. Chitris in an exploratory study of senior department heads asked who are the work motivated managers in the hotel industry? The study concluded that the manager's work motivation is affected by education level, age, and length of employment with current firm. Characteristics unrelated to work motivation are gender, marital status and length of time in current position. Charles and Marshall examined the motivational preferences of hotel workers in the Caribbean, with the aim of advising hotel managers of the best way in which they can motivate their staff.

The study concluded that Caribbean hotel workers may have different motivational preferences from others in developed countries, and hotel managers should consider the individual differences among their employees when proposing appropriate motivational strategies for them. What these miscellaneous themes show is applied research that could improve industry selection, motivation and successful operational outcomes.

To conclude, research which explores issues relating to managerial research in the studies shows that within the hospitality literature there exists a body of work relating to hotel managers that draws from established theoretical foundations of managerial theory and psychology. The research aims to contribute to a deeper understanding of the nature of the occupation in terms of work roles, effectiveness, leadership styles and empowerment issues. The research is both applied and theoretical. Clearly despite the variety there is room for expansion of alternative aspects of management theory into hospitality research.

THE CAREERS OF HOTEL MANAGERS

The second category within the hospitality literature for exploration focuses on the careers of hotel managers and draws upon the theoretical foundations of career theory. At the macrolevel there are a number of studies that have specifically examined hotel general managers' careers. The first, by Guerrier, examined hotel managers careers and their impact on the cultures of hotel organisations in Britain. A number of characteristics of the hotel industry were identified, for example the insularity of hotel managers who tend to be trained separately from managers in other industries, and the emphasis of mobility within hotel managers' careers, which helps to define the character of the industry.

The paper explored ways of understanding careers; the careers of hotel managers; the hotel industry; and finally, the implications of the traditional approach to career development. Although largely descriptive, the paper provides a useful explanation of hotel managers' careers. As with the nature of managerial work, again the idea that hospitality management is different from general management practices is raised.

Three main stages in a hotel manager's career are identified by Guerrier. First is the training stage, which usually begins with specific hotel and catering education. Second is the assistant manager stage, where the employee is usually given some kind of functional responsibility, the two main functions identified as front of house and food and beverage. The final stage is the general manager stage, characterised by increased mobility as managers move through an increasing size of hotel, which increases pay and prestige. Guerrier argued that the careers of hotel managers are best understood from an occupational perspective rather than an organisational perspective, as managers become moulded to an occupation rather than an organisation.

Finally, the differences between the traditional hotel manager and the modern hotel manager were identified. This study cited the characteristics of the traditional career path of managers as a barrier to the development of female general mangers. Similarly Baum through a wider study of the hotel industry in Ireland gives an account of the career paths of Irish hotel managers, and examined the needs for training and human resource development in the Irish hotel industry.

Building on the work of Guerrier and continuing the theme of career patterns and mobility, a study of the career paths of hotel managers in the UK was provided by Ladkin and Riley. Here the use of age distributions is tested and the notion of career logics is introduced for the first time as a method of interpretation of a career sequence. Issues of job mobility, length of time to general manager, and the salience of specific jobs to career development are explored. Food and beverage was found to be the most salient function in career development.

In updated research the focus moves to concentrate on the number of job moves in terms of whether they are internal or external to the company, and whether the individual or the company initiated the moves. In this research a whole range of variables are tested to see how they influence the shape of a career. An American perspective of the same topic was provided by Nebel *et al.*, who explored hotel general manager career paths in the USA.

A number of key findings are addressed, the most notable being that most general managers have a narrow career path before their first general manager job. A reported 87.5% spent their time in only one department.

Nearly 80% had held assistant manager positions and two major hotel operational departments, 'food and beverage' and 'rooms' accounted for three-quarters of general managers' career paths. It was reported that this trend is increasing, as the figures were higher for younger managers. These studies show that there is still an importance of traditional craft training in hotel management.

The manpower and labour market components of careers are also addressed. A study of career paths of hotel general managers has been explored from a manpower planning perspective by Riley and Turam. In this study of 115 UK hotel managers, the authors identified the length of time taken to reach general manager status and the stages of development involved in progressing to reach this target job. The study produces a number of interesting findings with regard to functions, mobility, and locus of career control. These findings are supported by Guerrier and Lockwood, who distinguish between company core and unit core staff in the hotel industry in terms of positioning in the labour market.

Related to the manpower planning approach is the labour market perspective, which has been explored by Ladkin and Riley. Here there is an examination of the career paths of hotel managers in relation to the bureaucratic model, which dominates career theory. The argument put forward is that the opportunity structure of the industry encourages a form of career management that involves, in addition to jobs and organisations, the labour market as an entity in its own right. The study explored mobility, skills, knowledge and personal planning strategies in relation to career advancement. With respect to career advancement and continuing with the labour market theme, two types of contrasting career paths for hotel managers have been outlined by Beck. This study compared the corporate-paved route and the self-planned route to industry management.

The paper postulates that for graduates who do not join planned traditional corporate training schemes, an alternative route is available to them whereby the graduate works his/her way up through the ranks of the industry. The object concluded by presenting opinions from an industry with regard to the best way for an ambitious graduate to develop his/her own route to management. Swanljung identified five broadly defined career routes of hotel executives: the operations route, the accounting and finance route, the marketing route, the food and beverage route, and the non-hospitality route. Taking a psychological stance, the perceptions of hotel managers' careers from the perspective of supervisory employees are examine by Williams and Hunter.

This chapter examined the transition from being a supervisor to a hotel manager, and identifies the hesitancy and difficulty in making such a career shift. What this collection of papers represents is research that examines career paths and the variables that influence the shape and form of a hotel managers' career. The most recent research draws heavily from career theory, and has a practical application in so far as it sends messages to the industry concerning labour market behaviour, established career routes and skill development.

The subject of labour markets in the tourism and hospitality industry is explored in career research. Two major lines of enquiry are identified. The first labour market issue that has been examined is labour market trends in the tourism and hospitality industry. For example, Boella described a background of the hospitality industry's workforce, and examines changes in the hospitality industry and the industry workforce.

Hornsey and Dann examined the nature of organisations in the hotel and catering industry, and classify the nature of jobs in the hotel and catering industry. Issues of conditions of employment, hours of work and pay are also discussed. Baum reviewed a range of books that focuses on human resource issues, and examines tourism labour markets. Wood researched the British and international experience of hospitality industry labour trends, and Lucas examined recent trends in hospitality employment, and looks at the possible developments in the 1990s. The American hotel and catering labour market trends are reviewed by Tanke. One of the emergent key findings in these reviews of labour market trends is a shortage of labour. This has direct implications for the industry.

Addressing this labour shortage, an examination into core and peripheral employees in the hotel industry was undertaken by Guerrier and Lockwood. This flexible working approach attempted to alleviate problems of recruitment and retention of staff in hotel operations, in addition to responding to pressures for delivering a high quality service, therefore improving the performance of employees. A model of core and peripheral staff within hotels was proposed. Human resource needs and priorities for the hospitality and tourism industry were outlined by Teare and Brotherton and the job opportunities offered to hotel and catering graduates were explored by Jameson and Hargreaves. Problems of seasonality for workers in the tourism labour market have been examined by Ball.

The second labour market issue looks at the subject of labour turnover. Bonn and Forbringer examined the issue of reducing turnover in the hospitality industry, and present an overview of recruitment, selection and retention. Riley presented the relationship between recruitment, labour turnover and occupational rigidity in the hospitality industry. Hornsey and Dann examined labour turnover in the hotel and catering industry, and Johnson focused on labour turnover specifically in hotels.

The labour retention strategies of UK hotel managers are illustrated by Riley. Finally, in a review of labour turnover, Riley identified six themes evident from the literature. These are; the extent of labour turnover, attributed causes, solving the labour problems, labour turnover and labour economics, images and perceptions, and informed opinions. Riley argued for a change in the paradigm from these approaches to one that addresses the relationship between commitment, job satisfaction, and the intention to leave. The idea that the high rates of turnover is a damaging feature to the industry is questioned by Riley, who argues that labour mobility plays an important role is the development of skills.

In addition to the dominant research themes of career theory and labour markets, a number of specific career issues drawing from career theory have received attention in the hospitality literature. The importance of career planning in the hospitality industry was addressed by Antil. The author stated that career planning is a continual process, and stresses the importance of not leaving career opportunities to occur by chance. The main thrust of the argument is the importance of individuals and organisations making the right match. The means of achieving this match is said to be through career planning. Although not specific to hotel managers, Ross examined management values, work preference ideals and personality needs as predictors of hospitality industry career anchors. Using Schein's conceptualisation of career anchors, these are considered as explanatory variables among Australian hospitality industry employees. Ross argued that despite the rapidly growing importance of the hospitality industry in terms of economic benefits, little is known about personality and socio-demographic variables of hospitality employees. Murphy and Ross have found that certain groups of people appear to develop much more positive attitudes to the tourism industry in any tourism-related community.

In this study, 274 employees within the hospitality industry in Cairns, Australia were sampled to test their management values, work preference ideals and personality needs in relation to career anchors. Using a range of measurements to define career anchors, the career anchors of job satisfaction, job security and continuing employment were identified as the most predominant anchors.

The major career anchors suggest that many employees' fundamental motivation is associated with feelings of work satisfaction within an employment environment offering both stability and continuity. The implications for hospitality industry management and human resource managers are discussed. Authors drawing from Schein represent key ways the work of a theorist has been applied to the hotel management literature. Similar to Mintzberg, Schein has been adapted by researchers in an attempt to explain personal variables in career paths.

Career development issues have also been covered in the literature concerning hotel managers. Tanke offered a definition of career development, and examined the role and the intricacies of career development programmes for hospitality management. The career development of hotel managers has been researched by a number of authors.

For example, Ruddy in a study of 31 hotel managers in Hong Kong addressed the issue of what general managers believe are the key influences in helping them to become successful. The conclusions drawn from this study are that the managers place qualities related to their behaviour and personal characteristics highest on their list of career influences. The less important factors were external to the managers and consisted of family support, mentor relationships and education. A further study as part of on-going research to focus on the patterns of hotel management development in South East Asia, focused on the factors that have influenced the success of a sample of hotel general managers.

The respondents place qualities related to their personal characteristics and behaviour highest on their list of career influences. The respondents gave an importance to human relations and communication skills when asked what others should do to become successful hotel managers. The author argued that the future direction of research in this area should be to determine what it takes to become a 'high flyer' in the hotel industry.

Dodrill and Riley examined hotel worker's orientation to work, to see if a unique orientation to work can be identified. Five attitudes were measured; ambitions, the desire for scope in the job, mobility, security and autonomy. No distinctive attitudes towards work by hotel workers were found. Damonte and Vaden undertook a study to examine the nature of career decisions in the hospitality industry by looking at the experiences affecting career decisions, characteristics important in a career, and sources of career satisfaction.

The career plateau receives specific attention in research by Reed and Evans. This study urges the hospitality industry to recognise when career plateau's exist, and examines ways in which the industry can respond to the problem of people who can no longer be promoted. The 'career plateau' is a concept taken directly from career theory.

A comprehensive review of the organisational commitment literature as applied to the hospitality industry has been provided by Paxon. The research states that few studies of organisational commitment relate to the hospitality industry in contrast to the number of studies that exist in organisational behaviour and organisational psychology literature.

CAREER PROBLEMS

A further specific topic of investigation with regard to the careers of hotel managers is the problems associated with the job, and the effects that these problems have on hotel managers. In a study by Larmour the problems faced by managers in the hotel and catering industry were examined. The study revealed that managers in the hotel and catering industry rate their problems as different from managers in other comparable businesses. Within this, the problems are different for managers of different sectors within the hotel and catering industry. Again we see the recurrent theme of hotel management being perceived as different from general management.

Specific attention is given to job stress. Managerial job stress in the hospitality industry is examined in detail by Brymer *et al.*. This study stated that despite the large range of research into managerial job stress, little research has been undertaken with a specific focus on the hospitality industry. This study aimed to rectify this situation, and examine three types of stress on middle and upper level managers in the hotel industry in the USA. The results of the study indicate that perceived job stressors are positively related to overall strain, and the use of negative coping mechanisms have a positive relationship with overall strain.

The study concluded that perceived job stressors were related to self-reported psychological strain and behavioural strain. The authors call for stress management programmes and employee assistance programmes to attempt to reduce stress at work, in view of the financial cost to organisations in employee sickness and layoffs. Sarabakhsh *et al.* examined the personal cost of hospitality management by investigating how hospitality manager's working conditions affect their overall quality of life. The study consists of 42 managers in food service operations, 41 hotel general managers and 68 blue cross/blue shield employees. The research reveals that the three measures of life stress; career interference with social life and career interference with a happy marriage all scored significantly higher for hospitality groups. The self-esteem and anxiety ratings are not significantly different amongst the three groups. The disturbing conclusion from this study reports that the situation was much worse for hotel managers, who repeatedly scored the highest in all three stress factors.

The author argues for more emphasis on teaching staff how to delegate and to give managers assistance by not short-staffing organisations in an attempt to alleviate these problems. Brymer and Pavesic examined job satisfaction in an attempt to determine why so many young managers are leaving the hospitality industry. The study states that the concept of the traditional career path has become inconsistent with the living styles of junior executives. The young managers state that although they like the people aspect of the job and the challenge that the career presents, they are not happy with the long hours. The respondents can point to no single motivator for leaving the industry, and are more likely to be unhappy with the job rather than the career.

The authors concluded that more help is needed in the critical time three to four years after graduation if the substantial loss of young talent is to be curbed. In a similar study, Reichel and Pizam compared the job satisfaction, lifestyle and demographics of hospitality workers in the USA against employees in four other industry groupings. In all three areas the hospitality workers were different from the other groups. The findings revealed that the employees were less satisfied with their jobs than the other workers.

Although not concerned directly with hotel managers, a number of related specific functions are examined in relation to job stress and manager's burnout. For example, Krone *et al.* examined 'manager burnout' for a sample of food service managers. Using the Maslash burnout inventory of the 532 respondents, the results showed that 20±25% of the managers fell into the high burnout range, over 25% showed high levels of emotional exhaustion, and 33% demonstrated levels of emotional exhaustion in the middle range. The factors cited for this burnout were role overload, role ambiguity, and role conflict.

Whitney examined the attention styles and stress factors of hotel sales and marketing managers. A range of attention styles are presented and the study shows that effective performance depends upon a good match between situational demands and attention styles, which reduces stress and overload.

What these studies have in common is an attempt to understand the problems of hotel management as an occupation, and how these problems can be alleviated. This has obvious implications for industry.

MENTORING

As an attempt to alleviate job stress and career problems, a subject that has received increasing attention in the management literature relating to organisations is mentoring. Research that specifically focused on the role of mentoring in the careers of hotel managers is evident from Roche and Schmidt. In a survey of 200 general managers, Rutherford and Wiegenstein examined findings with regard to mentoring in the hotel industry.

A number of variables were examined, for example, the role of a mentor in enhancing career success and satisfaction, and aiding career moves. The authors conclude that although the presence or absence of a mentor cannot be proved to distinguish managers on the basis of job satisfaction, career success or managerial effectiveness, mentoring has a positive influence on the careers of hotel general managers, specifically with regard to career moves and confidence building. Williams and Hunter in their study of supervisory hotel employee perceptions of management careers identified an informal nature of career mentoring for supervisors.

Eighty per cent of the supervisors claimed that they could rely on the advice of a person higher in the organisation with regard to advice on career opportunities, although more than three-fifths of them claimed they were not in receipt of a formal mentoring system devised by the organisation. Mentoring represents one way in which the industry could reduce labour turnover and alleviate some of the difficulties faced by those in the hospitality professions.

To summarise, the literature relating to the careers of hotel managers focuses on a range of issues drawing from career theory, for example, career planning, career development, job satisfaction and career anchors. The issue of labour turnover and job mobility is a recurrent theme that shows the importance of mobility for the industry and in shaping career paths.

It is perhaps in this regard that the hotel manager's literature makes the most of established theory as a means to understand the ways in which managers develop their careers, and the structures and characteristics of the industry that facilitate career development. However, like the hospitality research that comes from management theory and Mintzberg, there is a dominance of only one key theorist, in this case Schein. There is clearly room for expansion.

In an attempt to address this, one of the most comprehensive attempts to integrate career theory, hospitality and tourism is provided by Riley and Ladkin, who developed a basic analytical framework for integrating career theory and tourism.

Following an overview of the main areas of research on careers, a framework is devised for analysing careers in tourism using a structural±technical perspective. There are three structural±technical determinants of a career; organisation size and structure, technological specificity, and dispersion of knowledge. In addition, career behaviour affects the career path, which sits within the structural variables. Sequence analysis is suggested as a way to research careers paths, and the variable of the labour market is introduced.

MANAGERIAL WORK

The first prominent research theme evident in the literature concerning hotel managers for exploration is that of managerial work. Three divisions are evident; the nature of managerial work *per se*, empowerment, and managerial effectiveness. In addition, a number of miscellaneous managerial studies are identified.

The Nature of Managerial Work

There is a collection of literature concerning hotel management that exists within the theoretical body of knowledge relating to managerial work. It is beyond the scope of this chapter to examine management literature, and for a concise summary the reader is directed towards Hales. What is important in this context is to show how the hospitality management literature draws upon the theoretical concepts appropriate to management research.

On a broad scale an appropriate starting point is with Guerrier and Lockwood, who provided a detailed review of the current research with regard to managers in hospitality. Their paper begins with a review of the last 30 years of management literature, and explains that there have been few studies that focus on the problems of management and organisation in the hospitality industry. The authors reviewed themes in management research, and postulated that the research which has been carried out into hospitality management falls within four main areas.

1. The first, what do hospitality managers do? cites studies by:
   - Nailon,
   - Ley,
   - Ferguson and Berger,
   - Arnaldo
   - Shortt.
2. Second, who hospitality managers are; cites studies by:
   - Melrose-Wood-man,,
   - The HCITB, and
   - The HCIMA.
3. Third, managers' careers in hospitality cites large-scale studies by:
   - Nicholson and West

- Small-scale studies of Levinson,
- Gunz,
- Riley and Turam, and
- Guerrier.

4. Finally identifying managerial competencies, includes studies by:
   - The HCIMA,
   - Johnson,
   - Jones and
   - Gamble and Messenger.

The authors concluded that a recurrent theme in the hospitality management literature is the consistent focus on the traditional style of operations in the hospitality industry. This style is biased towards high levels of visible managerial activity, with a focus on craft skills and operations. The authors have reviewed the limitations for this style, and note that there does appear to be a slow move towards a business orientation.

This early review by Guerrier and Lock-wood exemplifies the focus on craft operations, and pre-empts the managerial skills versus technical skills debate. The move towards a business orientation is defined here. Similarly, Dann provided a summary of the nature of managerial work in the hospitality industry along with a review of the general body of knowledge of managerial work, and attempted to link the two together.

The author shows that studies of managerial work in the hospitality industry have both replicated and developed the general framework of managerial studies. This object provided detail on a number of studies of managerial work in the hospitality industry that sit comfortably with the main body of research in the field.

The following studies are cited:

- Nailon,
- Ley,
- Arnaldo
- Ferguson and Berger,
- Koureas,
- Hales and Nightingale and
- Hales.

Clearly, these reviews by Guerrier and Lockwood and Dann show that there are a number of authors who have attempted to draw from management theory in hospitality research. These reviews show that predominately the research into the nature of managerial work is exploratory, using selective theoretical concepts to outline working practices.

Moving on from comprehensive reviews, managerial concepts and theories are applied to general managers at the microlevel by a number of authors. The dominant theorist drawn upon from management literature is Mintzberg. Nailon examined the nature of managerial work in terms of time and contact patterns, Arnaldo and Ferguson and Berger link the work of Mintzberg with the hospitality industry, and Hales and Nightingale and Hales provided a methodology which places the conduct of managerial work within the context of the total managerial processes. Dann proposed a model of research directions for managerial work in the hospitality industry, which divides the nature of managerial work into three distinct phases; inputs and demands, conduct and choices and ends.

The study argues for a better understanding of the processes that influence the nature of managerial work. These studies focus primarily on the process of management, and use management theory as a template. The work of Mintzberg is used again by two authors in the specific context of hotel managers.

Kim explored hotel managers in Korea using a method of analysis of hotel managers and examined the allocation of time to the ten Mintzberg managerial roles. Shortt mapped the work activities of hotel managers in Northern Ireland on to the set of ten managerial roles suggested by Mintzberg, and attempted to build upon Mintzberg's work by using his framework to explore the work of these hotel managers in Northern Ireland. Again, work activities are explored using a well-developed managerial theory.

Again drawing upon Mintzberg, Nebel attempted to better understand the nature of the general manager's job by developing a conceptual framework for the job. The author argued that we can better understand the job of a hotel manager by analysing the influences that shape it. This represents a changing emphasis away from a focus on process to explain a manager's job to exploring external factors that may be influential. By reviewing the hotel management literature and studying in depth ten successful general managers, Nebel identified two major contextual elements that influence the job, these are job demands and relationship issues.

These two elements differ just as to the time-frame that they are working in, either short, intermediate or long term. These give rise to three separate job functions for the general manager, which the author terms: operational controller, organisational developer and business maintainer.

The author then relates these three roles to the ten managerial work roles to explore managerial effectiveness and concludes that in order to be successful in the three roles the general managers must be effective in at least seven of the ten Mintzberg roles. This study is more complex and analytical than research, as it includes the variables of external factors, a time-frame and a measure of success.

Within the hospitality literature, the studies that draw upon the work of Mintzberg perhaps demonstrate the body of research which is most rooted in established theory. Moving away from theoretical issues, at the microlevel a call for managerial research to be more directly applicable to actual work activities was put forward by authors such as Dann, who examined strategy and managerial work in hotels.

His paper argued that although much has been written about specific managerial processes in the hospitality industry, it has been undertaken without an understanding of how these issues actually relate to the work that managers engage in. This call for applied research represents a shift in focus to address needs specifically for the industry.

Dann argued that given the lengthy socialisation process involved in becoming a hotel manager, it is not surprising that managers behave in a similar way despite having large areas of discretion in their work. He argued that it is the managerial strategies present in companies that shape the differing roles for general managers. Four roles are identified; entrepreneur, cost controller, marketer and finally service and quality assurance. Each of the operational strategies directs managers into certain roles, which are shaped through the process of socialisation. Here the additional external variable of corporate culture is influenced by Dann.

Attempts to further integrate general management theory with hospitality management are offered by a number of authors. Mullins introduced the open systems model of organisational analysis as a means of integrating general management theory with hospitality management. Mullins highlighted that managers in the industry tend to regard the industry as unique and special from other industries, rather than drawing from general principles of management. The validity of these claims is then examined, and the author postulates that the open systems framework provides a useful basis of analysis of the industry.

The theory in hospitality management has been examined by Nailon. His paper points to the absence of any commonly agreed theoretical framework concerning hospitality management. Nailon offers a model that identifies the interdependent and interrelated elements of hospitality management, and suggests that this might be used as a basis for research and management teaching. This research has received some criticism, most notably from Wood. What both of these authors claim is that hospitality management has sufficient differences from general management practice to warrant the development of its own concepts and theories.

To summarise, the research presented here shows that the nature of managerial work has undergone a number of changes in direction, and that it is closely related to general management theory. The research relating to Mintzberg is particularly comprehensive and further development along these lines drawing from other theorists is a possible way forward.

Empowerment

Within the general theoretical framework of managerial work, the subject of empowerment of employees has received extensive attention in the hospitality literature. This is not surprising owing to the growth and popularity of the subject as a management tool. Of particular interest is the recurrent theme of whether empowerment can lead to positive benefits for the company. Jones and Davies explored the role of empowerment in the UK hotel industry, and argued that more hotel companies will seek to empower their managers and employees.

The study examined feelings of empowerment, and attempted to identify a range of variables that may effect feelings of empowerment amongst hotel managers. The study concluded that the largest factor which influences feelings of empowerment appears to be the company that the manager works for, therefore corporate culture is the dominant force. Lashley examined the meanings and myths of empowerment in the hospitality industry, and outlined the benefits that organisations will gain if they empower their employees.

The benefits include increased employee motivation and satisfaction, and ultimately empowerment will help organisations meet their commercial objectives. It is interesting to note the positive approach of the authors to the subject of empowerment and the absence of a critique of the disbenefits.

Overwhelmingly the research advocates the advantages of empowerment as an employee motivator, and is not perceived as something that could create difficulties. Echoing these positive benefits, Sparrowe examined the issue of empowerment in the hospitality industry with the aim of assessing whether empowerment leads to positive employee outcomes, and if so, how managers can foster greater employee empowerment. A structural model was developed in order to test the antecedents and consequences of employee empowerment using 182 hospitality employees. The study concluded that empowerment would help to increase employee satisfaction with promotional opportunities, and turnover intentions would decrease.

The argument that empowerment leads to greater employee self-esteem and as a consequence, more satisfied guests, was echoed by Ninemeier. In this study, advice is offered as to how staff can be trained in empowerment so that hotel managers can delegate more tasks and decisions. Similarly the benefits that empowerment brings to employees have been examined by Zohar, who explored job stress in the hotel industry and identifies empowerment as a positive coping strategy in hospitality industries in the USA.

This positive approach also has influences outside the UK and the USA. Anastassova and Purcell evaluate current employment practices and management styles in the Bulgarian hotel industry, and consider to what extent the Bulgarian managers from a developing market economy may adopt from the current thinking about empowerment and staff development in the West. The authors conclude that the barriers to change are due to culturally entrenched practices, but state that the industry would be able to move into new markets if privatisation is handled appropriately and sensitively. More critical work in progress by Ghillyer and Lockwood argues that much of the research on empowerment focuses on the results achieved, with little attention being paid to the steps involved in getting there. As a result, the predominance of descriptive rather than prescriptive case studies supports the apparent potential of empowerment, without offering the specific information as to the processes involved.

The authors conclude that the concept of empowerment needs to be supported by far more empirical evidence of its potential, as those organisations seeking to improve commitment and employee performance need to be convinced before the capital is provided to implement the changes. Perhaps here the disbenefits of empowerment will be addressed.

STATUS OF HOSPITALITY MANAGEMENT EDUCATION IN INDIA

There has been no data, and no research has been conducted in India on the status of hospitality management or hotel management education. Although a large number of Government and private sector institutions are working in this area, there is no data about the number of students passing out from different programme every year. More than that, there is no data about the demand for trained manpower in the hotel, restaurant and catering industry in India. This research study has attempted to fill this gap and provide the necessary data and qualitative information on hospitality management education in India.

A questionnaire was sent out to 1200 FHRAI hotel members in different cities to provide the necessary data on the various parameters on which research was conducted.

The research revealed:

- There are, on the average, 2.28 staff members, including managers, supervisors and staff, per room in 5 star deluxe hotels in India. This staff to room ratio goes down to 1.84, 1.82, 1.84 and 1.30 in 5 star, 4 star, 3 star and 2 star hotels respectively.
- There is a ratio of 1 manager to 1.22 supervisors, 1 supervisor to 5.40 staff and 1 manager to 6.58 staff in the 5 star deluxe hotels. These ratios go up on the higher side, which means that there are more staff members and lesser number of managers and supervisors, as we go down the ladder to lower category star hotels. The ratio is 1 manager to 1.75 supervisors, 1 supervisor to 8.59 staff and 1 manager to 15.04 staff members in 2 star hotels.
- In India currently there are 13937 managers, 20707 supervisors and 128077 staff, all 3 categories totaling to 162721 employees in 1722 star category hotels (from 1 to 5 star deluxe) in the hotel industry in India.

- The average staff turnover in 5 star deluxe hotels in India is 24.14 per cent, going up to 28.96 per cent, 31.64 per cent, 42.97 and 45.63 per cent in the case of 5 star, 4 star, 3 star and 2 star hotels respectively.
- Figures on the number of trained manpower working in star category hotels in India indicate that there are total of 4668 trained persons working in 2 star to 5 star deluxe category hotels. (The definition of trained manpower is those persons who have qualified with a minimum of 1-year educational certificate or diploma in hotel management, which is mostly obtained before joining the service). Trained persons working in 1 star, government approved/ unapproved hotels, restaurants and other catering establishments and made the estimate that there are currently about 80,000 trained persons working in the hospitality and catering industry in India.
- There is a requirement of about 15000 additional trained persons in the star category hotels in India, which includes about 2700 managers, about 2500 supervisors and about 1000 staff members. The requirement given for manager and supervisor categories which totals to 5200 and will be filled by 3 or 4 years diploma and degree holders. In 1 star, government approved/unapproved hotels, restaurants and other catering establishments, it is estimated that there is an additional requirement every year for about 7500 diploma/degree holders in the country and about 15000-20000 one year certificate holders.
- In trained manpower, which means certificate/ diploma/ degree hotels coming out of hotel management institutions, 5171 students passed from 3 or 4 years diploma/degree courses in private hotel management institutions in 2004. In addition 1658 students passed from the 25 institutes of hotel management (IHMs) under the National Council of Hotel Management and Catering Technology under the Ministry of Tourism. This makes a total of 6829 such graduates who came out in the market for jobs in 2004. Similarly 989 students passed from one or two years postgraduate diploma courses from private institutions and a much smaller number of 218 qualified from Government institutions, making a total of 1207 numbers passing out from such programmes.
- Many institutions that offer one year certificate courses where the entry qualification is 10th grade, these persons are absorbed in lower level jobs in hotels, restaurants and catering establishments. The data shows that 3786 persons qualified from private institutions through such courses in 2004 and 1275 persons passed out from 12 Food Craft Institutes of the government, making a total of 5061 students who qualified with certificate in hotel management in 2004.

- Although the numbers passing out from diploma/degree courses match with the demand side statistics collected, there is a strong evidence, that not more than 60 per cent of diploma/ degree holding students are joining the Indian hospitality industry.

For a qualitative assessment of the status of hospitality education in India and to obtain certain estimated data from the key players, FHRAI also conducted field interviews among the three key stakeholders - the hotel managers, faculty of hotel management institution and students.

- 21 managers from hotels and restaurants in Delhi, Bangalore and Kolkatta stated that the current status of hospitality management education in India and faculty is poor or that it is satisfactory but needs tremendous improvement. A lot of emphasis is laid on theory rather than practical training of hotel operations.
- Many interviewees felt that the objective of majority of private sector institutions is to make money and they are not spending enough funds in providing the basic infrastructure, qualified faculty and quality education.
- Mushrooming of private sector institutions in hotel management and additional numbers are opening up every year. They usually do not have any infrastructure or labs and have poor faculty and standards. A number of them also said that there should be a curb on such institutions from the Government, who should only allow quality institutions to come up
- On the question on the quality of students joining the hotel management institutions, many managers said that it is still the last resort or a low priority programme, and bright students go for medical, engineering, IT, business management and other programmes. However, the situation is improving. This is because of opening up of job opportunities for hotel management graduates in many other sectors like call centres, airlines, banks, shopping malls, cruise ships, multiplexes and others. A large number of them are also able to find jobs abroad.
- On the complaints from the institutions on the quality of industrial training for students in the hotels, majority of the interviewed managers said that there are problems in this, and the fault lies on both sides. While many hotels consider such trainees as cheap labour and fill more seats than they can manage, some fault also lies with the institutions. They do not monitor the training and do not make sure that the students are sent only to such hotels which have a training department and have also earned a high reputation for imparting good industrial training in the past. This is also a numbers game as the number of aspiring students is much more than the

reasonable number of slots which can be filled in good hotels and restaurants.

- Faculty members of some Government and private institutions of hotel management contradicted the views of the hotel managers and felt that the standard of hotel management education in India is satisfactory and is going up over the years. This is because of better job prospects for hotel management graduates, not only in hotels and restaurants but also in many other sectors and abroad.
- Many faculty also said that the quality of industrial training in the hotels is poor. They all squarely blamed the hotels for it, which treat these students as cheap labour and do not give them satisfactory training or a comprehensive exposure to the operations. There are just a few hotels that take good care of the students and have structured and meaningful training programmes for them. Many faculty members said that these practices are lowering the image of the industry in the eyes of the students and this spreads far and wide through word of mouth. Many of these disenchanted students leave their education before finishing it.
- Many faculty members felt that hotels should co-operate more with the institutions in areas like curriculum development, guest lecturers and training of faculty members in the hotels. They appreciated some of the hotels who are inviting the faculty members for a brief exposure of about two weeks where they get to see the working in key departments of the hotel and also get exposed to latest trends in operations, equipment and procedures.
- It is now a known fact that hotel management graduates and certificate holders have much wider job prospects and less than half of them join hotels and restaurants after passing out. Some faculty members said that only about 15 per cent of those passing out from diploma/ degree programmes are joining any hotels and restaurants in India. This appears to be too small a number and could perhaps apply to a few upper end institutions from where majority of students are able to afford higher studies or go abroad or have the personality profile to join the higher paying jobs in other service sectors. The other view expressed by some faculty members, which could perhaps apply to majority of the institutions was that about 60 per cent of students passing out from hotel management institutions are joining the hospitality industry in India and the remaining numbers are accounted for by jobs in other sectors like call centers, higher studies and going abroad. It was the general view that a much higher number of students who do one year certificate courses in India, are able to go abroad for jobs as there is

a greater demand for such persons in cruise ships and places like the Middle East. Some interviewees said that about 70 per cent of certificate holders are able to go abroad after passing out and a brief job in India.

- Majority of interviewed faculty members felt that there is a over capacity in students passing out of diploma/ degree programmes in India. A majority of them are not able to get good jobs and feel frustrated after doing an expensive professional course. Some persons also felt that there is an over capacity in certificate holders also, but most of them felt that there is a need for more seats in the certificate courses and training of larger numbers in this segment.
- Majority of students said that they were happy with their studies and the institute. On the question as to whether they would still join hotel management education after seeing the working conditions in hotels, particularly in terms of long hours and low pay, majority of them said that they had known about this in advance and were enthusiastic about doing their careers in the hospitality industry. Some of them were happy that such a course had helped them in personality development, communication skills and grooming, which they would not have received from an ordinary BA course. These remarks and those appearing in the following paragraphs may again be taken in the context that we did the interviews only in a small number of upper end institutions in India.
- While hotel managers and faculty members were critical of the state of industrial training for students for different reasons, surprisingly the students all appeared to be happy with their industrial training. They said that this gave them a rare insight into operations in the hotels, which they could not have received while studying in the institute. Majority of them considered the exposure and training in the hotels to be highly valuable to their education and for their job prospects
- While hotel managers said that institutes have a theoretical curriculum and many of the things they taught are not in keeping with modern trends in hotels operations, the students did not mind it. They said that they were getting good and useful education, even if it was theoretical. They were getting some practical training in the hotels during their education and they would get more of it when they joined the industry. Some of them did feel that the institutes should revise their curriculum, add more practical hours and also buy some new and latest equipment being used in the hotels.
- While hotel manages and some faculty members said that many

institutions have poor faculty with low skills and practical exposure, the interviewed students did not agree with this view. Majority of them praised their faculty and said that they were getting good education. Many of them said that their faculty had past experience of working in the industry and this was not an issue. As clarified earlier, this could perhaps apply to a few upper end institutions in India.

- On the question of fees being charged in the institutions and whether they were satisfactory or high, the students gave the reply on the basis of where they were studying. Those who were in Government IHMs said that the fees were adequate and should not be increased further.

Through this survey on hospitality management education in India, it was found that many institutions are stuck in the syndrome of low fee, low quality of faculty, lower infrastructure and standards resulting in lower quality of students.

In some cases the fee is being mandated by institutions like AICTE and Universities to which the institutions are affiliated. In other cases it is competitive market pressures that influence the fee structure. They are also essentially playing a numbers game. Such inadequate fee revenues lead to poor infrastructure, lab facilities and lower emoluments for faculty. For example a senior lecturer (even in Government IHMs) gets a salary in the range of Rs 8000 to 12,000. Hotel management institutions are thus getting teachers who are unable to find a job in good hotels and restaurants or in other service sectors.

Such teachers, mostly without any working experience in hotels, are providing poor quality of teaching and academic inputs. This is leading to a situation where a majority of students passing out from the institutions are not considered employable by the hotel industry. This scenario is also leading to lower quality of students coming into these programmes, most of whom cannot get admission in good colleges, either for normal degrees or professional courses. It is indeed becoming a vicious circle.

There is a need for serious thinking on this matter whereby the institutions should be willing to increase their fees by a substantial margin and spend more money on infrastructure, operational expenses and hiring of faculty. Once the overall fee level goes up, the students and parents will gradually accept it. Moreover, loans are easily available from the banks and paying a higher fee for good education should not be a problem.

However this will only be possible with a change in the mindset of officials in the affiliating institutions like AICTE, universities and the concerned agencies/ departments in the government.

However this may be read with a caveat. Even with current level of fees, many institutions are still making good surpluses. This is also true of many government IHMs where the surpluses are visible on the records. Some IHMs have reserves of many crores of rupees piled up with them, but they still pay a pittance as salary to the faculty and have a dismal placement record.

Therefore, it is also a question of vision and commitment of management, in private or Government sector institutions, to analyse the reasons for their near failure and do something about it.

As our solution, if top 50 institutions in the country, both government and private, raised their faculty salaries to the level of managers in 5 star hotels, and concurrently raised expenses on other things, the face of hospitality management education in India will change drastically for the better, over the next five years.

PERSONALITY CHARACTERISTICS OF HOTEL MANAGERS

The third predominant research area, which draws from psychological theory and has received substantial treatment in the hospitality literature, consists of studies that focus on the personality characteristics of hotel managers. Although it is not clear why so much research has been undertaken in this area, it is perhaps because the popular perception of hotel managers is that they are a particular personality type. Arnaldo provided a profile of hotel managers and identified the personal characteristics of general managers, and the general managers' allocation of time and importance to Mintzberg's ten managerial roles.

The study examined general managers' education, job satisfaction, effective measures of success and the future for the managerial training. Kim provided a profile of hotel general managers in Korea, again using Mintzbergs' managerial roles. Arnaldo examined the general managers' allocation of time to the ten Mintzberg managerial roles. In addition the study identified the demographic characteristics of the general managers, and aspects of the general managers' job satisfaction. The paper makes recommendations for the future training of managers, such as increasing training in personnel management, accounting and finance.

The managerial roles of leader, monitor, disseminator and entrepreneur are judged to be important, and it is crucial they are included in training programmes. Brownell examined the gender differences of hotel managers in relation to personality and career development. The focus of the study was on how the personality traits of hotel managers influence career development in the hotel industry. The study identified that women are more in agreement than men about the characteristics they believe contributed to their career development. Most often mentioned by women are interpersonal skills, determination and hard work. Men responded with integrity, hard work, and interpersonal skills. The diverse backgrounds of hotel managers were also identified by Bentivegna and Sluder, who give a detailed demographic breakdown of a sample of 237 hotel general managers in the USA.

Worsfold examined the personality profiles of a group of UK hotel managers. The personality profile of hotel managers are described, and differences are identified between the personality profile of hotel managers and managers in other industries.

Worsfold compared the managers' self ratings against their personality profile, as measured through Cattell's 16PF test. Compared with the general management norms provided by Cattell, the personality characteristics of the managers are shown to be more assertive, more venturesome, more competitive and more tough minded, more independent and to have lower levels of anxiety than Cattell's management sample. Again, the trend towards showing that hotel managers are unique and different from other managers is evident here.

Swanljung's paper is one of the few studies published that attempts to identify common personality characteristics to the success of hospitality managers. Fourteen successful North American hospitality executives were interviewed and asked to identify their personal characteristics. Swanljung identified that the hotel executives have to be determined, hard working, fair, and able to motivate others. Stone also replicated this study.

Here personality characteristics are related to effective hospitality management using a survey of 140 UK general managers. Stone postulates that hotel managers demonstrate particular forms of behaviour, and identifies a number of factors that identify them from non-hotel managers. For example, compared with other managers, hotel general managers are more assertive, stubborn, cheerful, competitive, active, independent, cynical, calm, socially bold and spontaneous, harder to fool, and more concerned with self. Seymour in a study of 30 managers of small hotels in France found that the first thing in common with all the managers was their belief that they were somehow different or individualistic.

In a similar study by Nebel the background and the personality characteristics of a small sample of ten general managers are examined. The study focuses on five separate categories of personal characteristics: needs and drives, attitudes and values, interpersonal orientation, temperament and cognitive orientation.

The study concludes that although the personality characteristics of successful hotel managers are varied, there is evident consensus of what characteristics are required in order to successfully carry out the hotel managers' job. What these research objects show are strong commonalities in the sense that somehow personal characteristics are the dominant measure of success in a managers' career, rather than other external variables put forward by authors such as Ladkin and Riley.

An additional use of personality characteristics is evident in the research by Dickinson and Ineson. This research identified personality characteristics by the use of biodata as a means of assessment in the selection of operative staff in hotels. The authors conclude that the use of biodata to determine personality characteristics holds potential for the selection of reliable operative staff whose job involves a degree of customer interaction. Finally, the personality characteristics and profiles of hospitality management graduates in the USA were detailed by Brymer and Pavesic. This research attempts to show through the use of personality traits why some graduates remain in the industry, and why others take the decision to leave. The study concluded that quality of life issues and academic preparation are important to industry retention of hospitality graduates.

In summary the literature concerning the personality characteristics of hotel managers has common aims insofar as the research focuses on whether there are particular personality traits that set hotel managers apart from other professions and whether specific personality traits result in career success. The fact that many of the studies are not conclusive means that there is scope for more research here. However, the research calls upon psychological theory to help better understand the people who become and are successful hotel managers. There is a practical application here for industry, as research identifying the right type of individuals for the job may have benefited in terms of successful hotel management.

FUNCTIONAL RESPONSIBILITY, SKILLS AND COMPETENCIES

The fourth area to be reviewed contains literature on functional responsibility in a general manager's job, and the use of different skills and competencies. There is no shortage of literature that examines the role of the various functional activities of hotel departments contained within a hotel organisation. Within the literature regarding hotel managers, there are a number of authors who have examined the role of specific functions in the hotel industry. The research is applied as the main theme to determine the importance of the functions for both hotel companies and the development of hotel managers, which has implications for the hotel industry.

FUNCTIONS

Beginning with the personnel function, research by Kelliher and Johnson made empirical observations regarding the personnel function, and related these observations to the performance of the personnel function within hotels. The status of the personnel function is very low in the majority of hotels; many of the personnel managers are not trained specifically in personnel management and have worked their way up from line management, the individual responsible for personnel in many hotels does this as part of their 'other' job, for example in their assistant manager role; most personnel managers have a very limited view of what their role is, and finally, personnel work is well down the list of priorities in terms of time assigned to the role in any working day.

The object concluded that theory and practise in the role of the personnel function are discordant, as these findings contrast the optimism and growth of the importance of personnel departments stated by recent literature. These findings are worrying because they indicate that industry fails to recognise the importance of the personnel function with regard to recruitment and retention policies in hotels, along with career development and labour market analysis.

The second function to have received attention in the literature is that of food and beverage. The food and beverage function is cited as important in the career development of hotel general managers in a number of studies. For example, Nebel *et al.*, Knutson and Patton, Guerrier, Ruddy, Williams and Hunter, Guerrier and Lockwood, and Ladkin and Riley. The importance of the food and beverage function is highlighted from the American perspective in an object by Nebel *et al.*. Food and beverage management is recognised as a difficult and complex aspect of hotel management, and that hotels are often judged by the quality of their food and beverage operation.

This research examined the career histories of food and beverage directors, and highlights through a number of findings the importance of the food and beverage function in the career paths of hotel managers. In contrast to the personnel function, this study shows that the food and beverage department is given high status within hotels. The contrast between the importance of food and beverage function compared with the low status of the personnel function adds evidence for the debate between managerial and craft skills. It would appear that in terms of career development, the food and beverage craft route continues to dominate.

The third function that receives attention in the literature is sales and marketing. Plunkett and Berger examined the sales skills required for the hospitality industry. They began by explaining the unique nature of hospitality sales, and then identified important sales skills obtained from the opinions of hotel general managers.

The study indicated that communication skills are considered to be the most important, followed by product knowledge. The authors relate these finding to hotel company training schemes, and argue for a balance to be struck between the two mostused sales training techniques, off the job or on the job training. Wagner, identified the importance of developing employees who are competent in sales and marketing skills.

Wagner argued that many hotel sales people are incompetent, and urges them to become aware of the needs of their customers. With regard to training, Feiertag accused hotels of being negligent when it comes to sales and marketing training. The reason for this is identified as being that many general managers come from operational backgrounds, for example, food and beverage or front office, and they have little or no knowledge of selling or the selling side of the business. The call for a more business orientation is given here. Transferable skills are acknowledged as being important with regard to the hiring of sales employees, rather than specific marketing importance. The literature concerning sales and marketing contains evidence of a number of case studies that outline the successes of hotel marketing managers, for example, Wolchuck and Lawson and Stevenson.

The fourth functional area to receive specific attention in the literature is housekeeping. Rutherford and Schill explored a proposed model for restructuring knowledge constructs and activities of hotel housekeeping departments. A national sample of housekeeping directors was administered, using 400 rooms as the minimum size limit. The results indicated that the most important skills fundamental to housekeeping management are those generally related to broad organisational talents, relations with the key departments of sales, security and front office and the department's primary mission of cleaning functions. The research has implications for structuring the importance of housekeeping activities, industry training programmes and hospitality educators.

The research on functions attempts to explore both the functional roles in the hotel industry, and the importance of these to individuals' careers. It is important to see how the function relates to a career in hotel management from the perspective of manpower planning, as it has direct application for industry training. The career development approach makes them worthy of future research.

SKILLS AND COMPETENCIES

Related to the importance of the different functions in terms of career advancement, a further area of research into hotel managers is the relative importance of skills and competencies essential to their careers. The terminology evident in the literature concerning skills and competencies means that usually the two terms are used interchangeably and taken to mean the same. It is perhaps useful to begin this part by highlighting the existing research into trends of skill development in the hospitality industry. Skill and competency development forms a large aspect of research in this area. Riley identified a decline in the standards of skills in British hotels, and postulates two theories to explain this. The first relates to the labour market and the trading-down of skills, and the second to hotel culture and the 'European tradition'. Central to the theories is the notion of hotel employees gaining their skills through mobility, and moving through a hierarchy of establishments. This provided a useful insight into the skill acquisition of hotel workers, and illustrated evidence of the existence of a dual labour market operating in the hotel industry.

Staying with skill development, the importance of international career moves to a hotel managers' career and for skill development is a theme examined by Gliatis and Guerrier. This study argued for the importance of working abroad as vital training for a hotel manager, and stressed that the most important trait of an executive manager with an international hotel chain is that the manager is an internationalist. Training for the multicultural workplace was a topic investigated by Shames, who argued that, as hotel employees move from one country to another, they will benefit from developing cultural awareness and skills.

These benefits also remain relevant up the hierarchy to the hotel manager, as most hotels are multicultural workplaces due to the mix of nationalities within a hotel, as staff and/or guests. In all these studies, mobility is clearly the vehicle used to skill development. Similarly, one of the key areas of research that has received increasing attention is the importance of a range of skills to a career in hospitality management, and the ways in which the balance of skills is changing.

European management skills in the hospitality industry have been examined by Gamble *et al.*. This chapter explored the nature of management development and management roles in Europe, and highlights the changing emphasis of European management skills. The top managers identify a move towards a more business-oriented hospitality manager, the importance of specific functional abilities, and the move towards a team facilitator. There are calls away from the traditional craft approach, despite evidence that in terms of career development, this is not yet the case.

The changing balance of the importance of management skills versus operational skills is contested by Carper. This research reported on a round table discussion between hotel managers from nine countries at Cornell University, New York. Although there was continued support for the importance of operational skills and craft training, the managers acknowledged the growing importance of managerial skills in the careers of hotel managers. In research that examined the practices for developing hotel managers by Guerrier and Lockwood, the authors identified managers who adopt an operational perspective and managers who adopt a business perspective to their work.

The authors argued that the way in which hotel managers are trained and developed acts to reinforce an operational perspective rather than a business perspective to hotel management. The operational perspective stresses the importance of technical skills and the 'being there and doing it' style of management.

The current practice is for managers to spend apprenticeships at operative level, with specific emphasis on the food and beverage and front of house operations. Managers adopting a business approach would be concerned with strategic planning and business skills. As the current emphasis is on operational styles of management, the importance of technical rather then managerial skills will remain apparent as evidenced by Ladkin and Riley and Nebel *et al.*.

Guerrier and Lockwood, in their review of the current research of managers in hospitality, note that a recurrent theme is the traditional styles of operations in the hospitality industry. The authors reviewed the current limitations of this approach, and conclude that there is a slow move towards the business orientation. This trend is further noted and supported by Ruddy. The debate and lack of agreement looks set to continue.

The debate between managerial skills and technical skills again is outlined by specifically exploring the increasing importance of managerial competencies. This has received increased coverage in recent years. For example, Hay examined core managerial competencies and managerial characteristics that are essential in today's rapidly changing world. O'Driscoll *et al.* examined the manager and subordinate perceptions of managerial activities, competence and effectiveness. As identified by Morri0073, job competencies are those activities and skills judged essential to perform the duties of a specific position.

Guerrier and Lockwood argued that there is a need for specific research into the knowledge and competencies that hospitality employees require in order to be effective in their work. One of the most extensive studies of managerial competencies in relation to the hotel and catering industry has been undertaken by Tas. This study identified the most important competencies for hotel general manager trainees, as determined by 75 general managers of the top 75 USA hotels. The research listed specific competencies that are needed by trainee managers, and then relates these competencies to curriculum design in order to determine appropriate training and educational programmes for schools of hotel and restaurant administration.

The study undertaken by Tas is repeated in the context of the UK by Baum. Here the same competencies are used, with a number of modifications to allow for differences in language and terms. The opinions of 118 hotel general managers are obtained whereby they were asked to identify the importance of each competency, and again these results are applied to curriculum design.

This study also compared the two sets of results for the USA and the UK, and identifies the similarities and differences. Interestingly, both of the surveys identified what Baum calls 'soft' or human relations associated competencies as the most significant within the top rated groupings. These involve the traditional skills of hotel keeping, such as employee relations, guest care, professionalism and communication.

Jones argued that the concept of managerial competencies may provide a framework for structured training for managers in the hospitality industry, preferably leading to a qualification in hospitality management. This study reviewed the Manpower Services Commission study. The report suggests four major areas of competence that are relevant to management; competencies pertaining to dealing with people, competencies concerned with managing activities, competencies reflecting a sensitivity to environment or external factors and competencies reflecting personal effectiveness.

It is argued that this is the way forward for managerial development and training in the hospitality industry. A perspective from Taiwan is given by Hsu and Gregory, who investigate from the industry professional's viewpoint a range of competencies needed for hotel managers. The top 11 competencies identified were human relations skills. The authors postulate that the competencies identified in the survey as important by entry level managers could be used as a foundation for development of hospitality management curricula in Taiwan. This has obvious implications for training but it is worth considering if this is the best way forward. Clearly further research is critical.

A further trend evident in the skills and competency literature is studies that focus on specific skills and competencies. This research is concerned with examining the skills relevant to employees working in the hotel and catering industry. For example, Basker has examined the importance of presentation skills for trainee managers. The importance of managerial accounting skills to lodging managers has been examined in detail by Damitio, who investigates how hotel managers view the importance of selected managerial accounting skills. The added dimension of the views of hospitality accounting educators is examined by Damitio and Schmidgall.

A similar study is again repeated by Damitio and Schmidgall, which compares hospitality executives', educators' and students' views on the importance of accounting skills. This research supports the all three groups consider certain accounting skills to be important for lodging managers, and there is general agreement that the top 15 skills should be emphasised in hospitality and accounting courses.

The changing role of the financial controller is examined by Ferri. This study indicated that the job of the financial controller has changed over the years, the controller can no longer be a specialist, but has to incorporate a knowledge of computers, financial management skills, and operational analysis skills. The study adds that more non-accounting people have entered the field of financial controller, and that more financial managers are moving into hotel general management. Tarpey urged hoteliers to improve their language skills if they wish to capitalise on the predicted increase of European visitors to Britain.

Effective communication is an essential component of business success, and improved language skills is seen as a way forward for employees in the hotel industry.

Haywood examined the value of the skill of thinking for managers, and states that thinking is a critical human resource skill which is important in solving the range and depth of problems that managers face. The author argues that the issue is for educators to encourage clear thinking through the development of critical thinking courses.

Brownell stated that communication will play an increasingly vital role for hospitality managers, and argues that hospitality managers' communication practice is particularly important. Clark examined the communications and social competencies of hospitality managers.

Here, primary, research undertaken in the UK obtains the views of hotel managers who were asked to identify what they considered to be the essence of managerial communications and interpersonal or social skills. The studies by Tas and Baum are cited as a justification for the importance of this study, as they reveal that 40% of the required competencies emphasise the human or 'people skills' element of management in the hotel and catering industry.

Taking a different stance the perception of the importance of various skills has also been explored. The importance of skills for Canadian hospitality managers has been examined by Shaw and Patterson in their assessment of what hoteliers want from management development programmes. The results from 365 respondents indicated that the highest rated subject areas were service quality, motivation and training, and communication skills. Strategic planning, budgeting and forecasting were also rated as important by lodging sector managers.

An examination of the importance of skills that hospitality students feel they will need to be successful managers is provided by Knutson and Patton. The results of this study indicated that hospitality students feel that because they need to be able to manage employees and interact with guests, the 'people' skills are important, specifically, effective communication skills. With regard to skill development in education, Purcell and Quinn examined recent graduates and HNDs from hospitality management education. The respondents were asked to evaluate the development of skills on supervised work experience placements. The overall picture indicates that supervised work experience is good, or at least adequate, in terms of the development of practical skills and teamwork, but the development of management or supervisory skills is poor.

Appropriate management learning opportunities are inadequate within the work experience period of hospitality education. Furthermore, the study revealed that there is a strong positive correlation between perceived opportunity to develop practical skills and enthusiasm for the industry. The top transferable skills that the respondents felt they had developed were presentation skills, team working skills, critical analysis and written communication. The bottom ones were leadership skills, numerical data and computer skills.

The research relating to skills and competencies focuses upon the importance of the different areas for success in the hotel management profession, and upon what are considered important to the industry. Although the research has no clear theoretical foundations, the studies provide a valuable insight into where skills and knowledge are learnt. Clearly, there is scope here for the integration of theory and for more conclusive research. One thing which is certain is that the debate between managerial skills and competencies and technical skills and competencies looks set to continue. This needs to be related more closely to educational research in order for the training needs to be addressed.

ACHIEVEMENT OF WOMEN CAREER IN HOTEL MANAGERS

The fifth research theme evident in the hospitality literature concerns women hotel general managers. The research relating to women hotel managers highlights attempts to shed light on the marked differences between the careers of males and females, and to explore why so few females reach general manager status. A number of research studies have been carried out that specifically examine the role of women in hotel management careers. Although these studies vary in focus, the general theme common to all was the lack of women in general manager positions, despite the high percentage of female hotel and catering graduates.

A number of reasons are suggested for this. McKenna and Larmour postulated that contributing causes are the attitudes and behaviour of women, the personnel procedures and career paths of women, and the organisational climate. Guerrier cited three possible causes of the lack of success for women; the career paths to becoming a hotel manager, the role of the hotel manager and the attitudes and aspirations of women in the hotel and catering industry.

Guerrier highlighted the lack of opportunity for women in hotel management, and postulates that the arguments which state women are to blame for their lack of progress reinforces the notion that what men do and think is best. The food and beverage route to management is seen as a barrier to the development of female general managers.

Hicks argued that language provides key clues to the attitudes of women and towards women in the hospitality industry, and argues that male hotel managers have the power to restrict entry into their own rank. Women are at a disadvantage in the informal route to hotel general manager, which uses the 'old boy' network. Brownell supports this claim. Common to the studies is the agreement that the lack of experience acquired in the food and beverage function is a hindrance to the career advancement of women hotel general managers.

The importance of the food and beverage function is presented as a contributing factor in the lack of success of women in a hotel management career. Food and beverage is still regarded as traditionally a male domain, with women often pushed towards work in either housekeeping, sales and marketing or front office positions. Because of the importance of the craft and technical skills learnt in the food and beverage function, women are excluded to an extent that it becomes a hindrance to their careers. This argument is supported by Guerrier.

Evidence by Purcell and Quinn indicated that even in the early years, female hospitality graduates achieve less in career terms than their male counterparts. Males on average are significantly better paid, have superior fringe benefits, and more intrinsic employment satisfaction. This suggests that their average career progression has been steeper and they have achieved more responsible and higher status posts. A study by Stacey interviewed women who have succeeded in obtaining a hotel general manager position in order to gain insight into their careers.

They reported that one of the barriers to career development was a reluctance to be considered for food and beverage posts, the traditional roles of entering into the housekeeping sector, and managing a career and a family. However, evidence of female success particularly in the contract catering sector is reported.

Finally, Brownell explored women's career development in the hospitality industry from a general managers' perspective. The purpose of the study was to test if there were any differences in the views of male and female managers with regard to the communication skills and job-related activities that had contributed most to individual career advancement, and to the various obstacles to women's career development.

In terms of skills and job activities, little difference between the two groups was identified, and both groups regarded listening as the most important competence. However, there were significant differences between the two groups with respect to the degree to which various obstacles were a hindrance to women's career development. Males felt that the obstacles were less severe.

The importance of this area of research is that it sends messages to the industry in terms of identifying career barriers faced by females who are trying to succeed in the profession. The evidence presented by the research outlines this lack of success. What is not clear is why this is so.

EMERGING THEMES

The final category to be explored represents a number of research issues that are referred to repeatedly in the hotel manager's literature; ethics, technology, hotel security, and the problems of AIDS related to hotel staff. They are largely descriptive pieces that update the industry on recent development in operational practice, and warn of new issues managers need to be considered.

ETHICS

The ethics of hospitality managers have come under scrutiny in recent years. Hall argued that the delivery of service excellence requires not only quality, but a sense of morality, and urges hotel managers to become ethical decision makers. In this chapter, the barriers to ethics are examined, and an ethical code for hotel management is proposed. The study showed that from a survey of nationwide hotels of over 300 rooms in the USA, it was revealed that hoteliers believed they needed more education in ethics, and that hotel schools were doing an inadequate job of teaching the subject.

Schmidgall outlined that the topic of ethics and cheating in the business community has become the subject of a heated debate in the USA. Schmidgall acknowledged that the hotel community is not immune from ethical concerns, and undertook a survey of 400 lodging managers to gain an insight into the industry's code of ethics and to ascertain what is acceptable and what is not. Damitio and Schmidgall examined responses to ethical situations in a survey of general managers, controllers and club managers. The intention was to discover if there was any agreement in what is and what is not acceptable behaviour. After considering a number of scenarios, the authors conclude that there is a reasonable consensus of agreement across the groups as to what consititues ethical behaviour.

Drawing upon ethical theories and the philosophy of ethical decision making, Upchurch and Ruhland investigated ethical work climates, and explore the relationship between ethical decision making and leadership style amongst lodging managers.

They identified that benevolence is the primary dimension of ethical climate in lodging organisations, the local level of analysis is the primary determinant of ethical decisions in the organisation, and the primary leadership style is the high-task and high-relationship orientation. Turning their attention to the classroom, Enghagen and Hott have attempted to ascertain students' perception of ethical issues in the hospitality industry.

It is the turn of hospitality financial managers to be scrutinised by Schmidgall and Damitio in an attempt to ascertain how ethical hospitality financial managers are. The authors prepared a questionnaire of 16 scenarios, and the managers were asked to rate whether or not they agreed with the proposed action. The scenarios were in three groups; personal scenarios, scenarios involving other employees, and scenarios involving outsiders. The purpose of the study was to determine how hospitality managers feel about ethical dilemmas in a number of business situations.

The ethics in the hospitality industry with a focus on hotel managers was examined by Whitney. Here, the difficulties encountered in applying ethical principles to business realities are discussed, followed by the formation of a model that identifies ethical orientations as basic values which influence ethical decision making. The study concludes that the hotel managers reflect strong traditional values. Whitney builds upon this first study and discusses the problems encountered by hotel managers when applying ethical principles to business realities. Ethics clearly represent an important issue for the hospitality industry, and it is the subject of increasing research.

TECHNOLOGY

There have been a number of objects that identify the increasing importance of technology in the hospitality professions. For example, Coulton investigated the future direction of lodging technology and argues that technology will play an increasingly important role in the everyday functions of hotel operations.

Wolff argued that technology is turning the world into a single network, and identifies a number of ways that hoteliers can cope with ever increasing computer technology applications. The difficulties faced by small hotels with the technological advancement of CRS is identified by Boyce, who argued that the small hotelier will have to adapt in order to remain competitive.

Van Hoof *et al.* argued that hospitality managers need to be made aware of the importance of technology, and explore technology needs and perceptions of managers. Computer technology is seen as a way in which guest satisfaction could be improved, if managers could be persuaded to try it. Sheel looks at the advantages of the Monte Carlo simulations and scenario analysis as an important decision making tool for hotel managers. The consensus of agreement amongst researchers is that hotel managers in the future are likely to become more competent with technological advancement in response to this dynamic situation. Given the dynamic nature of the technology, it is likely that research into this area will continue.

HOTEL SECURITY

A further aspect of the hotel manager's job which has received an increasing amount of attention is that of hotel security. For example, Loyd argued that in a world where litigation is becoming increasingly important, hotel managers must at the minimum provide warnings about dangers that may be present and the hotels' relevant legal liabilities, and recognise their basic obligations of providing protection and security for guests. Gailly argued that managers are responsible for client and staff security as well as the protection of the hotel building and its equipment. They must be aware of the risk of fire, theft, vandalism and illegal intrusion in their hotels, and urges managers to be vigilant about such aspects.

THE PROBLEMS OF AIDS

Finally, there is a new issue facing managers and employees in the hotel and catering industry, the threat of AIDS. Gatty reported the legal issues facing employees with the illness, and outlines the educational efforts that are under way to attempt to reduce alarm and prejudice. Palmer examined the legal, operational and medical concerns for the hospitality industry with regard to employees suffering from AIDS, and Adam Smith and Goss examine the implications of perceived risk for hotel and catering employees suffering from AIDS. What these studies clearly show is the growing number of employees and employers who have to face the issue, and the implications this has for employee relations and legal matters. These issues have no theoretical basis, but offer a commentary on some practical themes related to general managers.

CONCLUSIONS AND THE WAY FORWARD

In pursuit of its aims, this review has identified six prominent research themes that explore the profession of the hotel general manager. The review demonstrates three important traits. First, although there is a wealth and diversity of literature concerning hotel general managers, common themes are evident. Within the broad groups research is often comprehensive and well documented.

However, there is clearly little interaction between the groups, which results in individual themes running parallel, rather than in collaboration. Increased interaction between these themes could improve the quality and dimensions of the research. Second, the issues covered vary in their approach, ranging from research that contains elements of established theory from the disciplines of psychology, career theory and management theory, to the descriptive reporting style of issues such as changing technology. This is not surprising, as some research often leans towards a theoretical or practical approach, and there is a valid need for both The way forward here lies in two directions; to integrate theory as an attempt to explain best practice and to develop a greater use of other key theorists in particular areas to offer new insight and a balanced approach.

There is an emphasis on the work of Mint berg from management theory and Schein from career theory, but as yet other key theorists have been ignored. This represents a possible way forward. Third, the review demonstrates that research has gone a long way into revealing the nature and characteristics of the hotel manager's job, and the type of people who undertake and are successful in this profession. We know something about the careers of hotel managers, barriers to female career development, where managers gain skills and competencies, the nature of the job, and the personality types of hotel general managers. This research has obvious benefits for the hotel industry, which can use the findings to identify best practice in terms of recruitment, training, career development and operational success.

At this juncture, it is appropriate to suggest areas for future research. Given the variety of research themes evident, this is not an easy task, as there are many avenues for exploration. However, there are a number of specific areas where immediately further research may be appropriate. The first is to take the area of skills and competencies, and explore where and how these are developed. Past research has identified what skills and competencies are important for a general manager's job, but we know little about how these skills and competencies are accumulated.

There is a continued debate within the industry concerning the relative importance of managerial versus operational skills, and how these relate to managerial effectiveness. It is important to understand how and where skills are accumulated if educationalists and the industry wish to train managers in an effective way. There is strong evidence to suggest the importance of the food and beverage function and further exploration into this specific function would be beneficial. Related to the issue of skill and competency accumulation, the second area for further exploration is mobility.

Research has identified that manager's use mobility to develop their skills, and general manager's careers demonstrate a high level of mobility. We know that managers use both the internal and external labour market for mobility, and we know they display a high degree of self-direction in the job moves. What remains unsolved is to what extent mobility is central to a successful career, and which job moves are seen as particularly significant and salient towards enhancing career development. An understanding of salient jobs and job moves would enhance our understanding of career progression. In addition, the variables that influence a career require further examination.

For example, is it personality traits, corporate culture, or the labour market that determines career advancement? Finally, the lack of female general managers signals to the industry an under utilized resource. Career barriers that hinder females from reaching general manager status have been identified, and further research could be undertaken to ascertain what measures could be used to alleviate this.

To conclude, past research into hotel general managers has answered a range of questions, but has opened the door to many avenues for further research. There exists an enormous potential to enhance our understanding of the general manager job and profession, which would benefit individuals and the hotel industry alike.

4

Career in Hotel Front Desk Management

FRONT DESK RECEPTIONIST

The Front Desk Receptionist is responsible for assisting and directing tenants/guests/owners, monitoring incoming enquiries and ensuring proper check in procedures are followed. This position also provides customer service support to the guests and owners. This ever smiling happy person has administrative skills and needs limited supervision to take the decision in every parties interest.

Front Desk/Concierge Cast Members work in an environment with a high level of Guest interaction. These roles involve the use of computer based systems, resolving challenging Guest situations and cash handling.

Responsibilities may include checking Guests in and out of resorts, assisting Guests with itinerary planning and ticket sales, tagging and delivering luggage, and providing information to Guests. Cast Members receive Theme Park admission and discounts at select dining, merchandise and recreation locations. Full-time Cast Members may be eligible to receive medical, dental and vision benefits, plus paid vacation and sick days.

The purpose of the Front Desk Lead is to handle the daily operation of the Front Desk activities, reservations, and their coordination with other departments. Responsibilities include training and scheduling of Front Desk personnel as directed by the Front Office Manager. Must be willing and able to work any shift as necessary as dictated by the needs of the Resort to insure adequate coverage at all times. Assist in maintaining proper working relationships between the Front Desk, Housekeeping, Maintenance, and Sales departments. Prepare daily reports as directed by Front Office Manager. Track and maintain housekeeping/maintenance reports on a daily basis. Ensure the satisfaction of all guests by implementing and maintaining proper Guest/ Owner relation programmes. Respond to Guest/Owner Issues. Assist in maintaining continued training for Front Desk staff. Assist in coaching, counseling, and developing of Front Desk staff as necessary.

The award-winning Nickelodeon Family Suites Resort has welcomed guests to the Orlando area for the past 4 years. With a management team that has always been on the cutting edge with innovative ideas designed to make family travel more enjoyable, they are poised once again to make their mark on the hotel industry.

Partnering with the number one kid's television network, Nickelodeon, the first-ever Nickelodeon themed hotel premiered in Spring 2005. The Nickelodeon Family Suites showcases a 25 million dollar infusion of water park attractions, Nickelodeon themed suites, banquet space, character breakfasts and a show room hosting Nickelodeon entertainment nightly. The hotel is a world class resort destination - a virtual city where "Kids Rule."

At the first-ever Nickelodeon Family Suites, We are seeking positive, energetic employees who desire to be part of an industry leading team, and are prepared to exceed our guest's expectations daily. Our Human Resources Department looks forward to helping you soak up the Nickelodeon Family Suites Values. Become part of our world-class team where we live by the motto: It's a cool place for families, a hot place for kids, where employees make IT happen! The first-ever Nickelodeon Family Suites by Holiday Inn is seeking "A" level talent for our Front Desk Team.

Hotel, motel, and resort desk clerks perform a variety of services for guests of hotels, motels, and other lodging establishments. Regardless of the type of accommodation, most desk clerks have similar responsibilities. Primarily, they register arriving guests, assign rooms, and check guests out at the end of their stay. They also keep records of room assignments and other registration information on computers. When guests check out, they prepare and explain the charges, as well as process payments.

Front desk clerks are always in the public eye and, through their attitude and behaviour, greatly influence the public's impressions of the establishment. When answering questions about services, checkout times, the local community, or other matters of public interest, clerks must be courteous and helpful. Should guests report problems with their rooms, clerks contact members of the housekeeping or maintenance staff to correct them.

In some smaller hotels and motels, clerks may have a variety of additional responsibilities usually performed by specialized employees in larger establishments. In these places, the desk clerk is often responsible for all front office operations, information, and services. These clerks, for example, may perform the work of a bookkeeper, advance reservation agent, cashier, laundry attendant, and telephone switchboard operator.

WORKING CONDITIONS

Working conditions vary for different types of information clerks, but most clerks work in areas that are clean, well lit, and relatively quiet. This is especially true for information clerks who greet customers and visitors and usually work in highly visible areas that are furnished to make a good impression. Reservation agents and interviewing clerks who spend much of their day talking on the telephone, however, commonly work away from the public, often in large centralized reservation or phone centres. Because a number of agents or clerks may share the same work space, it may be crowded and noisy. Interviewing clerks may conduct surveys on the street, in shopping malls, or go door to door.

Although most information clerks work a standard 40-hour week, about 3 out of 10 work part time. Some high school and college students work part time as information clerks, after school or during vacations. Some jobs—such as those in the transportation industry, hospitals, and hotels, in particular—may require working evenings, late night shifts, weekends, and holidays. This is also the case for a growing number of new accounts clerks who work for large banks with call centres that are staffed around the clock. Interviewing clerks conducting surveys or other research may mainly work evenings or weekends. In general, employees with the least seniority tend to be assigned the less desirable shifts.

The work performed by information clerks may be repetitious and stressful. For example, many receptionists spend all day answering telephones while performing additional clerical or secretarial tasks. Reservation agents and travel clerks work under stringent time constraints or have quotas on the number of calls answered or reservations made. Additional stress is caused by technology that enables management to electronically monitor use of computer systems, tape record telephone calls, or limit the time spent on each call.

The work of hotel, motel, and resort desk clerks and transportation ticket agents also can be stressful when trying to serve the needs of difficult or angry customers. When flights are canceled, reservations mishandled, or guests are dissatisfied, these clerks must bear the brunt of the customers' anger. Hotel desk clerks and ticket agents may be on their feet most of the time, and ticket agents may have to lift heavy baggage. In addition, prolonged exposure to a video display terminal may lead to eye strain for the many information clerks who work with computers.

HOTEL MANAGEMENT SERVICES

BMC provides the full spectrum of hospitality management services to owners, investors, and lenders of hotels, resorts, conference centers, and condominium hotels. Our comprehensive scope of hotel management services includes:

- Sales & Marketing, with comprehensive assistance in the form of direct sales, blitzes, database marketing, travel agent contacts, affinity marketing programs, and cross referral initiatives
- Revenue and yield management, as well as electronic distribution strategies
- Comprehensive food and beverage services, with expertise in managing multiple outlets, extensive meeting, conference, and

catering operations, and casual dining and franchised restaurant operations.

- Management of Ancillary Revenue Producing Departments, (such as Executive Meeting Centre, Golf, Marina, Retail, Spa and Fitness)

Centralized purchasing services:

- Hotel accounting and financial management, risk management and loss-control support
- Facilities/ engineering services and preventative maintenance programs

Cash management services:

- IT applications and support, with a 24-hour centralized help desk that provides for uniform and controlled processing of accounting, sales and catering, payroll, and time and attendance systems.
- Centralized recruiting services, encompassing management identification, placement, and relocation services of employees.
- Human resources management, including training and career development.
- Strict internal controls, resulting in improved accuracy, accountability, and control of cash and financial reporting to owners

Management oversight and coordination of hotel renovation programs:

- Hotel brand relations and ownership support, through the evaluation and negotiations of license agreements, product improvement plans, and balancing the objectives of the owner and brand
- Market analysis and development consulting
- Condominium hotel management services
- Quality assurance and internal control audits, to ensure the proper maintenance of books and records.

CONDOMINIUM HOTEL MANAGEMENT

BMC provides a comprehensive range of consultative services to developers of condominium hotel and resort properties. As an experienced owner and operator of condominium hotels, BMC has a proven track record and unique skill base setting the company apart from traditional hotel operators. Through a highly coordinated management approach, BMC professionals provide value-added assistance to developers in the following areas:

- Development and design considerations
- Assembling the project team
- Working with project consultants on programme elements and operational requirements

- Providing input on the declaration of condo-minium and other legal documents
- Structuring of the rental management agreement
- Preparation of pre-opening and hotel and rental programme operating budgets
- Development of marketing, advertising and public relation campaigns
- Assisting with the purchase of FF&E and technology solutions including the PMS, PBX, Point of Sale, Guestroom/Entertainment Services, and Telecommunications
- Assisting with selection of reservation and property management systems, telecommunications and all other system requirements
- Providing direction on operational requirements for project elements including: administrative office, front desk details and equipment, kitchen, employee facilities, laundry and valet layout, public and meeting/conference space, business centre, spa/fitness facilities, guest rooms and bathrooms, purchasing and receiving offices, room service areas, and other guest areas
- Development and implementation of the owners' relations programme

HOTELIER

Hotel Management System is an ideal software solution for Hospitality Industry that can be used at hotels, motels, inns, resorts, lodges, hostel, military guest houses, ranch, suites, apartments, medical centres and bed, breakfast operations.

Our product Hotelier Hotel Management Systemis a comprehensive software suite consisting of integrated modules for various aspects of hotel management. The software is often referred to as Property Management System in the Hotel industry.

Hotelier includes all the features required in a Hotel Management Software, Hotel Reservation Software, Hotel Reception Software (Front Office), Call Accounting, Hotel Point of Sales (Restaurant, Bar, Room Service, House Keeping or any other outlet), Inventory Management System and Hotel accounting software.

In our lodging software all modules are tightly integrated and all hotel programs are included in one price, meaning all modules are included at no additional cost regardless of your hotel size.

Our Motel management software is developed for Microsoft Windows operating system using latest software developing techniques. Hotelier is hospitality software designed for full service luxury inns, bed, breakfasts, and resorts. It emphasizes the highest level of individual guest services through our comprehensive features seamlessly integrating rooms, dining, and retail, with information contained in reservations till back office general ledger.

OPPORTUNITIES FOR HOSPITALITY GRADUATES

Global growth and development of tourism have opened up innumerable openings, as a result graduate can look forward to career opportunities as:

- Management Trainee in Hotel and allied industry
- Guest/ Customer Relation Executive in Hotel and other Service Sectors
- Kitchen Management/ House keeping Management Trainee in Hotels
- Flight Kitchens also offer opportunities for career building
- Executive multi skilled in Fast Food Chains
- Hospital and Institutional Catering Executives
- Faculty in Hotel Management/ Food Craft Institutes(after earning industry work experience)
- Cabin Crew in National and International Airlines
- Catering Officer or Chef in Cruiselines
- Marketing/ Sales Executive in Hotel
- Executive in Tourism Development Corporations and Resort properties
- Self employed entrepreneurs

India has been ranked the second fastest growing travel and tourism economy in the world. As per a recent estimate, over the next ten years, the annualized real growth in demand for travel and tourism is expected to grow by 8.8 per cent for India. Travel and tourism within the country is also increasing.

This has resulted in increased occupancy levels at hotels and holiday resorts as well as increased interest in the course of hotel management. Needless to say, growth in travel and tourism industry has translated into growth in hospitality industry, with increase in job opportunities for those who want to make a career in this booming industry.

National Council for Hotel Management and Catering Technology, a registered Society functioning as the apex body for education and training in Hotel Management and Catering Technology is the premier institute imparting education and training in the field. It was set up by the Central Ministry of Tourism in the year 1982 for development of human resources for the Hotel and Catering Industry. The Council performs a key role in creating a modern and model training system to meet the varied and changing manpower needs for different segments of the Hotel and Catering Industry. The council has various affiliated colleges which conduct a number of courses in different aspects of the hospitality sector, catering to the needs of various sections of the industry.

Courses such as B.Sc. Hospitality and Hotel Administration, M.Sc. Hospitality Administration, P. G. Diploma in Accommodation Operation & Management, P. G. Diploma in Dietetics and Hospital Food Service, Craftsmanship course in Food Production, Craftsmanship course in Food and Beverage Service, Diploma in Food Production, Diploma in Food & Beverage Service, Diploma in Front Office Operation, Diploma in House Keeping Operation, Diploma in Bakery and Confectionery are some of the courses conducted by the institutes which may be pursued to carve a career in the hotel management industry.

There are different admission criteria for gaining admission to these courses. For example, Bachelor of Science (B.Sc.) in Hospitality and Hotel Administration is a 3 year Programme and minimum eligibility is 10 + 2 of Indian education system or equivalent with 50 % marks. For Master of Science (M.Sc) in Hospitality Administration, which is a 2 year Programme eligibility is 50% marks in B.Sc (H.M) or 3 year Diploma in H.M. with Graduation. The Craftsmanship course in Food Production involves 1 Year + 6 months Internship and minimum eligibility is 10th Class Pass (of 10+2 system) and so on. The competition to gain admission is stiff as demand is very much.

Hospitality industry thrives on the concept of service. Hence attitude and aptitude for service is the key element for success in the field. Patience and perseverance and ability to maintain cool and composure even in adverse conditions is the key to success in the field. More often, candidates are required to put long hours and hence ability to work hard is also very important for success.

This is a rewarding career and compensation packages are very good. Starting salary in most start hotels is around 35000/- to 50000/- per month which also shoots up with right experience and talent. Perks of offices such as subsidized accommodation and free food are other added attractions of the profession.

(PGSHM) POST GRADUATE DIPLOMA IN HOSPITALITY MANAGEMENT

In the UK, there are three main levels of postgraduate study: postgraduate certificates and diplomas, master's degrees and doctorates.

Most of them take only one academic year to complete, compared to two years in many other countries. Post graduate diplomas or certificates are offered in a huge variety of subjects, from education to management to network engineering. These are often accepted as professional qualifications in their field. It is often similar to a master's, the only difference being that it doesn't require you to write a dissertation.

At some institutions, you might be asked to register for a post graduate diploma as the first stage of a master's programme, and some diploma courses enable you to transfer to a master's when you've completed them.

Valuable insights into the course:

- Duration of ONE academic Year Only
- Qualification from UK's largest awarding body
- Part of Pearson plc, world's largest education services company
- Age and work experience considered towards entry
- Progression to an MBA/Master's programme (with exemptions)
- Automatic membership from Chartered Management Institutes(MCMI)
- Gain up to 2 yrs of Post Study Work
- Study in one of the most cosmopolitan cities of the world and leading Tourism capital

Hotel and Motel Management Schools prepare students for careers in hotel, motel, and restaurant management. Students learn about hospitality, food and beverage management, catering services, marketing and sales, and much more.

Whether the lodge is small or large, services can include coffee and tea, daily newspapers, shoe shines and more. Workers may be required to take care of swimming pools, golf courses, tennis courts, health spas, and game rooms. The hotel and motel industry includes lodging and services to customers in five-star hotels to the most rudimentary campgrounds. Graduates can choose to enter into management of luxury spas, motels, commercial establishments, resorts, residential or extended-stay hotels, guest ranches, RV parks, boarding houses, or quaint homes offering bed and breakfast.

Managers of hotels, resorts, and motels must be sure all aspects are functioning at optimum levels. Hotel and motel management is responsible for the quality of food, hotel supplies, catering, and customer services. They also oversee conference room scheduling, valet and ride service, and all special services for provided to guests. An associate degree (AHM) from Hotel and Motel Management Schools can be accomplished in about 18 months.

Graduates will be ready for small and large worldwide companies for entry-level management in hotels, motels, and restaurants. Hotel and motel management students will take business courses along with classes in English, communications, and general studies, and many Hotel and Motel Management Schools provide hands-on management experience for their students. Some bachelor degree (BMH) programs in hotel and motel management are designed for students seeking opportunities to advance their careers in hotel and motel management.This degree allows specializations that prepare students with tools for advancing to upper levels in the industry in areas of food and beverage services, marketing hospitality services, accommodations, business and accounting, human resources, as well as others.Master (MMH) level Hotel and Motel Management Schools students may choose to study areas of entrepreneurship, marketing, information systems management, operations management, and real estate and investment. These programs of study provide solid knowledge and skills for preparedness in upper-level positions in areas of hotel and motel management.

Hotel and motel management are allowed opportunities to enjoy discounts in lodging and travel amenities, which makes hotel and motel management careers attractive for those who enjoy travel.

RESTAURANT MANAGER

Job Purpose

To be responsible for the image of the restaurant and increasing its sales (from preparation through to service).

Key Responsibilities:

- Be the host and communicate with guests
- Organise the restaurant team: their tasks, schedules and information meetings
- Staff management: recruitment, training, evaluation and promotion
- Monitoring customer service levels
- Ensure the quality of service and service provision
- Maximise restaurant occupancy
- Ensure on-going profitability and have knowledge of financial matters
- Increase restaurant sales

Entry Requirements

Skills:

- Management: managing priorities, the ability to listen, stress management, team motivation
- Recruitment
- Sales ability
- Ability with figures and the ability to manage a profit centre
- Multi-skilled
- Sensitivity to customers
- Able to deliver training at all levels
- Have understanding of IT issues in relation with the post

- Thoroughness
- Dynamism/good relationship skills: maintaining the image of the restaurant

Qualifications:

- 2 years further education in hotel/food and beverage studies to BTS/ HND standard or similar
- Significant experience of restaurant management

ASSISTANT RESTAURANT MANAGER

Job Purpose

To assist the Restaurant Manager in maintaining the image of the restaurant and increasing its sales (from preparation through to service).

Key Responsibilities:

- Be a host and communicate with guests
- Organise the restaurant team: their tasks, schedules and information meetings
- Assist the Restaurant Manager in staff management: recruitment, training, evaluation and promotion
- Monitor customer service levels
- Ensure the quality of service and service provision
- Take full responsibility for the Restaurant during allocated shifts
- Maximise restaurant occupancy
- Organise of the restaurant team
- Increase restaurant sales

Entry Requirements

Skills:

- Management: managing priorities, the ability to listen, team motivation
- Recruitment
- Sales ability
- Ability with figures
- Sensitivity to customers
- Able to deliver training at all levels
- Have understanding of IT issues in relation with the post
- Thoroughness: a good supervisor

- Dynamism/good relationship skills: maintaining the image of the restaurant

Qualifications:

- 2 years' further education in hotel/food and beverage studies to BTS/ HND standard or similar
- Significant experience of restaurant supervision

CONFERENCE & BANQUETING MANAGER

Job Purpose

To organise and monitor the quality of customer events on behalf of the entire Conference and Banqueting Department: He or she:

- Supervises Food and Beverage services as they relate to his or her department
- Manages the reservation schedules
- Helps in the preparation of the department's annual budgets

Key Responsibilities:

- To supervise the quality of services offered to customers, in terms both of production and service
- To recruit, manage and motivate the members of his or her team
- To ensure that the brand standards are applied
- To ensure that health and safety rules are applied and respected
- To control and manage the staff cafeteria

Entry Requirements

Skills:

- Sales ability
- The ability to listen: detecting customer needs
- Team leadership
- Teaching skills
- Creativity
- Reactivity
- Organisation
- Thoroughness

Qualifications:

- 2 years' further education in hotel, food and beverage or sales to HND standard or similar

- Significant experience in the Banqueting and Conference trade (5 years)
- Good general level of education

CONFERENCE & BANQUETING SALES MANAGER

Job Purpose

To handle requests for seminars, weddings, conference, etc. From the first telephone call through to invoicing, he or she:

- Identifies precisely the expectations of the customer
- Checks the availability of meeting rooms and bedrooms
- Prepares costed proposals
- Follows up customers and confirms reservations
- Passes on instructions to the various departments (reception, food and beverage and kitchen)

Key Responsibilities:

- Ensuring the success of the event
- Delivering customer satisfaction
- Making sure that customer promise is kept
- Handling any complaints and following-up debtors

Entry Requirements

Skills:

- Using the Windows environment
- Sales ability: negotiating and selling the product
- Hospitality
- Adaptability: coping with the diversity of customers and their needs
- Availability
- Reactivity
- Organisation
- Good relationship skills
- Self-control: handling complaints

Qualifications:

- 2 years' further education to HND standard or similar in Hotel studies, Tourism or Sales
- Previous food and beverage experience would be an advantage

FRONT OFFICE MANAGER

Job Purpose

Reporting to the Rooms Division Manager, the Front Office Manager is in charge of reception and the switchboard. To be responsible for welcoming guests and handling any complaints.

In doing so, he or she:

- Supervises reservations and the allocation of bedrooms with the Executive Housekeeper
- Monitors the customer accounts and till accounts
- Applies and ensures the application of the sales strategy to maximise occupancy and average room price
- Co-ordinates the reception team, organising its work and schedules

Key Responsibilities:

- To monitor the quality of welcome extended to guests
- To recruit, train and motivate the members of the his or her team
- To ensure that all hotel standards and procedures are applied
- To manage daily billing and payments

Entry Requirements

Skills:

- Use of Windows
- The ability to train and motivate a team
- The ability to be available to work nights, weekends or public holidays
- Sales ability
- Hospitality
- Adaptability: coping with the diversity of customers and their needs
- Self-sufficiency
- Self-control: handling complaints
- Good relationship skills
- Team leadership
- Good memory: remembering guests
- Taking the initiative
- Discretion

Qualifications:

- From A-levels to 2 years' further education to HND standard or similar in Hotel or Tourism studies
- 4 years' experience of reception
- Fluency in a second language is an advantage
- Good general level of education
- Significant experience of Fidelio (reservations system)

RESERVATIONS MANAGER

Job Purpose

To organise the reservations system and take responsibility for the quality of the service it provides, whilst maximising occupancy rates and average revenue per room.

Key Responsibilities:

- To ensure that all telephone, fax and Internet enquiries received from customers are handled to a high quality standard
- To ensure that customers are offered high quality services and a high quality service
- To ensure the continuation of the resources supplied for his or her use
- To ensure that the brand standards are applied

Entry Requirements

Skills:

- Using the Windows and Tars on-line environment
- Self-control
- Thoroughness
- Organisation
- Readiness to take the initiative

Qualifications:

- From A-levels (Technology) to HND or similar
- 2 to 5 years' experience in a hotel environment
- Good general level of education
- Fluency in a second language is an advantage
- Significant experience of Fidelio (reservations systems)

FRONT-OFFICE/BACK OFFICE RELOCATION FRENZY

Restructuring, re-engineering, downsizing, rightsizing, merger mania, unbundling, outsourcing - all of these expressions are 1990s corporate jargon for workplace changes that are sweeping the nation. At the local level, these changes are remapping the regions of growth and decline.

Like the movement of U.S. manufacturing companies overseas during the past 20 years, today's corporate wanderlust is driven by a search for lower operating costs. But unlike the flight of manufacturing, many of today's corporate moves remain on home soil. Today's relocation manager is looking for lower costs but also requires an English speaking, well-educated workforce, advanced technology, excellent telecommunications, stable utility service, and extensive air transport to make a move successful.

State and local incentives to attract footloose companies are part and parcel of the relocation equation. The bidding war has pitted state against state, municipality against municipality, in a game of chicken that no local government alone can afford to give up.

Relocation frenzy, makes local tax bases more volatile. The receiving community, is likely to expand infrastructure, increase borrowing, and make some tax changes to accommodate the newcomer. The losing community is faced with higher unemployment, excess infrastructure capacity fixed costs to finance that infrastructure, and lower revenues. Whichever side of the market we are on, these changes will affect our work, our portfolio, and our decision making. By, taking a walk through the land of relocation, we can get a look at the trends that are out there.

THE FRONT OFFICE

The journey, begins with a comparison of the relocation of Fortune 100 headquarters in 1985 and 1995. Among this group, National Municipal Research found a few moves, mostly from New York City to other locations and mostly, among oil and gas companies. Exxon moved from New York City to Irving, Texas; Mobil moved from New York to Fairfax, Virginia; and Texaco from New York to White Plains, New York.

The Oil and Gas Journal, restructuring ill the oil industry, is far from over. The Quaker State Corporation recently moved its headquarters from Oil City, Pennsylvania, to the Dallas area. Quaker State had been a loyal resident of Pennsylvania since 1931.

Other companies moved their headquarters from urban centres to suburban locations. Sears, for example, moved from downtown Chicago to a huge facility in distant Hoffman Estates, Illinois. JC Penney moved its headquarters from Dallas to the northern suburb of Plano, Texas. And United Parcel Service has moved twice in recent history: from New York City to Greenwich, Connecticut, and later to Atlanta. Companies also are moving their headquarters to smaller metropolitan areas, as did Thrifty, Payless, Inc., which moved from Los Angeles to Wilsonville, Oregon, near Portland. The New York metropolitan region is home to the highest percentage of large corporate headquarters, followed by Chicago, Los Angeles, Philadelphia, Boston, San Francisco, Dallas, Fort Worth, Houston, Detroit, Minneapolis, Cleveland, and Atlanta, just as to a report in Economic Development Review by Growth Strategies Organization (GSO), Inc. In 1993, Los Angeles, Philadelphia, Boston, and Houston enhanced their shares of corporate headquarters at the expense of New York, Chicago, and Detroit. GSO also found a "modest shift of headquarters from the largest metropolitan areas to MSAS with populations in the 1 to 3 million range." These communities seem to offer the best compromise between lifestyle quality and availability of needed services. Hub airports were cited as one locational advantage for moving to a smaller MSA.

On the whole, large corporate headquarters tend to be loyal to the communities they grew up in. WalMart has stayed in Bentonville, Arkansas, and Coca-Cola in Atlanta. Dennis Donovan, senior manager of the Wadley-Donovan Group, Ltd., has explained why there are so few headquarters moves. "Corporate CEOs" he said, "are looking for specialized locations for their headquarters, and only a few places fit the bill. The location must be part of the global community with extensive international connections. Air service must be excellent and nearby, and which services as banking, courier services, and other support functions help anchor a large corporate headquarters. The image of the location also is important."

Headquarters relocation most commonly occurs within a metropolitan area or when there is a merger, downsizing, or decentralization of functions. More common today is the decentralization trend because it has become easier to locate certain back-office functions in remote locations. Donovan cited Metropolitan Life, which broke up its divisions and moved into six or seven locations.

THE BACK OFFICE

Such back-office functions as accounting, check processing, payroll, data processing, and information management are being spliced and diced and moved around the geographic chess board. Advances in technology and telecommunications also are creating new clusters of back-office functions.

Vast storehouses of information about corporate assets - inventory control, accounting, sales, production, and market conditions - have expanded the potential for corporate data and information centres. Systems for organizing and analysing this information have become standardized to the point at which companies can outsource, or contract with other companies for a service. M. Ross Boyle wrote in Economic Development Review that "until recently, these centres were always found within or near the corporate office building. Some companies now are concluding that this proximity to the corporate decision-makers is unnecessary and may not be cost-effective. They can be located in communities with outstanding telecommunications and mail service, plus at least adequate air service."

Boyle continued: "The justification for shifting these facilities to a location some distance from the corporate headquarters lies in the lower operating costs and greater productivity, that can sometimes be achieved by, such a move." The "help desk" function that grew up with the computer industry is one example of a back-office function that is finding new applications for companies that are willing to implement the technology.

For example, Taco Bell uses a system wide help desk that is available to answer questions about hardware, software, procurement, and asset management for its corporate operations, as well as for its 4,00 restaurants. The help desk is credited with cutting costs so low that the chain is able to continue to offer its 59-cent taco and free drink refills without compromising profitability.

Colleen McCormick, research as sociate at the Gartner Group, specializes in covering 22, large help-desk outsourcers. These companies handle calls from around the world for large international corporations. McCormick cited the South, Midwest, and California as areas for help centres. Texas, she noted, has a lot of call centres. Some hot back-office locations have become so overcrowded that the job market is tight or nonexistent. Mark Klender of Deloitte and Touche told the Wall Street Journal last year that Sacramento is one such market. Phoenix, Omaha, suburban San Francisco, Salt Lake City, Tucson, Des Moines, and Seattle are other frequently mentioned back-office locations.

In Florida, Tampa, Orlando, and Jacksonville, as well as newcomers Pensacola and Tallahassee, are strong back-office markets. In February, the Walt Disney Corporation announced that it is looking at Tampa for 500 back-office jobs. Insurance company USF&G chose Tampa for 500 back-office jobs, and American Express Travel Service will be adding 100 jobs there.

In investigating the criteria used to choose new back-office locations, one repeatedly hears "education, education, education." Employees who work computers or toil on a "telephone assembly line,, need to be articulate and to think on their feet in order to provide service to the customers at the other end. Winning locations tend to be those with good schools, colleges, and universities or specialized training programmes. For example, Fitch Investors Service recently moved its corporate and municipal database operations to Powell, Wyoming. Aside from the fact that Chairman Russell Frazer lives a drive away, Fitch had struck a deal with Powell's Northwest College, part of the state University, system. The two organizations will design courses so that students can work at the facility.

Donovan underscored the importance to a successful back-office move of a good supply of well-educated, entry-level labour with solid basic skills and moderate wage levels. Air service is important, although it need not be as extensive as for corporate headquarters. The prestige of the address is less important than other factors. "The nation's urban centres missed the boat in the early 1990s" commented Donovan. That was a time when high office vacancies had shrunk the cost of office space in many localities to levels comparable to those in suburban and exurban locations. However, "nobody stepped up to the plate to address three key ingredients: parking facilities, increasing available floor sizes, and, most important, improving the skills attainment of the workforce." The urban centres lost their advantage to savvier locations.

THE INCENTIVES WAR

The price tag for company moves has increased over the past five to six years, according to Bill Schweke of the Corporation for Enterprise Development. Today, it has become easier to move goods and services around, which has led to companies, playing off one jurisdiction against another. Schweke has attributed the increase in competition to "economic insecurity" on the part of local officials. "Politicians don't want to be caught napping by not offering the same incentives as their neighbours," he said. Bidding wars have become more press worthy, and the politics of competition in the sweepstakes for corporate moves are more visible than ever before. "Today," he added, "every company that is locationally mobile expects to be given some kind of tax break to make a move."

When Columbia Healthcare Corporation merged with Nashville based Hospital Corporation of America, it decided to move the new company headquarters to Louisville, Kentucky. Following repeated complaints about Kentucky's provider tax and Tennessee's repeal of its hospital services tax (Tennessee has no provider tax), the company chose in 1994 to move its headquarters to Nashville. Modern Healthcare commented that Tennessee dropped its antitrust investigation into the company one day, after the company announced its move. The attorney general's office cited the "transaction's pro-competitive effects."

There is a growing trend towards rolling back some of the incentive competition. Factions on both the left and right ends of the political spectrum support limits on tax incentives. Criticisms range from the wastefulness of "corporate welfare" to the desire to keep government entirely of the way of enterprise. Some states have made it harder for local governments within them to use tax incentives to lure companies around the state. Ohio passed SB19 in 1994 to clarify the use of its urban enterprise zones. Ohio's enterprise zones may carry distressed designation," which gives them certain privileges. Bob Stempfer, manager of the tax incentives office of the Ohio Department of Development, there are 319 enterprise zones in the state and about 40 with the "distressed" designation.

At issue in Ohio were a number of communities that essentially were raiding each other's companies using tax incentives. A year ago, Cleveland's Mayor White attempted to block the move of a toolmaking company that was leaving for suburban Solon (he failed). Stempfer, the law generally prohibits movements from a distressed enterprise zone (Cleveland) to a nondistressed enterprise zone (Solon), but waivers may be granted with the director's approval if certain conditions are met.

The lack of control that states have over each other has led some observers to suggest federal constraints on the bidding war. Schweke has commented that today's bidding battles are analogous to those of, an earlier era in this country when the adversarial competition among states served to harm the economy giving rise to the Constitution's interstate commerce clause. Melvin Burstein and Art Rolnick have written a number of reports for the Minneapolis Federal Reserve that have criticize tax incentives as harmful to the overall economy. Burstein and Rolnick have been especially critical of intrastate bidding, in which local communities lure businesses away from each other, often with the help of state dollars. It will not be surprising if the bidding war receives attention in Washington when interstate commerce issues are addressed.

Landing a new corporate headquarters or back-office operation can be the ticket to a community's economic success. Locational changes have created new wealth in communities where little affluence existed before. Losers are faced with tax-base shock and the task of meeting public needs with fewer resources. For the foreseeable future, corporate wanderlust is likely to keep underwriters, analysts, portfolio managers, and public officials on their toes.

MERCHANT AGREEMENT TO ACCEPT VISA CARDS

ACCEPTING VISA CARDS AT HOTELS

If you have signed a merchant agreement to accept Visa cards, you should accept all Visa cards, irrespective of which bank issued them. Banks right around the world offer their customers a range of different Visa cards. This includes Classic cards, Gold cards, Infinite cards, Visa Electron cards, Visa Business cards and Visa Purchasing – as well as cards issued in conjunction with other major corporations.

These cards may look different, but they all:

- Have the same basic card elements and security features
- Guarantee payment to you when Visa acceptance procedures are correctly followed

HOW TO IDENTIFY A VISA CARD

There are many different kinds of Visa cards. All share the same essential card elements and security features. The unembossed Visa card is the new Visa product which has the card number and information printed on the front of the card, making the surface of the card smooth instead of being raised. The unembossed Visa card does not share some of the card elements as the normal Visa card. Visa Electron cards also have slightly different features, can only be accepted at an electronic terminal and always require authorization.

- *Visa flag symbol*: Always on the front, right hand side, but can be above or below the hologram.
- *Microprinting:* Should be visible around the Visa flag symbol.
- *Dove hologram:* Always on the front right hand side, and the dove appears to fly when the card is tilted back and forth. The Visa Infinite card, issued by some banks to their very best customers, has a different hologram design.
- *Four-digit number:* Printed above or below the account number. This should always begin with a '4', and should match the first four digits of the account number. If it does not, or if it is missing, the card may be counterfeit.
- *Account number:* Must be even, clear and straight, with all numbers the same size and shape. May be embossed or unembossed.
- *Embossed letter V:* Will be present on embossed Visa cards. On some cards, it may be shown as CV, BV, or PV. For unembossed Visa cards, this feature will not be present.
- *Cardholder name:* Letters must be even and straight. Whenever you are processing a transaction, this should be compared with the cardholder's signature. For unembossed Visa cards and for some prepaid Visa cards, a cardholder name may not be present.
- *Dates:* Whenever you are processing a transaction, you should check the dates are valid. If you are presented with a card where the dates are not valid, you must obtain authorization.
- *Signature Panel*: Look for the signature on the signature panel. You should see the repeated word "Visa" printed diagonally in blue and gold.
- *CVV2*: There should be a unique three-digit code printed after the account number on the signature panel.
- *Chip:* Many Visa cards now have a chip. If you still have a magnetic stripe terminal, these can be accepted in the normal way. If you have a chip-capable terminal, the card should be inserted into the chip reader for the duration of the transaction.

VISA ELECTRON CARD

- *Visa Electron symbol*: Always on the front, right hand side at either the top or bottom of the card. These cards may have a Dove hologram. Occasionally they may also have the Visa flag symbol and well as Visa Electron symbol.

- *Last four digits:* A full account number will not always be printed on the card. Check that the last four digits on the card correspond to the last four digits shown on your terminal.
- *Electronic use only:* Printed on the front of the card to remind you that Visa Electron cards cannot be used with manual systems. This may appear in other languages.
- *Signature panel*: May appear on the front or back of the card. You should see the repeated word "Electron" printed diagonally in blue, red and yellow.

The Visa reservation service helps you to guarantee room reservations and avoids losses from 'No Show' guests. However, whenever you are using the service, it is important that you correctly follow these simple steps. Failure to do so may result in unnecessary customer queries and complaints.

GUARANTEEING A RESERVATION

While speaking with the guest:

- Ask the guest for:
  - The Visa card account number
  - The card expiration date
  - The cardholder's name as it appears on the card
  - The billing address and phone number.
- Tell the guest:
  - The room rate (plus tax)
  - The hotel's address
  - The confirmation code for the guaranteed reservation
    Be sure to keep a record of the code for future reference.
- Be sure to explain:
  - Guaranteed rooms are held until check out time on the day following the scheduled arrival
  - The deadline for cancelling reservations is 6:00pm on the scheduled arrival date
  - If the room is not claimed or cancelled in time, the cardholder will be billed for one night's stay (plus tax).

Note: If your deadline is earlier than 6.00pm on the scheduled arrival date, tell the guest the date and time of your deadline, and send a follow up mailing with the cancellation policy.

- Following up...

If your guest requests a written confirmation, be sure to include:

- The Visa card account number
- The card expiration date
- The cardholder's name as it appears on the card

- The room rate with tax, and any other appropriate details about the accommodation
- The hotel's address
- The confirmation code
- The guest's rights and responsibilities under the Visa Reservation Service
- The date and time that the cancellation privileges expire.

HANDLING CANCELLATIONS

While speaking with the guest:

- Provide a cancellation code.
- Advise the guest to keep a record of the code for future reference. Following up...
- Write 'cancelled' on the reservation form and record the cancellation code provided to the guest.
- If requested, provide a written cancellation with:
  - The Visa card account number
  - The card expiration date
  - The cardholder's name as it appears on the card
  - The cancellation code.

HANDLING 'NO SHOW' TRANSACTIONS

If a guest fails to cancel a reservation or claim the room, you may submit a Visa sales draft for one night's accommodation, plus any applicable tax. Simply write 'No Show' on the signature panel of the sales draft and complete all parts of the sales draft normally.

HANDLING OVERBOOKINGS

If the guaranteed accommodation is not available when the guest arrives, you must at least provide the following at your hotel's expense:

- Comparable accommodation at a hotel of at least equal quality for one night
- Transportation to that establishment
- Forwarding of all messages and calls to the establishment
- A three-minute telephone call

THE VISA ADVANCE DEPOSIT SERVICE

Visa cards may be used when your hotel requires an advance deposit to guarantee a reservation.

This service also avoids the delay and confusion of handling personal or foreign cheques. However, whenever you are using the service, it is important that you correctly follow these simple steps. Failure to do so may result in unnecessary customer queries and complaints.

While speaking with a guest:

- Ask the guest for:
  - The Visa card account number
  - The expiration date
  - The cardholder's name as it appears on the card
  - The cardholder's billing address and telephone number
  - The expected arrival date and length of stay.
- Tell the guest:
  - The room rate (including tax)
  - The amount of the advance deposit that will be billed on their Visa card. This must not exceed the cost of 14 nights accommodation
  - That the deposit will be deducted from the final bill
  - That you will hold the accommodation for the period covered by the advance deposit
  - The hotel's address
  - The confirmation code of the reservation
  - To keep a record of the confirmation code for their future reference.
- Be sure to explain:
  - Your hotel's cancellation requirements
  - That all or part of the deposit may be forfeited if cancellation requirements are not met
  - The date and time the cancellation privileges expire
  - That a written copy of the cancellation policy will be mailed to the guest Following up.
- When filling out the Advance Deposit sales draft, be sure to include:
  - The Visa card account number, expiration date, and the cardholder's name
  - The cardholder's billing address and telephone number
  - The hotel identification
  - The words 'Advance Deposit' in the signature panel of the sales draft
  - The scheduled arrival date
  - The reservation confirmation code
  - The transaction date
  - The authorization code, if the transaction is above the floor limit
  - The date and time the cancellation privileges expire
  - The amount of the advance deposit.
- Mail a written reservation confirmation, along with a copy of the sales draft, within three business days.

The confirmation should include:

- The hotel's cancellation policy
- The guest's rights and responsibilities under the Advance Deposit Service
- The hotel's refund policy, which must allow for a complete refund of the guest's deposit if a reservation is cancelled before the specified deadline.

HANDLING ADVANCE DEPOSIT CANCELLATIONS

While speaking with the guest:

- Provide a cancellation code.
- Advise the guest to keep a record of the code for their future reference. Following...
- Write the word "cancelled" on the reservation form, along with the cancellation code provided to the guest.
- Determine the refund amount and prepare a credit voucher. The voucher should include:
  - The Visa card account number, expiration date, and the cardholder's name
  - The cardholder's billing address
  - The hotel identification
  - The cancellation code
  - The words "Advance Deposit" on the signature panel of the sales draft
  - The transaction date
  - The amount of the advance deposit
- Mail the cardholder a copy of the credit vouchers within three business days.
- Include the credit voucher with your daily deposits.

HANDLING OVERBOOKINGS

If the guaranteed accommodation is not available when the guest arrives, you must at least provide the following at your hotel's expense:

- Comparable accommodation at a hotel of at least equal quality for one night
- transportation to that establishment
- Forwarding of all messages and calls to the establishment
- Two three-minute telephone calls
- In addition, you must complete a credit voucher for the total deposit amount and mail a copy to the guest.

AUTHORIZE THE VISA TRANSACTION

It is important for you to obtain authorization whenever possible, particularly in the following instances:

- If the total transaction amount is above your hotel's floor limit
- If the card is not signed
- If the transaction involves suspicious or unusual circumstances
- If the card is a Visa Electron card

Note: the Visa Electron card works like any other Visa card. Procedures at the point of sale do not change except that it must always be authorized through a POS terminal. The authorization will stay valid for the length of the guest's stay. For stays longer than two weeks, we recommend that you close out the guest folio and bill the guests every two weeks.

ESTIMATED AUTHORIZATIONS

The estimated authorization procedure allows you to estimate the final transaction amount and receive the protection of an authorization before the guest checks out. However, whenever you are using the service, it is important that you correctly follow these simple steps. Failure to do so may result in unnecessary customer queries and complaints.

When the guest checks in:

- Estimate the guest's total charges based on:
  - The expected length of stay
  - The room rate including tax
  - Any estimated miscellaneous charges
- Compare the estimate with your floor limit
- Proceed just as to the following procedures

Below the floor limit Check the current Visa Card Recovery Bulletin to ensure it has not been reported lost, stolen or fraud.

Above the floor limit:

- Obtain authorization for the estimated amount do not over-estimate the amount authorized, as this will result in customer complaints
- Record in the guest folio/sales draft the date, amount authorized and approval code. Authorization reversal
- If the authorized amount is higher than the value of the guest's final bill, it is important that you process an authorization reversal for the difference between the authorized amount and the value of the cardholder's final bill.

REVISING ESTIMATED AUTHORIZATIONS

You may want to monitor charges to the guest's account to determine whether you need to revise your estimate. If the revised estimate exceeds the floor limit and:

Do this:

- No previous authorization was obtained
- Authorize the total amount
- Previous authorization was obtained
- Obtain authorization approval for the additional incremental amount(s) separately
- For all revised estimates
- Record on the guest folio/sales draft the date, amount authorized and approval code

When the Guest Checks out:

- When the guest is ready, you should determine the final bill and proceed just as to the following procedures.
- If the estimated amount is:

Do this:

- Below the floor limit
- No need for authorization Above the floor limit and no previous authorization was obtained
- Authorize the total amount

Above the floor limit and previous authorizations have been obtained, you are protected for the sum of the authorized amounts plus 15% of that sum.

To determine whether an additional authorization is required:

- Add up the sum of all authorized amounts
- To that sum add 15%
- Compare this figure to the final transaction amount
- Authorize the total amount

Then do one of these three things:

1. If the final transaction amount is less than the sum of all authorized amounts plus 15%
2. If the final transaction amount is greater than the sum of all authorized amounts plus 15%.
3. No need for authorization

Obtain an additional authorization for the difference between the final transaction amount and the sum of the authorizations already received.

THE VISA PRIORITY CHECK OUT SERVICE

The Visa Priority Check Out Service is a quick and convenient procedure for you and your guests – allowing them and you to avoid delays at peak check-out times. However, whenever you are using the service, it is important that you correctly follow these simple steps. Failure to do so may result in unnecessary customer queries and complaints.

CHECK OUT PROCEDURES

During the guest's stay:

- Describe the convenience of the Visa Priority Check Out Service. Then, if the guest requests Priority Check Out:
  - Ensure that you have recorded the Visa card account number, expiration date, and cardholder name on a Visa sales draft
  - Give the guest a Visa Priority Check Out agreement
  - Inform the guest of your policy regarding any charges discovered after check out
  - Ask the guest to return the completed signed agreement any time before check out.
- When the guest returns the agreement, verify that:
  - It is signed
  - The mailing address is included so that you can send a copy of the final bill after the guest's departure
  - The cardholder account number on the check out agreement matches the account number of the sales draft.
- After the guest's stay:
  - Complete the sales draft by entering the total charges incurred during the stay, including any restaurant, telephone or miscellaneous charges
  - Consult your authorization procedures to determine whether authorization is required at this time, and if so, obtain an authorization.
- If requested, mail to the guest within three business days after check out:
  - A completed sales draft indicating the final amount with the words "Priority Check Out" on the signature panel, or a printout of the Visa billing
  - The itemized hotel bill
  - Another copy of the Visa Priority Check Out agreement.

Retain a copy of the itemized bill and completed check out agreement for at least six months.

ADD CHARGES TO A VISA CARD AFTER CHECK OUT

This procedure allows you to bill Visa cardholders for any additional charges which are discovered after they have checked out – such as room service, telephone or mini bar charges. However, whenever you are billing guests for additional charges, it is important that you correctly follow these simple steps.

AFTER THE GUEST CHECKS OUT

You may deposit a separate sales draft for delayed charges, with the words "Signature on File" on the signature panel of the sales draft. Note: You should only do so if the guest has agreed to be responsible for such charges. You may not submit a separate or amended sales draft for loss, theft or damage to the room. Mail the guest a copy of the sales draft with a detailed explanation of the additional charges. Failure to do so will almost certainly result in customer queries and possible complaints. The cash disbursement service lets your hotel offer Visa Gold/Premier cardholders free access to extra cash whenever they need it.

To offer this service to your guests, use a Cash Disbursement sales draft and take the following steps:

- When they check in, the guest must confirm that they will use their Visa card to pay for the hotel stay
- The guest may receive a maximum cash disbursement of US$250 during their stay at the hotel
- Before disbursement, ask the cardholder for identification that includes an identification number
- Imprint the Visa card
- Verify the expiration date.

TERMS AND CONDITIONS

Brief guide to the terms and conditions of stay at a Hotel, and the terms and conditions for the usage of this internet site. Please allow 12 hours notice prior to your expected arrival to process the booking.

Confirmation of a booking by the client is deemed acceptance of these terms:

- *Prices:* All published rates include VAT or local service charges at the current rate. Accommodation rates are per room per night with meal plans as indicated. The Hotel reserves the right to alter prices for any reason up to the date of booking or up to 12 weeks prior to arrival, whichever is the later. After such dates, prices may only be altered to reflect a change in the rate of VAT or local service charge and taxes or for any other reason outside of the control of the Hotel, in which case the changes will be notified to the Client. In the latter event, the Client may cancel the booking without cost.
- *Availability:* All rooms and rates offered by the Hotel are subject to availability and the discretion of the Hotel manager. Limited

numbers of suitable rooms may be allocated to individual rates, packages or promotions and, when these allocations are taken up, remaining available rooms may be offered to the Client at a higher price.

- *Bookings:* Bookings must be guaranteed for the first night's accommodation by a major credit or debit card, by payment of a deposit or by agreement in writing with a company, travel agent or hotel booking agency. At the discretion of the Hotel, full pre-payment may be required. At least 3 working days are required to process credit and debit card payments and 5 working days to process cheque payments.
- *Arrival and departure:* Bedrooms are usually available from 2pm local time on the day of arrival. Check out is by 12 noon local time. There may be occasions, at times of high demand, when clients can check in and use the entire hotel facilities, but the bedroom is still being prepared.
- *Car parking:* Most Hotels have their own car park, which is usually free to residents. Some Hotels, however, have limited on-site parking and Clients are advised to check with the Hotel whether there is a charge for off-site parking. The Hotel does not accept responsibility for damage to, or for theft from, or for theft of vehicles parked on Hotel premises.
- *Cancellations, amendments and non-arrivals:* When the booking is confirmed, a reservation number and access code will be supplied. This must be retained for access to the booking in the event of the need for cancellation and/or amendment. There is no charge, and any deposit paid will be returned, if a guaranteed reservation is cancelled at any time up to 2pm local time on the day of arrival.

In the event of non-arrival or cancellation after 2pm local time and where the booking has been guaranteed, a charge equivalent to one night's accommodation at the package rate at which the reservation was made will be levied. Normal terms of payment apply to these charges. For this purpose the Hotel reserves the right to set-off the amount payable for such cancellation against the Client's credit card without prior notice or approval of the Client, where applicable.

If the Hotel cancels before 2pm local time on the scheduled day of arrival, the Hotel's liability to the Client will be no greater than the amount paid by the client in respect of any booking. If the Hotel cancels after 2pm local time on the day of arrival, the Hotel's liability will be limited to the charge for one night's accommodation. Where possible the Hotel may but is not obliged nor will it be liable to find alternative accommodation for the Client in the event that the Hotel is unable to accommodate the Client. A cancellation number will be provided at the time of cancellation and this should be retained for future reference.

PAYMENT

Settlement of the bill in full, less any advance payments must be made prior to departure from the Hotel. Upon arrival the Hotel reserves the right to request preauthorisation of the Client's credit or debit card or where payment is to be by cash, request the Client to place cash up to an amount of 1.5 times the room rate multiplied by the number of nights booked. All major credit and debit cards are accepted. Company cheques are not accepted without prior clearance.

Please contact the Hotel prior to arrival. Accounts may only be forwarded for payment on completion by the Client and formal acceptance by the Hotel of an application for credit facilities, which may be withdrawn at any time. Credit facilities are not offered to private individuals. All sums are due for payment on presentation of the invoice. In the event of any query relating to the invoice, the Client must notify the Hotel within 7 days of the invoice date and the Client's obligation to pay all outstanding balances immediately will not be affected.

Personal Information and payment details may be used by the system to determine automatically the appropriate way to fulfil your order. In order to process a booking, your Personal Information and payment details may be passed to third party service providers and, where we are lawfully requested to do so, regulatory authorities. Such third party service providers will have access to the Personal Information needed to perform the relevant service. They may not, however, use your Personal Information for any other purposes and are required to process your Personal Information in accordance with the Data Protection Act 1998.

Hospitality is an exciting and multifaceted industry that offers a variety of career opportunities to those who have earned a hotel/restaurant management degree. Careers with hotel, restaurant, airline, cruise line, gaming, and wine and spirit companies are readily available to such graduates. In addition, careers with service firms that support hospitality companies in the areas of accounting, consulting, real estate development, architecture, interior design, real estate brokerage, hotel valuation, investment banking, mortgage brokerage, insurance, advertising, and technology are also available to those with hospitality degrees.

Although dynamic and interesting, the business of hospitality presents many challenges. For example, hospitality businesses operate on low profit margins with fluctuating sales volumes. The ability to forecast revenues and control expenses is critical to achieving budgeted profits and a favourable return on investment for the owners of the company. Also, because hospitality businesses are labour intensive, scheduling employee hours so they are consistent with forecasted revenues and monitoring payroll cost daily are just two major management challenges. While a hospitality business typically requires a relatively low level of operating inventories, it requires a relatively high level of capital for its real estate component. This component often includes buildings, operating systems, guest room furniture, and restaurant equipment. Securing financing to acquire these assets is a continuing challenge for management.

Finally, hospitality businesses rely heavily on the discretionary income of their customers. During a weak economy, when household discretionary income is low, the hospitality industry usually suffers. High-end establishments, such as resorts and fine dining restaurants, normally feel the effects of a weak economy first, but eventually, the entire industry feels the financial pain.

However, as soon as the economy takes a turn for the better, consumers return, discretionary spending increases, and the industry prospers. Accurately predicting these economic fluctuations, and knowing when to buy and sell hospitality assets, can be financially lucrative for the astute hospitality investor. The financial tools utilized by modern-day management to address these challenges and opportunities are the focus of this book. Understanding of these financial tools and applying them to the challenges and opportunities they will soon face when they take jobs in the industry will serve hospitality graduates well throughout their business careers.

Children aged 15 years and under must be accompanied by a responsible adult to ensure that the children's behaviour is appropriate for other guests within the Hotel. Subject to the availability of suitable accommodation, children aged 15 years and under stay free when sharing a room with two adults, on the basis of one child per adult. Children sharing with one adult or in their own room pay 50% of the adult rate.

At the discretion of the Hotel, children may be excluded from certain events or promotions where deemed unsuitable or inappropriate.

Where Hotels have health and leisure facilities, children aged 15 years and under must be accompanied by an adult at all times and they are not permitted to use gymnasium equipment or the sunbed/tanning equipment. Under 5's are excluded from the sauna, spa pools and solaria areas and must be accompanied in the swimming pool by an adult at all times. Clients must read and follow the conditions of use displayed at such facilities.

In the interest and safety of children, some health and leisure clubs may be subject to specific time allocations for use of the facilities by children. Clients are advised to check with the Hotel beforehand. The Client is responsible for controlling the pet and will be liable for any damage, soilage or injury however caused by the pet.

The Hotel reserves the right to judge acceptable levels of noise or behaviour of Clients, guests or representatives, who must take all steps for corrective action as requested by the Hotel. In the event of failure to comply with management requests, the Hotel may terminate the booking or stop any event immediately without being liable for any refund or compensation.

It is the policy of the hotel not to discriminate on the grounds of race, colour, nationality, creed, sex, marital status, age, ethnic origin or disability. Clients, their employees, guests and all sub-contractors engaged by or on behalf of the Client are expected to adhere to this policy and the Hotel may, without incurring any liability to the Client, remove from the Hotel any person or persons offending against this policy.

5

Career in Hotel, Motel, and Resort Desk Clerks

Hotels are open around the clock creating the need for night and weekend work. Extended hours of operation also afford the many part-time job seekers an opportunity to find work in these establishments, especially on evenings and late-night shifts or on weekends and holidays. About half of all desk clerks work a 35 to 40 hour week—most of the rest work fewer hours—so the jobs are attractive to persons seeking part-time work or jobs with flexible schedules. Most clerks work in areas that are clean, well lit, and relatively quiet, although lobbies can become crowded and noisy when busy. Many hotels have stringent dress guidelines for desk clerks.

Desk clerks may experience particularly hectic times during check-in and check-out times or incur the pressures encountered when dealing with convention guests or large groups of tourists at one time. Moreover, dealing with irate guests can be stressful. Computer failures can further complicate an already busy time and add to stress levels. Hotel desk clerks may be on their feet most of the time and may occasionally be asked to lift heavy guest luggage.

Hotel, motel, and resort desk clerks deal directly with the public, so a professional appearance and a pleasant personality are important. A clear speaking voice and fluency in English also are essential, because these employees talk directly with hotel guests and the public and frequently use the telephone or public-address systems. Good spelling and computer literacy are needed, because most of the work involves use of a computer. In addition, speaking a foreign language fluently is increasingly helpful, because of the growing international clientele of many properties.

Most hotel, motel, and resort desk clerks receive orientation and training on the job. Orientation may include an explanation of the job duties and information about the establishment, such as the arrangement of sleeping rooms, availability of additional services, such as a business or fitness centre, and location of guest facilities, such as ice and vending machines, restaurants and other nearby retail stores. New employees learn job tasks through on-the-job training under the guidance of a supervisor or an experienced desk clerk. They often receive additional training on interpersonal or customer service skills and on how to use the computerized reservation, room assignment, and billing systems and equipment. Desk clerks typically continue to receive instruction on new procedures and on company policies after their initial training ends.

Formal academic training generally is not required so many students take jobs as desk clerks on evening or weekend shifts or during school vacation periods. Most employers look for people who are friendly and customer-service oriented, well groomed, and display the maturity and self confidence to demonstrate good judgment. Desk clerks, especially in high-volume and higher-end properties should be quick-thinking, show initiative, and be able to work as a member of a team. Hotel managers typically look for these personal characteristics when hiring first-time desk clerks, because it is easier to teach company policy and computer skills than personality traits.

Large hotel and motel chains may offer better opportunities for advancement than small, independently owned establishments. The large chains have more extensive career ladder programmes and may offer desk clerks an opportunity to participate in a management training programme. Also, the Educational Institute of the American Hotel and Motel Association offers home-study or group-study courses in lodging management, which may help some obtain promotions more rapidly.

Hotel, motel, and resort desk clerks held about 195,000 jobs in 2004. Virtually all were in hotels, motels, and other establishments in the accommodation industry. Few were self employed.

Employment of hotel, motel, and resort desk clerks is expected to grow about as fast as the average for all occupations through 2014, as more hotels, motels, and other lodging establishments are built and occupancy rates rise. Job opportunities for hotel and motel desk clerks also will result from a need to replace workers, because many of these clerks either transfer to other occupations that offer better pay and advancement opportunities or simply leave the workforce altogether. Opportunities for part-time work should continue to be plentiful, because these businesses typically are staffed 24 hours a day, 7 days a week.

Employment of hotel and motel desk clerks should benefit from an increase in business and leisure travel. Shifts in preferences away from long vacations and toward long weekends and other, more frequent, shorter trips also should boost demand for these workers, because such stays increase the number of nights spent in hotels. While many lower budget and extended-stay establishments are being built to cater to families and the leisure traveller, many new luxury and resort accommodations also are opening to serve the upscale client. With the increased number of units requiring staff, employment opportunities for desk clerks should be good.

Growth of hotel, motel, and resort desk clerk jobs will be moderated by technology. Automated check-in and check-out procedures reduce the backlog of guests waiting for desk service and may reduce peak front desk staffing needs in many establishments. Nevertheless, the front desk remains the principal point of contact for guests at most properties and most will continue to have clerks on duty.

Employment of desk clerks is sensitive to cyclical swings in the economy. During recessions, vacation and business travel declines, and hotels and motels need fewer desk clerks. Similarly, employment is affected by special events, business and convention business, and seasonal fluctuations.

The restaurant and hotel industries consist of establishments that are open to the public or are operated by membership organizations that furnish meals or lodging. The restaurant industry is composed of establishments that prepare and serve meals and beverages and includes, but is not limited to, restaurants, cafeterias, caterers, cocktail lounges, diners, fast food places, and takeout or delivery businesses.

Establishments in the hotel industry provide lodging to their customers or members and include, but are not limited to, hotels, motels, hostels, inns, rooming and boarding houses, fraternity or sorority residential houses, and residential clubs.

JOBS IN HOTEL, MOTEL, AND RESORT DESK CLERKS

Hotel, motel, and resort desk clerks held about 159,000 jobs in 1998. This occupation is well suited to flexible work schedules, as over 1 in 4 desk clerks works part time. Because hotels and motels need to be staffed 24 hours a day, evening and weekend work is common.

Although hiring requirements for information clerk jobs vary from industry to industry, a high school diploma or its equivalent is the most common educational requirement. Increasingly, familiarity or experience with computers and good interpersonal skills are often equally important to employers. For new account clerk and airline reservation and ticket agent jobs, some college education may be preferred.

Many information clerks deal directly with the public, so a professional appearance and pleasant personality are important. A clear speaking voice and fluency in the English language also are essential because these employees frequently use the telephone or public address systems. Good spelling and computer literacy are often needed, particularly because most work involves considerable computer use. It also is increasingly helpful for those wishing to enter the lodging or travel industries to speak a foreign language fluently.

With the exception of airline reservation and transportation ticket agents, orientation and training for information clerks usually takes place on the job. For example, orientation for hotel and motel desk clerks usually includes an explanation of the job duties and information about the establishment, such as room locations and available services. New employees learn job tasks through on-the-job training under the guidance of a supervisor or an experienced clerk. They often need additional training in how to use the computerized reservation, room assignment, and billing systems and equipment. Most information clerks continue to receive instruction on new procedures and company policies after their initial training ends.

Receptionists usually receive on-the-job training which may include procedures for greeting visitors, operating telephone and computer systems, and distributing mail, fax, and parcel deliveries. Some employers look for applicants who already possess certain skills, such as prior computer and word processing experience, or previous formal education.

Most airline reservation and ticket agents learn their skills through formal company training programmes. In a classroom setting, they learn company and industry policies, computer systems, and ticketing procedures. They also learn to use the airline's computer system to obtain information on schedules, seat availability, and fares; to reserve space for passengers; and to plan passenger itineraries.

They must also become familiar with airport and airline code designations, regulations, and safety procedures, and may be tested on this knowledge. After completing classroom instruction, new agents work on the job with supervisors or experienced agents for a period of time. During this period, supervisors may monitor telephone conversations to improve the quality of customer service. Agents are expected to provide good service while limiting the time spent on each call without being discourteous to customers. In contrast to the airlines, automobile clubs, bus lines, and railroads tend to train their ticket agents or travel clerks on the job through short in-house classes that last several days.

Most banks prefer to hire college graduates for new account clerk positions. Nevertheless, many new accounts clerks without college degrees start out as bank tellers and are promoted by demonstrating excellent communication skills and motivation to learn new skills. If a new accounts clerk has not been a teller before, he or she will often receive such training and work for several months as a teller. In both cases, new accounts clerks undergo formal training regarding the bank's procedures, products, and services.

Advancement for information clerks usually comes about either by transfer to a position with more responsibilities or by promotion to a supervisory position.

Most companies fill office and administrative support supervisory and managerial positions by promoting individuals within their organization, so information clerks who acquire additional skills, experience, and training improve their advancement opportunities. Receptionists, interviewers, and new accounts clerks with word processing or other clerical skills may advance to a better paying job as a secretary or administrative assistant. Within the airline industry, a ticket agent may advance to lead worker on the shift.

EMPLOYMENT OF HOTEL, MOTEL, AND RESORT DESK CLERKS

Additional training is helpful in preparing information clerks for promotion. In the lodging industry, clerks can improve their chances for advancement by taking home or group study courses in lodging management, such as those sponsored by the Educational Institute of the American Hotel and Motel Association. In some industries—such as lodging, banking, or the airlines—workers commonly are promoted through the ranks. Positions such as airline reservation agent or hotel and motel desk clerk offer good opportunities for qualified workers to get started in the business. In a number of industries, a college degree may be required for advancement to management ranks.

Employment of hotel, motel, and resort desk clerks is expected to grow about as fast as the average for all occupations through 2008, as more hotels, motels, and other lodging establishments are built and occupancy rates rise. Job opportunities for hotel and motel desk clerks will result from an unusually high turnover rate.

These openings occur each year as thousands of workers transfer to other occupations that offer better pay and advancement opportunities or simply leave the work force altogether. Opportunities for part-time work should continue to be plentiful, as nearly all front desks are staffed 24 hours a day, 7 days a week.

Employment of hotel and motel desk clerks should be favourably affected by an increase in business and leisure travel. Shifts in travel preference away from long vacations and towards long weekends and other, more frequent, shorter trips also should increase demand as this trend increases the total number of nights spent in hotels. The expansion of smaller, budget hotels relative to larger, luxury establishments reflects a change in the composition of the hotel and motel industry. As employment shifts from luxury hotels to more "no-frills" operations, the proportion of hotel desk clerks should increase in relation to staff such as waiters and waitresses and recreation workers.

However, the growing effort to cut labour costs while moving towards more efficient service is expected to slow the growth of desk clerk employment. The role of the front desk is changing as some of the more traditional duties are automated. New technologies automating check-in and check-out procedures now allow guests to bypass the front desk in many larger establishments, reducing staffing needs. The expansion of other technologies, such as interactive television and computer systems to dispense information, should further impact employment in the future as such services become more widespread.

Employment of desk clerks is sensitive to cyclical swings in the economy. During recessions, vacation and business travel declines and hotels and motels need fewer clerks. Similarly, desk clerk employment is affected by seasonal fluctuations in travel during high and low tourist seasons.

Earnings vary widely by occupation and experience. Annual earnings ranged from less than $11,750 for the lowest paid 10 per cent of hotel clerks to over $39,540 for the top 10 per cent of reservation agents in 1998. Salaries of reservation and transportation ticket agents and travel clerks tend to be significantly higher than for other information clerks, while hotel, motel, and resort desk clerks tend to earn quite a bit less, as the following tabulation of median annual earnings shows.

Reservation and transportation ticket agents and travel clerks	$22.120
New accounts clerks	21,340
Receptionists	18,620
Interviewing clerks	18,540
Hotel, motel, and resort desk clerks	15,160

Earnings of hotel and motel desk clerks also vary considerably depending on the location, size, and type of establishment in which they work. For example, clerks at large luxury hotels and those located in metropolitan and resort areas generally pay clerks more than less exclusive or "budget" establishments and those located in less populated areas.

In early 1999, the Federal Government typically paid salaries ranging from $16,400 to $18,100 a year to beginning receptionists with a high school diploma or 6 months of experience. The average annual salary for all receptionists employed by the Federal Government was about $22,700 in 1999. In addition to their hourly wage, full-time information clerks who work evenings, nights, weekends, or holidays may receive shift differential pay. Some employers offer educational assistance to their employees. Reservation and transportation ticket agents and travel clerks receive free or reduced rate travel on their company's carriers for themselves and their immediate family and, in some companies, for friends.

AN EMPLOYEE

A worker is a common law employee when the employer has the right to direct and control the manner and means of accomplishing the work. Types of employees that are typical in the restaurant and hotel industries are:

- Chefs
- Cooks
- Dishwashers
- Kitchen Helpers

- Bus Persons
- Waiters and Waitresses
- Maitre d's
- Hosts and Hostesses
- Cashiers
- Managers
- Delivery Persons
- Bartenders
- Valets
- Clerical and Office Staff
- Maids
- Switchboard Operators
- Laundry Persons
- Repair and Maintenance
- Desk Clerks
- Persons
- Bellhops

Other services that may be performed by an employee under common law rules include, but are not limited to, those of bookkeepers, janitors, and entertainers.

Wages

Wages are payments made to an employee for services performed during employment. The payment may be made in cash or some medium other than cash. Types of payments typically considered to be wages are:

- Cash
- Lodging
- Meals and Beverages
- Tips

Employer-provided meals and lodging are subject to Unemployment Insurance (UI), State Disability Insurance (SDI), and Employment Training Tax (ETT). Meals are subject to personal income tax (PIT) withholding and reportable as PIT wages unless furnished for the employer's convenience and on the employer's premises.

If more than half of the employees receive meals that are for the convenience of the employer, all meals furnished by the employer are considered furnished for the employer's convenience and are therefore not subject to PIT withholding or reportable as PIT wages. If fewer than half of the employees receive meals which are for the convenience of the employer, only those meals actually provided for the employer's convenience would be exempt from the PIT withholding and wage reporting requirements.

Lodging is also subject to PIT unless furnished on the employer's premises, for the employer's convenience, and as a condition of employment.

The Values of Meals and Lodging

The taxable values of meals and lodging should not be less than the reasonable estimated values stipulated by the contract of employment or in a union agreement. If the cash values are not stipulated in the hiring or union agreement, the taxable values are established by regulation. The taxable value of lodging is 66 2/3 percent of the ordinary rental value to the public up to a maximum per month and not less than a minimum value per week.

The taxable values of meals and lodging are listed below:

The cash values of meals and lodging are subject to change each calendar year. This information is published in the Employment Development Department's (EDD) quarterly newsletter.

Employees who receive more than $20 in tips in a calendar month must report all tips in one or more written statements to the employer on or before the tenth day of the month following the month in which they are received from the customers. Tips are taxable when the employee's statement is furnished to the employer.

Banquet tips and tips controlled by the employer are treated as regular wages, and their taxability is not contingent upon employees reporting them to the employer. Tips that are included in a written statement furnished to the employer are wages and are subject to Ul, ETT, SDI, and PIT. Tips should be combined with regular wages when reported to EDD.

A Survey Report

Using specially developed models of service management, the researchers looked at five key service sectors: retail, hotels and catering, health care, utilities, and professional and financial services. "We identified the top 10 companies that have set the standard for service quality in America over the past decade and uncovered the secrets of the global leaders,". "Each excelled by systematically linking the drivers of service excellence: leadership, people, processes and performance management. We discovered that delivering service quality goes beyond simplistic prescriptions about people issues, and instead extends to strategic factors, such as organizational design, leadership and market acuity, to orchestrate the entire service encounter."

The researchers found vast differences among the service sectors. The retail and hotel industries were the two highest performing sectors in the survey; the researchers found they follow best practices, achieving good results. The hotel industry also paid more attention to customer service than any other sector, which paid off in hefty returns. Not all hotels are wonderful, but those that succeed manage the "evidence" of quality, such as how the hotel looks and how employees dress. These hotels also manage customer interactions and continuously communicate their high standards to employees, according to the study.

Other pacesetter sectors in the study are industrial service and telecommunications companies. The researchers found that financial-services companies satisfy customers, but they concluded that the institutions may be yielding good performance without being brilliant strategists. Many are riding a wave of low interest rates and a favourable economy.

For example, some financial institutions seemed complacent about managing customer interactions, compared to their counterparts in other service sectors. By stressing re-structuring and reducing their staffs at the expense of customer service, businesses like banks and insurance companies may be vulnerable to future market changes.

Professional services such as legal and architectural firms were found to be "surprisingly weak" in both practice and performance. Of the top 10 service practices emphasized by senior executives, half are customer-focused: accessibility, listening to customers, competitive positioning, consistently meeting customers' needs and customer orientation.

Accessibility is the new "location, location, location" of service. It refers to a customer's ability to contact someone in a company easily, and at many companies, 24 hours a day. The top 10 companies were described as having "global-service leadership," demonstrating world-class capabilities, regardless of the geographic market of a company's location. Nordstrom, the retail chain, was cited as a classic example of a company that maintained world-class standards in both practice (such as how they control quality and handle complaints) and service performance (such as value, quality, satisfaction, business performance and customer retention).

The study also found that managing change is one of the biggest hurdles to achieving global service leadership. However, by world standards, the top American service businesses enjoy a supremacy role similar to that of Japan's manufacturing sector. The researchers were involved an in-depth, year-long survey of medium- to large-size service companies in the United States.

They conducted three-hour interviews with senior executives who, besides responding to 80 questions about their own company, rated other American companies on their quality of service. Participants were not allowed to identify themselves in the "best company" category. A hotel, resort, casino, or other hospitality asset's positioning is uniquely complex among real estate property types.

Changing market factors, including outside economic forces, shifts in demand patterns, and changing competitor pressures can all influence a property's success and require an owner to constantly re-evaluate an asset's current positioning. A sound repositioning strategy is an effective way to maximize a property's future financial returns.

The results show that 39 percent of the 181 companies surveyed had the potential to become global leaders in delivering good customer service, although only 13 percent of these companies have achieved both world-class performance and world-class service management practices. The research team also surveyed 21 governmental and non-profit organizations.

The results clearly show a need for improvement in governmental agencies. With the exception of altruism and cost performance, the study found that productivity, quality service and customer growth and retention lagged behind private enterprises. The researchers found most government organizations do not measure value or are not striving sufficiently to create it. Major changes in management and the approach to customer are needed to produce better results.

Hospitality & Leisure practice is comprised of industry professionals with significant experience in successful product positioning. Knowledge of the local market, the latest in competitive product offerings, and effective branding strategies are vital to creating a successful repositioning strategy. The specialists possess the knowledge and skills to formulate a creative vision for a market-based, property-specific repositioning, and employ proven methods to analyze and quantify potential financial benefits to the owner.

The professionals will not simply recommend a plan to reposition a property, but take the next step to assist the owner in understanding how the repositioning strategy should be implemented so that optimal financial returns can be achieved. The specialists investigate a multitude of possibilities for a property's potential repositioning, based on historical and recently changing market conditions, and the property's past and current positioning in the market.

Conducting a thorough market analysis and obtaining a solid understanding of the local economy, area demographics, demand generators, market trends, and other related area-specific characteristics are only the first steps taken in formulating an effective repositioning strategy. Considers every aspect of a property's operations in relation to its local market competition and the needs of the local market, to determine a relevant solution with an optimal financial payback.

NATURE OF THE HOTELS AND OTHER ACCOMMODATIONS

Hotels and other accommodations are as diverse as the many family and business travellers they accommodate. The industry includes all types of lodging, from upscale hotels to RV parks. Motels, resorts, casino hotels, bed-and-breakfast inns, and boarding houses also are included. In fact, in 2004 nearly 62,000 establishments provided overnight accommodations to suit many different needs and budgets. Establishments vary greatly in size and in the services they provide. *Hotels* and *motels* comprise the majority of establishments and tend to provide more services than other lodging places. There are five basic types of hotels—*commercial, resort, residential, extended-stay,* and *casino.*

Most hotels and motels are *commercial* properties that cater mainly to business people, tourists, and other travellers who need accommodations for a brief stay. Commercial hotels and motels usually are located in cities or suburban areas and operate year round. Larger properties offer a variety of services for their guests, including a range of restaurant and beverage service options—from coffee bars and lunch counters to cocktail lounges and formal fine-dining restaurants.

Some properties provide a variety of retail shops on the premises, such as gift boutiques, newsstands, drug and cosmetics counters, and barber and beauty shops. An increasing number of full-service hotels now offer guests access to laundry and valet services, swimming pools, and fitness centres or health spas. A small, but growing, number of luxury hotel chains also manage condominium units in combination with their transient rooms, providing both hotel guests and condominium owners with access to the same services and amenities. Larger hotels and motels often have banquet rooms, exhibit halls, and spacious ballrooms to accommodate conventions, business meetings, wedding receptions, and other social gatherings.

Conventions and business meetings are major sources of revenue for these hotels and motels. Some commercial hotels are known as conference hotels—fully self-contained entities specifically designed for meetings. They provide physical fitness and recreational facilities for meeting attendees, in addition to state-of-the-art audiovisual and technical equipment, a business centre, and banquet services.

Resort hotels and *motels* offer luxurious surroundings with a variety of recreational facilities, such as swimming pools, golf courses, tennis courts, game rooms, and health spas, as well as planned social activities and entertainment. Resorts typically are located in vacation destinations or near natural settings, such as mountains, the seashore, theme parks, or other attractions. As a result, the business of many resorts fluctuates with the season.

Some resort hotels and motels provide additional convention and conference facilities to encourage customers to combine business with pleasure. During the off season, many of these establishments solicit conventions, sales meetings, and incentive tours to fill their otherwise empty rooms; some resorts even close for the off-season.

Residential hotels provide living quarters for permanent and semi permanent residents. They combine the comfort of apartment living with the convenience of hotel services. Many have dining rooms and restaurants that also are open to residents and to the general public.

Extended-stay hotels combine features of a resort and a residential hotel. Typically, guests use these hotels for a minimum of 5 consecutive nights. These facilities usually provide rooms with fully equipped kitchens, entertainment systems, ironing boards and irons, office space with computer and telephone lines, fitness centres, and other amenities.

Casino hotels provide lodging in hotel facilities with a casino on the premises. The casino provides table wagering games and may include other gambling activities, such as slot machines and sports betting. Casino hotels generally offer a full range of services and amenities and also may contain conference and convention facilities.

In addition to hotels and motels, *bed-and-breakfast inns, recreational vehicle (RV) parks, campgrounds,* and *rooming and boarding houses* provide lodging for overnight guests. *Bed-and-breakfast inns* provide short-term lodging in private homes or small buildings converted for this purpose and are characterized by highly personalized service and inclusion of breakfast in the room rate. Their appeal is quaintness, with unusual service and decor.

RV parks and campgrounds cater to people who enjoy recreational camping at moderate prices. Some parks and campgrounds provide service stations, general stores, shower and toilet facilities, and coin-operated laundries. While some are designed for overnight travellers only, others are for vacationers who stay longer. Some camps provide accommodations, such as cabins and fixed campsites, and other amenities, such as food services, recreational facilities and equipment, and organized recreational activities. Examples of these overnight camps include children's camps, family vacation camps, hunting and fishing camps, and outdoor adventure retreats that offer trail riding, white-water rafting, hiking, fishing, game hunting, and similar activities.

Other short-term lodging facilities in this industry include *guesthouses,* or small cottages located on the same property as a main residence, and *youth hostels*—dormitory-style hotels with few frills, occupied mainly by students traveling on limited budgets. Also included are *rooming and boarding houses,* such as fraternity houses, sorority houses, off-campus dormitories, and workers' camps.

These establishments provide temporary or longer term accommodations that may serve as a principal residence for the period of occupancy. These establishments also may provide services such as housekeeping, meals, and laundry services.

In recent years, hotels, motels, camps, and recreational and RV parks affiliated with national chains have grown rapidly. To the traveller, familiar chain establishments represent dependability and quality at predictable rates. National corporations own many chains, although many properties are independently owned but affiliated with a chain through a franchise agreement.

Many independently operated hotels and inns participate in national reservations services, thereby appearing to belong to a larger enterprise. Also, many hotels join local chambers of commerce, boards of trade, convention and tourism bureaus, or regional recreation associations in order support and promote tourism in their area.

Increases in competition and in the sophistication of travellers have induced the chains to provide lodging to serve a variety of customer budgets and accommodation preferences. In general, these lodging places may be grouped into properties that offer luxury, all-suite, moderately priced, and economy accommodations. The numbers of limited-service or economy chain properties—economy lodging without extensive lobbies, restaurants, or lounges—have been growing. These properties are not as costly to build and operate. They appeal to budget-conscious family vacationers and travellers who are willing to sacrifice amenities for lower room prices.

While economy chains have become more prevalent, the movement in the hotel and lodging industry is towards more extended-stay properties. In addition to fully equipped kitchenettes and laundry services, the extended-stay market offers guest amenities such as in-room access to the Internet and grocery shopping. This segment of the hotels and other accommodations industry has eliminated traditional hotel lobbies and 24-hour front desk staffing, and housekeeping is usually done only about once a week. This helps to keep costs to a minimum.

All-suite facilities, especially popular with business travellers, offer a living room or sitting room in addition to a bedroom. These accommodations are aimed at travellers who require lodging for extended stays, families traveling with children, and business people needing to conduct small meetings without the expense of renting an additional room.

Increased competition among establishments in this industry has spurred many independently owned and operated hotels and other lodging places to join national or international reservation systems, which allow travellers to make multiple reservations for lodging, airlines, and car rentals with one telephone call. Nearly all hotel chains operate online reservation systems through the Internet.

WORKING CONDITIONS

Work in hotels and other accommodations can be demanding and hectic. Hotel staffs provide a variety of services to guests and must do so efficiently, courteously, and accurately. They must maintain a pleasant demeanor even during times of stress or when dealing with an impatient or irate guest. Alternately, work at slower times, such as the off-season or overnight periods, can seem slow and tiresome without the constant presence of hotel guests. Still, hotel workers must be ready to provide guests and visitors with gracious customer service at any hour. Because hotels are open around the clock, employees frequently work varying shifts or variable schedules. Employees who work the late shift generally receive additional compensation. Many employees enjoy the opportunity to work part-time, nights or evenings, or other schedules that fit their availability for work and the hotel's needs.

Hotel managers and many department supervisors may work regularly assigned schedules, but they also routinely work longer hours than scheduled, especially during peak travel times or when multiple events are scheduled. Also, they may be called in to work on short notice in the event of an emergency or to cover a position. Those who are self-employed, often owner-operators, tend to work long hours and often live at the establishment.

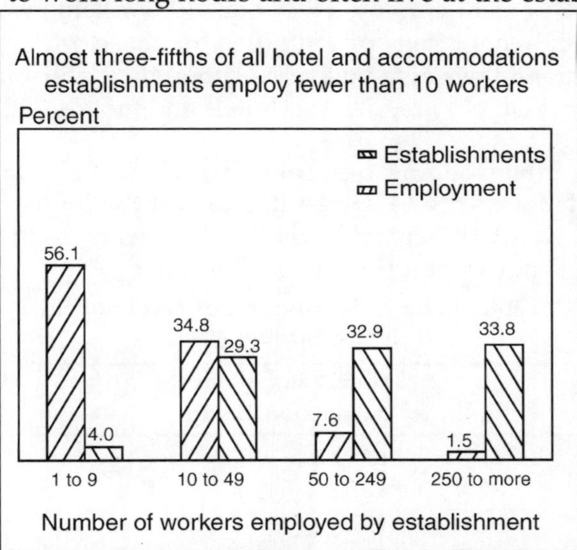

Food preparation and food service workers in hotels must withstand the strain of working during busy periods and being on their feet for many hours. Kitchen workers lift heavy pots and kettles and work near hot ovens and grills. Job hazards include slips and falls, cuts, and burns, but injuries are seldom serious. Food service workers often carry heavy trays of food, dishes, and glassware. Many of these workers work part time, including evenings, weekends, and holidays.

Office and administrative support workers generally work scheduled hours in an office setting, meeting with guests, clients, and hotel staff. Their work can become hectic processing orders and invoices, dealing with demanding guests, or servicing requests that require a quick turnaround, but job hazards typically are limited to muscle and eye strain common to working with computers and office equipment.

In 2003, work-related injuries and illnesses averaged 6.7 for every 100 full-time workers in hotels and other accommodations, compared with 5.0 for workers throughout private industry. Work hazards include burns from hot equipment, sprained muscles and wrenched backs from heavy lifting, and falls on wet floors.

EMPLOYMENT IN RESORT AREAS

Hotels and other accommodations provided 1.8 million wage and salary jobs in 2004. In addition, there were about 33,000 self-employed and unpaid family workers in the industry, who worked in bed-and-breakfast inns, camps, and small motels.

Employment is concentrated in densely populated cities and resort areas. Compared with establishments in other industries, hotels, motels, and other lodging places tend to be small. About 91 percent employed fewer than 50 people; about 56 percent employ fewer than 10 workers (chart). As a result, lodging establishments offer opportunities for those who are interested in owning and running their own business. Although establishments tend to be small, the majority of jobs are in larger hotels and motels with more than 100 employees.

Hotels and other lodging places often provide first jobs to many new entrants to the labour force. As a result, many of the industry's workers are young. In 2004, about 19 percent of the workers were younger than age 25, compared with about 14 percent across all industries.

Table. Percent distribution of employment, by age group, 2004

Age group	Hotels and other Accommodations	All industries
Total	100.0%	100.0%
16-19	5.3	4.2
20-24	13.7	9.9
25-34	22.4	21.8
35-44	23.7	24.8
45-54	20.2	23.3
55-64	11.4	12.4
65 and older	3.3	3.5

Occupations in the Industry

The vast majority of workers in this industry—more than 8 out of 10 in 2004—were employed in service and office and administrative support occupations. Workers in these occupations usually learn their skills on the job. Postsecondary education is not required for most entry-level positions; however, college training may be helpful for advancement in some of these occupations.

For many administrative support and service occupations, personality traits and a customer-service orientation may be more important than formal schooling. Traits most important for success in the hotel and motel industry are good communication skills; the ability to get along with people in stressful situations; a neat, clean appearance; and a pleasant manner.

Service occupations, by far the largest occupational group in the industry, account for 65 percent of the industry's employment. Most service jobs are in housekeeping occupations—including maids and housekeeping cleaners, janitors and cleaners, and laundry workers—and in food preparation and service jobs—including chefs and cooks, waiters and waitresses, bartenders, fast food and counter workers, and various other kitchen and dining room workers. The industry also employs many baggage porters and bellhops, gaming services workers, and grounds maintenance workers.

Workers in *cleaning* and *housekeeping occupations* ensure that the lodging facility is clean and in good condition for the comfort and safety of guests. *Maids and housekeepers* clean lobbies, halls, guestrooms, and bathrooms. They make sure that guests not only have clean rooms, but have all the necessary furnishings and supplies. They change sheets and towels, vacuum carpets, dust furniture, empty wastebaskets, and mop bathroom floors. In larger hotels, the housekeeping staff may include assistant housekeepers, floor supervisors, housekeepers, and executive housekeepers. *Janitors* help with the cleaning of the public areas of the facility, empty trash, and perform minor maintenance work.

Table. Employment of wage and salary workers in hotels and other accommodations by occupation, 2004 and projected change, 2004-14. (Employment in thousands)

Occupation	Employment, 2004 Number	%	% change, 2004-14
Total, all occupations	1,796	100.0	16.9
Management, business, and financial occupations	99	5.5	26.6
Top executives	16	0.9	25.8
Food service managers	10	0.6	16.2
Lodging managers	28	1.6	27.4
Meeting and convention planners	7	0.4	27.3
Service occupations	1,169	65.1	16.0
Security guards and gaming surveillance officers	34	1.9	-2.3
Chefs and head cooks	13	0.7	16.9
First-line supervisors/managers of food preparation and serving workers	22	1.2	16.5
Cooks, restaurant	56	3.1	16.7
Food preparation workers	23	1.3	27.1
Bartenders	39	2.2	13.1
Fast food and counter workers	27	1.5	25.2
Waiters and waitresses	133	7.4	9.5

Food servers, nonrestaurant	39	2.2	11.9
Dining room and cafeteria attendants and bartender helpers	43	2.4	9.1
Dishwashers	38	2.1	8.3
Hosts and hostesses, restaurant, lounge, and coffee shop	21	1.2	9.1
Supervisors, building and grounds cleaning and maintenance workers	37	2.0	26.6
Janitors and cleaners, except maids and housekeeping cleaners	49	2.7	20.2
Maids and housekeeping cleaners	405	22.5	17.0
Landscaping and groundskeeping workers	23	1.3	20.3
Gaming supervisors	11	0.6	10.3
Gaming dealers	35	2.0	25.0
Baggage porters and bellhops	25	1.4	21.5
Concierges	7	0.4	17.0
Recreation and fitness workers	13	0.7	22.1
Sales and related occupations	54	3.0	18.3
Cashiers, except gaming	16	0.9	14.3
Gaming change persons and booth cashiers	10	0.6	7.6
Office and administrative support occupations	320	17.8	15.0
Supervisors, office and administrative support workers	22	1.2	7.7
Bookkeeping, accounting, and auditing clerks	24	1.4	14.6
Gaming cage workers	5	0.3	5.7
Hotel, motel, and resort desk clerks	183	10.2	17.4
Reservation and transportation ticket agents and travel clerks	13	0.7	15.7
Installation, maintenance, and repair occupations	75	4.2	26.8
Maintenance and repair workers, general	64	3.6	27.2
Production occupations	39	2.2	19.0
Laundry and dry-cleaning workers	32	1.8	18.0
Transportation and material moving occupations	24	1.3	7.0

Note: May not add to totals due to omission of occupations with small employment

Workers in the various food service occupations deal with customers in the dining room or at a service counter. Waiters and waitresses take customers' orders, serve meals, and prepare checks. In restaurants, they may describe chef's specials and suggest appropriate wines. In smaller establishments, they often set tables, escort guests to their seats, accept payment, and clear tables. They also may deliver room service orders to guests. In larger restaurants, some of these tasks are assigned to other workers.

Hosts and hostesses welcome guests, show them to their tables, and give them menus. Bartenders fill beverage orders for customers seated at the bar or from waiters and waitresses who serve patrons at tables. Dining room and cafeteria attendants and bartender helpers assist waiters, waitresses, and bartenders by clearing, cleaning, and setting up tables, replenishing supplies at the bar, and keeping the serving areas stocked with linens, tableware, and other supplies. Counter attendants take orders and serve food at fast-food counters and in coffee shops; they also may operate the cash register.

Cooks and food preparation occupations prepare food in the kitchen. Beginners may advance to more skilled food preparation jobs with experience or specialized culinary training. Chefs and cooks generally prepare a wide selection of dishes, often cooking individual servings to order. Larger hotels employ cooks who specialize in the preparation of many different kinds of food. They may have titles such as salad chef, grill chef, or pastry chef.

Individual chefs may oversee the day-to-day operations of different kitchens in a hotel, such as a fine-dining full-service restaurant, a casual or counter-service establishment, or banquet operations. Chef positions generally are attained after years of experience and, sometimes, formal training, including apprenticeships.

Larger establishments also employ executive chefs and food and beverage directors who plan menus, purchase food, and supervise kitchen personnel for all of the kitchens in the property. Food preparation workers shred lettuce for salads, cut up food for cooking, and perform simple cooking steps under the direction of the chef or head cook.

Many full-service hotels employ a uniformed staff to assist arriving and departing guests. Baggage porters and bellhops carry bags and escort guests to their rooms. Concierges arrange special or personal services for guests. They may take messages, arrange for babysitting, make restaurant reservations, provide directions, arrange for or give advice on entertainment and local attractions, and monitor requests for housekeeping and maintenance. Doorkeepers help guests into and out of their cars, summon taxis, and carry baggage into the hotel lobby.

Hotels also employ the largest percentage of gaming services workers because much of gaming takes place in casino hotels. Some gaming services positions are associated with oversight and direction—supervision, surveillance, and investigation—while others involve working with the games or patrons themselves, by tending the slot machines, handling money, writing and running tickets, dealing cards, and performing related duties. Office and administrative support positions accounted for 18 percent of the jobs in hotels and other accommodations in 2004. Hotel desk clerks, secretaries, bookkeeping and accounting clerks, and telephone operators ensure that the front office operates smoothly. The majority of these workers are hotel, motel, and resort desk clerks. They process reservations and guests' registration and checkout, monitor arrivals and departures, handle complaints, and receive and forward mail.

The duties of hotel desk clerks depend on the size of the facility. In smaller lodging places, one clerk or a manager may do everything. In larger hotels, a larger staff divides the duties among several types of clerks. Although hotel desk clerks sometimes are hired from the outside, openings usually are filled by promoting other hotel employees such as bellhops and porters, credit clerks, and other administrative support workers.

Hotels and other lodging places employ many different types of *managers* to direct and coordinate the activities of the front office, kitchen, dining room, and other departments, such as housekeeping, accounting, personnel, purchasing, publicity, sales, security and maintenance. Managers make decisions on room rates, establish credit policy, and have ultimate responsibility for resolving problems. In smaller establishments, the manager also may perform many of the front-office clerical tasks. In the smallest establishments, the owners—sometimes a family team—do all the work necessary to operate the business.

Lodging managers or *general and operations managers* in large hotels often have several assistant managers, each responsible for a phase of operations. For example, *food and beverage managers* oversee restaurants, lounges, and catering or banquet operations. *Rooms managers* look after reservations and occupancy levels to ensure proper room assignments and authorize discounts, special rates, or promotions. Large hotels, especially those with conference centres, use an executive committee structure to improve departmental communications and coordinate activities. Other managers who may serve on a hotel's executive committee include *public relations* or *sales managers, human resources directors, executive housekeepers,* and *heads of hotel security.*

Workers at vacation and recreational camps may include camp counselors who lead and instruct children and teenagers in outdoor-oriented forms of recreation, such as swimming, hiking, horseback riding, and camping. In addition, counselors at vacation and resident camps also provide guidance and supervise daily living and general socialization. Other types of campgrounds may employ trail guides for activities such as hiking, hunting, and fishing.

Hotels and other lodging places employ a variety of workers found in many other industries. Maintenance workers, such as stationary engineers, plumbers, and painters, fix leaky faucets, do some painting and carpentry, see that heating and air-conditioning equipment works properly, mow lawns, and exterminate pests. The industry also employs cashiers, accountants, personnel workers, entertainers, and recreation workers. Also, many additional workers inside a hotel may work for other companies under contract to the hotel or may provide personal or retail services directly to hotel guests from space rented by the hotel. This group includes guards and security officers, barbers, cosmetologists, fitness trainers and aerobics instructors, valets, gardeners, and parking attendants.

TRAINING AND ADVANCEMENT IN HOTEL OPERATIONS

Although the skills and experience needed by workers in this industry depend on the specific occupation, most entry-level jobs require little or no previous training. Basic tasks usually can be learned in a short time. Almost all workers in the hotel and other accommodations industry undergo on-the-job training, which usually is provided under the supervision of an experienced employee or manager. Some large chain operations have formal training sessions for new employees; many also provide video or on-line training.

Hotel operations are becoming increasingly diverse and complex, but all positions require employees to maintain a customer-service orientation. Hoteliers recognize the importance of personal service and attention to guests; so they look for persons with positive personality traits and good communication skills when filling many guest services positions, such as desk clerk and host and hostess positions.

Many hotel managers place a greater emphasis on customer service skills while providing specialized training in important skill areas, such as computer technology and software. Vocational courses and apprenticeship programmes in food preparation, catering, and hotel and restaurant management, offered through restaurant associations and trade unions, provide training opportunities. Programmes range in length from a few months to several years. About 800 community and junior colleges offer 2-year degree programmes in hotel and restaurant management. The U.S. Armed Forces also offer experience and training in food service.

Traditionally, many hotels fill first-level manager positions by promoting administrative support and service workers—particularly those with good communication skills, a solid educational background, tact, loyalty, and a capacity to endure hard work and long hours.

People with these qualities still advance to manager jobs but, more recently, lodging chains have primarily been hiring persons with four-year college degrees in the liberal arts or other fields and starting them in trainee or junior management positions. Bachelor's and master's degree programmes in hotel, restaurant, and hospitality management provide the strongest background for a career as a hotel manager, with nearly 150 colleges and universities offering such programmes. Graduates of these programmes are highly sought by employers in this industry. New graduates often go through on-the-job training programmes before being given much responsibility. Eventually, they may advance to a top management position in a hotel, a corporate management opportunity in a large chain operation, or an investment or financial analysis position in the financial services sector.

Upper management positions, such as general manager, lodging manager, food service manager, or sales manager, generally require considerable formal training and job experience. Some department managers, such as comptrollers, purchasing managers, executive housekeepers, and executive chefs, generally require some specialized training and extensive on-the-job experience. To advance to positions with more responsibilities, managers frequently change employers or relocate within a chain to a property in another area.

For office and administrative support and service workers, advancement opportunities in the hotel industry vary widely. Some workers, such as housekeepers and janitors, generally have few opportunities for advancement. In large properties, however, some janitors may advance to supervisory positions. Hotel desk clerks, hospitality workers, and chefs sometimes advance to managerial positions. Promotional opportunities from the front office often are greater than those from any other department, because this vantage point provides an excellent opportunity to learn the establishment's overall operation. Front-office jobs are excellent entry-level jobs and can serve as a steppingstone to jobs in hospitality, public relations, advertising, sales, and management.

Advancement opportunities for chefs and cooks are better than those for most other service occupations. Cooks often advance to chef or to supervisory and management positions, such as executive chef, restaurant manager, or food service manager. Some transfer to jobs in clubs, go into business for themselves, or become instructors of culinary arts.

Nature of the Work

A comfortable room, good food, and a helpful staff can make being away from home an enjoyable experience for both vacationing families and business travellers. While most lodging managers work in traditional hotels and motels, some work in other lodging establishments, such as camps, inns, boardinghouses, dude ranches, and recreational resorts. In full-service hotels, lodging managers help their guests have a pleasant stay by providing many of the comforts of home, including cable television, fitness equipment, and voice mail, as well as specialized services such as health spas. For business travellers, lodging managers often schedule available meeting rooms and electronic equipment, including slide projectors and fax machines.

Lodging managers are responsible for keeping their establishments efficient and profitable. In a small establishment with a limited staff, the manager may oversee all aspects of operations. However, large hotels may employ hundreds of workers, and the general manager usually is aided by a number of assistant managers assigned to the various departments of the operation. In hotels of every size, managerial duties vary significantly by job title.

General managers have overall responsibility for the operation of the hotel. Within guidelines established by the owners of the hotel or executives of the hotel chain, the general manager sets room rates, allocates funds to departments, approves expenditures, and ensures expected standards for guest service, decor, housekeeping, food quality, and banquet operations. Managers who work for chains also may organize and staff a newly built hotel, refurbish an older hotel, or reorganize a hotel or motel that is not operating successfully. In order to fill entry-level service and clerical jobs in hotels, some managers attend career fairs.

Resident or hotel managers are responsible for the day-to-day operations of the property. In larger properties, more than one of these managers may assist the general manager, frequently dividing responsibilities between the food and beverage operations and the rooms or lodging services. At least one manager, either the general manager or a hotel manager, is on call 24 hours a day to resolve problems or emergencies.

Assistant managers help run the day-to-day operations of the hotel. In large hotels, they may be responsible for activities such as personnel, accounting, office administration, marketing and sales, purchasing, security, maintenance, and pool, spa, or recreational facilities. In smaller hotels, these duties may be combined into one position. Assistant managers may adjust charges on a hotel guest's bill when a manager is unavailable.

An Executive Committee made up of a hotel's senior managers advises the general manager, assists in setting hotel policy, coordinates services that cross departmental boundaries, and collaborates on efforts to ensure consistent and efficient guest services throughout the hotel. The Committee may be comprised of the department heads for housekeeping, front office, food and beverage, security, sales and public relations, meetings and conventions, engineering and building maintenance, and human resources. Executive committee members bring a different perspective of guest service to the total management objective reflecting the unique expertise and training of their positions.

Executive housekeepers ensure that guest rooms, meeting and banquet rooms, and public areas are clean, orderly, and well maintained. They also train, schedule, and supervise the work of housekeepers, inspect rooms, and order cleaning supplies.

Front office managers coordinate reservations and room assignments, as well as train and direct the hotel's front desk staff. They ensure that guests are treated courteously, complaints and problems are resolved, and requests for special services are carried out. Front office managers may adjust charges posted on a customer's bill.

Convention services managers coordinate the activities of various departments in larger hotels to accommodate meetings, conventions, and special events. They meet with representatives of groups or organizations to plan the number of rooms to reserve, the desired configuration of the meeting space, and banquet services. During the meeting or event, they resolve unexpected problems and monitor activities to ensure that hotel operations conform to the expectations of the group.

Food and beverage managers oversee all food service operations maintained by the hotel. They coordinate menus with the Executive Chef for the hotel's restaurants, lounges, and room service operations. They supervise the ordering of food and supplies, direct service and maintenance contracts within the kitchens and dining areas, and manage food service budgets.

Catering managers arrange for food service in a hotel's meeting and convention rooms. They coordinate menus and costs for banquets, parties, and events with meeting and convention planners or individual clients. They coordinate staffing needs and arrange schedules with kitchen personnel to ensure appropriate food service.

Sales or marketing directors and public relations directors oversee the advertising and promotion of hotel operations and functions, including lodging and dining specials and special events, such as holiday or seasonal specials. They direct the efforts of their staff to purchase advertising and market their property to organizations or groups seeking a venue for conferences, conventions, business meetings, trade shows, and special events. They also coordinate media relations and answer questions from the press.

Human resources directors manage the personnel functions of a hotel, ensuring that all accounting, payroll, and employee relations matters are handled in compliance with hotel policy and applicable laws. They also oversee hiring practices and standards and ensure that training and promotion programmes reflect appropriate employee development guidelines.

Finance (or revenue) directors monitor room sales and reservations. In addition to overseeing accounting and cash-flow matters at the hotel, they also project occupancy levels, decide which rooms to discount and when to offer rate specials.

Computers are used extensively by lodging managers and their assistants to keep track of guests' bills, reservations, room assignments, meetings, and special events. In addition, computers are used to order food, beverages, and supplies, as well as to prepare reports for hotel owners and top-level managers. Managers work with computer specialists to ensure that the hotel's computer system functions properly. Should the hotel's computer system fail, managers must continue to meet the needs of hotel guests and staff.

Because hotels are open around the clock, night and weekend work is common. Many lodging managers work more than 40 hours per week, and may be called back to work at any time. Some managers of resort properties or other hotels where much of the business is seasonal have other duties on the property during the off-season or find work at other hotels or in other areas.

Lodging managers experience the pressures of coordinating a wide range of activities. At larger hotels, they also carry the burden of managing a large staff and finding a way to satisfy guest needs while maintaining positive attitudes and employee morale. Conventions and large groups of tourists may present unusual problems or require extended work hours. Moreover, dealing with irate guests can be stressful. The job can be particularly hectic for front office managers during check-in and check-out times. Computer failures can further complicate processing and add to frustration levels.

Hotels increasingly emphasize specialized training. Postsecondary training in hotel, restaurant, or hospitality management is preferred for most hotel management positions; however, a college liberal arts degree may be sufficient when coupled with related hotel experience or business education. Internships or part-time or summer work experience in a hotel are an asset to students seeking a career in hotel management. The experience gained and the contacts made with employers can greatly benefit students after graduation. Most degree programmes include work-study opportunities.

Community colleges, junior colleges, and many universities offer certificate or degree programmes in hotel, restaurant, or hospitality management leading to an associate, bachelor, or graduate degree. Technical institutes, vocational and trade schools, and other academic institutions also offer courses leading to formal recognition in hospitality management. In total, more than 800 educational facilities provide academic training for would-be lodging managers. Hotel management programmes include instruction in hotel administration, accounting, economics, marketing, housekeeping, food service management and catering, and hotel maintenance engineering. Computer training also is an integral part of hotel management training, due to the widespread use of computers in reservations, billing, and housekeeping management.

More than 450 high schools in 45 States offer the Lodging Management Programme created by the Educational Institute of the American Hotel and Lodging Association. This two-year programme offered to high school juniors and seniors teaches management principles and leads to a professional certification called the "Certified Rooms Division Specialist." Many colleges and universities grant participants credit towards a post-secondary degree in hotel management.

Lodging managers must be able to get along with many different types of people, even in stressful situations. They must be able to solve problems and concentrate on details. Initiative, self-discipline, effective communication skills, and the ability to organize and direct the work of others also are essential for managers at all levels.

Persons wishing to make a career in the hospitality industry may be promoted into a management trainee position sponsored by the hotel or a hotel chain's corporate parent. Typically, trainees work as assistant managers and may rotate assignments among the hotel's departments—front office, housekeeping, or food and beverage—to gain a wide range of experiences. Relocation to another property may be required to help round out the experience and to help grow a trainee into the position.

Work experience in the hospitality industry at any level or in any segment, including summer jobs or part-time work in a hotel or restaurant, is good background for entering hotel management. Most employers require a bachelor's degree with some education in business and computer literacy, while some prefer a master's degree for hotel management positions. However, employees who demonstrate leadership potential and possess sufficient length or breadth of experience may be invited to participate in a management training programme and advance to hotel management positions without the education beyond high school.

Large hotel and motel chains may offer better opportunities for advancement than small, independently owned establishments, but relocation every several years often is necessary for advancement. The large chains have more extensive career ladder programmes and offer managers the opportunity to transfer to another hotel or motel in the chain or to the central office. Career advancement can be accelerated by the completion of certification programmes offered by various associations. These programmes usually require a combination of course work, examinations, and experience. For example, outstanding lodging managers may advance to higher level manager positions.

Lodging managers held about 58,000 jobs in 2004. Self-employed managers—primarily owners of small hotels, motels, and inns—held about 45 percent of these jobs. Companies that manage hotels and motels under contract employed many managers.

Employment of lodging managers is expected to grow about as fast as the average for all occupations through 2014. Additional job openings are expected to occur as experienced managers transfer to other occupations or leave the labour force, in part because of the long hours and stressful working conditions. Job opportunities are expected to be best for persons with college degrees in hotel or hospitality management.

Renewed business travel and domestic and foreign tourism will drive employment growth of lodging managers in full-service hotels. The numbers of economy-class rooms and extended-stay hotels also are expected to increase to accommodate leisure travellers and bargain-conscious guests. An increasing range of lodging accommodations is available to travellers, from economy hotels which offer clean, comfortable rooms and front desk services without costly extras such as restaurants and room service, to luxury and boutique inns that offer sumptuous furnishings and personal services.

The accommodation industry is expected to continue to consolidate as lodging chains acquire independently owned establishments or undertake their operation on a contract basis. The increasing number of extended-stay hotels will moderate growth of manager jobs because these properties usually have fewer departments and require fewer managers. Also, these establishments often do not require a manager to be available 24 hours a day, instead assigning front desk clerks on duty at night some of the responsibilities previously reserved for managers.

Additional demand for managers is expected in suite hotels, because some guests—especially business customers—are willing to pay higher prices for rooms with kitchens and suites that provide the space needed to conduct small meetings. In addition, large full-service hotels—offering restaurants, fitness centres, large meeting rooms, and play areas for children, among other amenities—will continue to provide many trainee and managerial opportunities.

HOTEL MANAGEMENT COURSE ADMISSIONS

Candidates seeking admission to the hotel management courses in India need to pass their 12th standard examination with English as a subject. Students with a bachelor's degree from any recognized university may also join some of the management training schemes offered by various institutions. Admission depends on the performance of the students in the written admission test, personal interview round and group discussion session. The time duration of the courses offered by several institutes may vary from six months to three years.

HOTEL MANAGEMENT COURSE SCOPE

Hotel management job opportunities exists both in the private and public sector. One can look for various openings available in the hotels of the nation. Most of the hotels in India offer lucrative pay packages to the suitable candidates. The jobs offered are satisfying as well as highly rewarding. The country's rapidly growing economy has led to a remarkable growth in the tourism sector. In line with this growth, the hotel industry has flourished and thus, the demand for human resources specializing in hotel management has increased as well.

While some hotel owners would gladly employ just any individual willing to be trained, the bigger and better star hotels only consider those who are specialized in their own hotel management related field. For this reason, more and more students are beginning to take up hotel management in hopes to build a successful career in the industry. In a general sense, hotel management as a course may sound fairly simple. However, taking into consideration the number of specializations in this field of work, it would be important for one to really decide on which field to focus on. Although dozens of career prospects are available in hotel management, the more common ones include Catering Management, Housekeeping, and Front Office Management.

NATURE OF WORK

Graduates of hotel management may end up filling positions of general hotel managers or assistant managers. The roles of these two are very significant because not only should they serve as leaders of the number of workers employed by the hotel but also ensure that all the hotel's guests enjoy a pleasant and comfortable stay. The role of general managers becomes increasingly important as they work with the hotel's owners and directors to foresee income and expenditures by setting room rates and budgets. They must also establish the hotel's identity in terms of the kind of service that they are able to provide. To help them fulfill their roles, general managers are able to delegate tasks to assistant managers that often exist for every department.

These assistant managers are more hands on when it comes to each department's daily operations and they must ensure that the standards set by the owners and directors as well as that of the general manager are always met. Managers of each department will also serve varying functions and will take responsibility for all the levels of employment in their departments.

Food and Beverage

The food and beverage manager is responsible for all operations under the Catering Department. Here, the food and beverage manager leads all employees under both the culinary section and the steward section. Under the culinary section, the Executive Chef who is in charge of all kitchen activities answers directly to the food and beverage manager. This section is composed of all employees who work in the kitchen including all chefs and dishwashers.

On the other hand, the steward section is composed of all waiters and waitresses who are in charge of taking orders and serving food.

Bartenders are also under the responsibility of the food and beverage manager. Apart from these responsibilities, the food and beverage manager must also work with the general manager to decide on the pricing of all items in the hotel's menu. In general, food and beverage managers must ensure that all the operations in the catering department contribute to the ultimate goal of providing not only the most delicious food or the most appealing facilities but the best kind of service as well.

Housekeeping

The Executive Housekeeper is responsible for all employees who work towards maintaining all rooms and the rest of the hotel facilities to make sure that everything is clean and tidy at all times. Under direct command of the Executive Housekeeper are floor supervisors who ensure that all rooms in their floor of responsibility are well-maintained. Other employees who are under the supervision of the Executive Housekeeper are the bays who are in charge of making beds and cleaning rooms, chamber boys and maids who clean the toilets and the shower areas, and the linen maids who collect and stock all sheets, towels, and napkins for laundry.

Front Office

The role of the Front Office Manager is vital to the hotel's existence because employees under this department are those first encountered by all guests. Apart from making sure that all reservations and room assignments are in order, they supervise receptionists, information clerks, reservation officers, bellboys and doormen. They must ensure that all employees under their supervision are not only efficient but polite and courteous as well.

PERSONALITY

A job in the hotel industry requires certain essential personality characteristics. An individual seeking employment in this dynamic sector needs excellent social skills. A pleasant personality, enthusiasm, discipline, a genuine interest in a customer's needs and a willingness and aptitude for public relations work are the basic traits employers watch out for in their applicants. In addition to these basic personality traits, hotel managers must be highly business oriented and flexible and exhibit exceptional leadership skills. Managerial positions in hotels require excellent organization skills and the quick thinking and adaptive capabilities needed to handle the pressures of dealing with guests from vastly different cultures. A career in the hotel industry can certainly be tough and demanding at times, but with the right personality, an individual will find this work rewarding and pleasurable.

PROFESSIONAL COURSES

To pursue a career in hotel management, university courses that take 3 to 4 years are recommended. Among these courses commonly offered by Indian colleges and universities are 3 years Diploma in Hotel Management, 3 years in Bachelor of Science in Hotel Management, 3 years in Bachelor of Arts in Hospitality and Tourism Management, and 4 years in Bachelor of Hotel Management and Catering Technology. In order to qualify for these courses, one must have a 12th or equivalent pass with a minimum aggregate performance of 50%.

COLLEGES, INSTITUTIONS AND UNIVERSITIES

Below are some of the popular choices among those who wish to pursue careers in hotel management:

- A.K. Hafizka College of Hotel & Tourism Management Studies & Research

Website: http://www.anjumanihmct.org/Index.html

Address: 92, Dr. D. N. Mumbai - 400 001 Maharashtra, India.

Courses Offered:

- 3 years - Bachelor of Science in Hospitality Studies
- 3 years - Bachelor of Science in Catering and Hotel Administration
- 3 years - Advanced Diploma in Culinary Arts

- Army Institute of Hotel Management and Catering Technology

Website: http://www.aihmctbangalore.com/index.html

Address: Vivek nagar, Agaram, Bangalore 560007

Courses Offered:

4 years - Bachelor of Hotel and Restaurant Management

- Banarsidas Chandiwala Institute of Hotel Management & Catering Technology

Website: http://www.bcihmct.ac.in/index.html

Address: Chandiwala Estate, Maa Anandamayee Ashram Marg, Kalkaji, New Delhi 110019

Courses Offered:

- 4 years - Bachelor in Hotel Management and Catering Technology

- FHRAI Institute of Hospitality Management

Website: http://www.fhraiinstitute.com/index.asp

Address: 45, Knowledge Park III, Greater Noida- 201 306

Courses Offered:

- 4 years - International Hospitality Administration
- 4 years - International Culinary Administration
- 3 years - Bachelor of Science in Hospitality, Catering, and Tourism
- 1 year - Diploma in Hotel Operations

- Heritage Institute of Hotel and Tourism

Website: http://www.hihtagra.com/

Address: 8, Vibhav Nagar, Taj Nagri, Agra-282 001

Courses Offered:

- 3 years - Bachelor of Science in Hotel Management, Catering Technology and Tourism

- Institute of Hotel Management

Website: http://www.ihmbangalore.com/

Address: S.D. Road (S.J.P. Campus) Bangalore G.P.O., Bangalore 560001

Courses Offered:

- 3 years - Bachelor of Science in Hotel Management

- Institute of Hotel Management, Catering Technology, & Applied Nutrition

Website: http://www.ihmctan.edu/
Address: Veer Savarkar Marg, Dadar (W), Mumbai 400 028
Courses Offered:

  - 3 years - Bachelor of Science in Hospitality and Hotel Administration

- Merit Swiss Asian School of Hotel Management

Website: http://www.meritworldwide.com/MSASH.html
Address: 22, Havelock Road, Ooty - 643001, Nilgiris, India
Courses Offered:

  - 3 years - Diploma in Hotel Administration

- Oberoi Centre of Learning and Development

Website: http://www.oberoihotels.com
Address: 7, Sham Nath Marg, Delhi - 110 054, India
Courses Offered:

  - 3 years - Diploma in Hotel Operations Managemenet

- Welcomgroup Graduate School of Hotel Administration

Website: http://www.manipal.edu/wgsha/index.htm
Address: WGSHA, Valley View International, Manipal - 576104
Courses Offered:

  - 4 years - Bachelor of Hotel Management

6

Career in Food and Beverage Industry

FOOD AND BEVERAGE SERVICES

Food and beverage services are among the most visible locations at ski areas, and a ski area's environmental commitment is often judged by the environmental practices within these establishments. Food and beverage services at ski areas range from fine dining establishments to bars and cafeterias. Numerous programs exist for the food and beverage service industry that help restaurants and their customers minimize environmental impacts.

These programs have established systematic approaches to help restaurants reduce their environmental impacts. Involvement in environmental programs is a good way for a restaurant to learn more about environmental best practice opportunities.

Food and beverage serving and related workers are the front line of customer service in restaurants, coffee shops, and other food service establishments. These workers greet customers, escort them to seats and hand them menus, take food and drink orders, and serve food and beverages. They also answer questions, explain menu items and specials, and keep tables and dining areas clean and set for new diners. Most work as part of a team, helping coworkers to improve workflow and customer service.

Waiters and waitresses, the largest group of these workers, take customers' orders, serve food and beverages, prepare itemized checks, and sometimes accept payment. Their specific duties vary considerably, depending on the establishment. In coffee shops serving routine, straightforward fare, such as salads, soups, and sandwiches, servers are expected to provide fast, efficient, and courteous service.

In fine dining restaurants, where more complicated meals are prepared and often served over several courses, waiters and waitresses provide more formal service emphasizing personal, attentive treatment and a more leisurely pace. They may recommend certain dishes and identify ingredients or explain how various items on the menu are prepared. Some prepare salads, desserts, or other menu items tableside. Additionally, they may check the identification of patrons to ensure they meet the minimum age requirement for the purchase of alcohol and tobacco products.

Waiters and waitresses sometimes perform the duties of other food and beverage service workers. These tasks may include escorting guests to tables, serving customers seated at counters, clearing and setting up tables, or operating a cash register. However, full-service restaurants frequently hire other staff, such as hosts and hostesses, cashiers, or dining room attendants, to perform these duties.

Bartenders fill drink orders either taken directly from patrons at the bar or through waiters and waitresses who place drink orders for dining room customers. Bartenders check identification of customers seated at the bar, to ensure they meet the minimum age requirement for the purchase of alcohol and tobacco products. They prepare mixed drinks, serve bottled or draught beer, and pour wine or other beverages. Bartenders must know a wide range of drink recipes and be able to mix drinks accurately, quickly, and without waste. Besides mixing and serving drinks, bartenders stock and prepare garnishes for drinks; maintain an adequate supply of ice, glasses, and other bar supplies; and keep the bar area clean for customers. They also may collect payment, operate the cash register, wash glassware and utensils, and serve food to customers seated at the bar. Bartenders usually are responsible for ordering and maintaining an inventory of liquor, mixes, and other bar supplies.

The majorities of bartenders directly serves and interact with patrons. Bartenders should be friendly and enjoy talking with customers. Bartenders at service bars, on the other hand, have less contact with customers. They work in small bars often located off the kitchen in restaurants, hotels, and clubs where only waiters and waitresses place drink orders. Some establishments, especially larger, higher volume ones, use equipment that automatically measures, pours and mixes drinks at the push of a button. Bartenders who use this equipment, however, still must work quickly to handle a large volume of drink orders and be familiar with the ingredients for special drink requests. Much of a bartender's work still must be done by hand to fill each individual order.

Hosts and hostesses welcome guests and maintain reservation or waiting lists. They may direct patrons to coatrooms, restrooms, or to a place to wait until their table is ready. Hosts and hostesses assign guests to tables suitable for the size of their group, escort patrons to their seats, and provide menus. They also schedule dining reservations, arrange parties, and organize any special services that are required. In some restaurants, they act as cashiers.

Dining room and cafeteria attendants and bartender helpers assist waiters, waitresses, and bartenders by cleaning tables, removing dirty dishes, and keeping serving areas stocked with supplies. Sometimes called backwaiters or runners, they bring meals out of the kitchen and assist waiters and waitresses by distributing dishes to individual diners. They also replenish the supply of clean linens, dishes, silverware, and glasses in the dining room and keep the bar stocked with glasses, liquor, ice, and drink garnishes.

Dining room attendants set tables with clean tablecloths, napkins, silverware, glasses, and dishes and serve ice water, rolls, and butter. At the conclusion of meals, they remove dirty dishes and soiled linens from tables. Cafeteria attendants stock serving tables with food, trays, dishes, and silverware and may carry trays to dining tables for patrons. Bartender helpers keep bar equipment clean and wash glasses. *Dishwashers* clean dishes, cutlery, and kitchen utensils and equipment.

Counter attendants take orders and serve food in cafeterias, coffee shops, and carryout eateries. In cafeterias, they serve food displayed on steam tables, carve meat, dish out vegetables, ladle sauces and soups, and fill beverage glasses. In lunchrooms and coffee shops, counter attendants take orders from customers seated at the counter, transmit orders to the kitchen, and pick up and serve food. They also fill cups with coffee, soda, and other beverages and prepare fountain specialties, such as milkshakes and ice cream sundaes. Counter attendants also take carryout orders from diners and wrap or place items in containers. They clean counters, write itemized checks, and sometimes accept payment. Some counter attendants may prepare short-order items, such as sandwiches and salads.

Some food and beverage serving workers take orders from customers at counters or drive-through windows at fast-food restaurants. They assemble orders, hand them to customers, and accept payment. Many of these are combined food preparation and serving workers who also cook and package food, make coffee, and fill beverage cups using drink-dispensing machines.

Other workers serve food to patrons outside of a restaurant environment, such as in hotels, hospital rooms, or cars.

Food and beverage service workers are on their feet most of the time and often carry heavy trays of food, dishes, and glassware. During busy dining periods, they are under pressure to serve customers quickly and efficiently. The work is relatively safe, but care must be taken to avoid slips, falls, and burns.

Part-time work is more common among food and beverage serving and related workers than among workers in almost any other occupation. In 2004, those on part-time schedules included half of all waiters and waitresses, and 40 percent of all bartenders.

Food service and drinking establishments typically maintain long dining hours and offer flexible and varied work opportunities. Many food and beverage serving and related workers work evenings, weekends, and holidays. Many students and teenagers seek part time or seasonal work as food and beverage serving and related workers as a first job to gain work experience or to earn spending money while in school. Around one-fourth of food and beverage serving and related workers were 16 to 19 years old—about six times the proportion for all workers. There are no specific educational requirements for food and beverage service jobs.

Many employers prefer to hire high school graduates for waiter and waitress, bartender, and host and hostess positions, but completion of high school usually is not required for fast-food workers, counter attendants, dishwashers, and dining room attendants and bartender helpers. For many people a job as a food and beverage service worker serves as a source of immediate income, rather than a career. Many entrants to these jobs are in their late teens or early twenties and have a high school education or less. Usually, they have little or no work experience. Many are full-time students or homemakers. Food and beverage service jobs are a major source of part-time employment for high school and college students.

Restaurants rely on good food and quality customer service to retain loyal customers and succeed in a competitive industry. Food and beverage serving and related workers who exhibit excellent personal qualities—such as a neat clean appearance, a well-spoken manner, an ability to work as a member of team, and a pleasant way with patrons—will be highly sought after.

Waiters and waitresses need a good memory to avoid confusing customers' orders and to recall faces, names, and preferences of frequent patrons. These workers also should be comfortable using computers to place orders and generate customers' bills. Some may need to be quick at arithmetic so they can total bills manually. Knowledge of a foreign language is helpful to communicate with a diverse clientele and staff. Prior experience waiting on tables is preferred by restaurants and hotels that have rigid table service standards. Jobs at these establishments often offer higher wages and have greater income potential from tips, but they may also have stiffer employment requirements than other establishments, such as prior table service experience or higher education.

FOOD AND BEVERAGE SERVING AND RELATED WORKERS

Usually, bartenders must be at least 21 years of age, but employers prefer to hire people who are 25 or older. Bartenders should be familiar with State and local laws concerning the sale of alcoholic beverages.

Most food and beverage serving and related workers pick up their skills on the job by observing and working with more experienced workers. Some full-service restaurants also provide new dining room employees with some form of classroom-type training that alternates with periods of actual on-the-job work experience. These training programs communicate the operating philosophy of the restaurant, help establish a personal rapport with other staff and instill a desire to work as a team. They also provide an opportunity to discuss customer service situations and the proper ways of handling unpleasant circumstances or unruly patrons with new employees. Additionally, managers, chefs and servers may meet before each shift to discuss the menu and any new items or specials, review ingredients for any potential food allergies, or talk about any food safety concerns, coordination between the kitchen and the dining room, or any customer service issues from the previous day or shift.

Some employers, particularly those in fast-food restaurants, use self-instruction or on-line programs with audiovisual presentations and instructional booklets to teach new employees food preparation and service skills. Some public and private vocational schools, restaurant associations, and large restaurant chains provide classroom training in a generalized food service curriculum. All employees receive training on safe food handling procedures and sanitation practices.

Some bartenders acquire their skills by attending a bartending or vocational and technical school. These programs often include instruction on State and local laws and regulations, cocktail recipes, proper attire and conduct, and stocking a bar. Some of these schools help their graduates find jobs. Although few employers require any minimum level of educational attainment, some specialized training is usually needed in food handling and legal issues surrounding serving alcoholic beverages and tobacco. Employers are more likely to hire and promote based on people skills and personal qualities rather than education.

Due to the relatively small size of most food-serving establishments, opportunities for promotion are limited. After gaining experience, some dining room and cafeteria attendants and bartender helpers advance to waiter, waitress, or bartender jobs. For waiters, waitresses, and bartenders, advancement usually is limited to finding a job in a busier or more expensive restaurant or bar where prospects for tip earnings are better. Some bartenders, hosts and hostesses and waiters and waitresses advance to supervisory jobs, such as dining room supervisor, maitre d'hotel, assistant manager, or restaurant general manager. A few bartenders open their own businesses. In larger restaurant chains, food and beverage service workers who excel at their work often are invited to enter the company's formal management training program.

EMPLOYMENT IN FOOD AND BEVERAGE SERVING

Food and beverage serving and related workers held 6.8 million jobs in 2004. The distribution of jobs among the various food and beverage serving workers was as follows:

Waiters and waitresses	2,252,000
Combined food preparation and serving workers, including fast food	2,150,000
Dishwashers	507,000
Bartenders	474,000
Counter attendants, cafeteria, food concession, and coffee shop	465,000

Dining room and cafeteria attendants and bartender helpers	401,000
Hosts and hostesses, restaurant, lounge, and coffee shop	328,000
Food servers, nonrestaurant	189,000
All other food preparation and serving related workers	64,000

The overwhelming majority of jobs for food and beverage serving and related workers were found in food services and drinking places, such as restaurants, coffee shops, and bars. Other jobs were found primarily in traveler accommodation (hotels); amusement, gambling, and recreation industries; educational services; grocery stores; nursing care facilities; civic and social organizations; and hospitals.

Jobs are located throughout the country but are typically plentiful in large cities and tourist areas. Vacation resorts offer seasonal employment, and some workers alternate between summer and winter resorts, instead of remaining in one area the entire year.

Job Outlook

Job openings are expected to be abundant for food and beverage serving and related workers. Overall employment of these workers is expected to increase as fast as the average over the 2004-14 period as population, personal incomes, and employment expand. While employment growth will create many new jobs, the overwhelming majority of openings will arise from the need to replace the high proportion of workers who leave the occupations each year. There is substantial movement into and out of these occupations because education and training requirements are minimal and the predominance of part-time jobs are attractive to people seeking a short-term source of income rather than a career. However, keen competition is expected for bartender, waiter and waitress, and other food and beverage service jobs in popular restaurants and fine dining establishments, where potential earnings from tips are greatest.

Projected employment growth between 2004 and 2014 varies somewhat by type of job; however, average employment growth is expected for almost all food and beverage serving and related occupations. Employment of combined food preparation and serving workers, which includes fast-food workers, is expected to increase as fast as the average in response to the continuing fast-paced lifestyle of many Americans and the addition of healthier foods at many fast-food restaurants.

Average employment growth is expected for waiters and waitresses and hosts and hostesses because increases in the number of families and the more affluent, 55-and-older population will result in more restaurants that offer table service and more varied menus. Employment of bartenders, dining room attendants, and dishwashers will grow more slowly than other food and beverage serving and related workers because diners increasingly are eating at more casual dining spots, such as coffee bars and sandwich shops, rather than at the full-service restaurants and drinking places that employ more of these workers.

Earning

Food and beverage serving and related workers derive their earnings from a combination of hourly wages and customer tips. Earnings vary greatly, depending on the type of job and establishment. For example, fast-food workers and hosts and hostesses usually do not receive tips, so their wage rates may be higher than those of waiters and waitresses and bartenders in full-service restaurants, who typically earn more from tips than from wages. In some restaurants, workers contribute all or a portion of their tips to a tip pool, which is distributed among qualifying workers. Tip pools allow workers who don't usually receive tips directly from customers, such as dining room attendants, to feel a part of a team and to share in the rewards of good service.

In May 2004, median hourly earnings (including tips) of waiters and waitresses were $6.75. The middle 50 percent earned between $6.04 and $8.34. The lowest 10 percent earned less than $5.60, and the highest 10 percent earned more than $11.27 an hour. For most waiters and waitresses, higher earnings are primarily the result of receiving more in tips rather than higher hourly wages. Tips usually average between 10 and 20 percent of guests' checks; waiters and waitresses working in busy, expensive restaurants earn the most.

Bartenders had median hourly earnings (including tips) of $7.42 in May 2004. The middle 50 percent earned between $6.34 and $9.26. The lowest 10 percent earned less than $5.72, and the highest 10 percent earned more than $12.47 an hour. Like waiters and waitresses, bartenders employed in public bars may receive more than half of their earnings as tips. Service bartenders often are paid higher hourly wages to offset their lower tip earnings.

Median hourly earnings (including tips) of dining room and cafeteria attendants and bartender helpers were $7.10 in May 2004. The middle 50 percent earned between $6.24 and $8.25. The lowest 10 percent earned less than $5.68, and the highest 10 percent earned more than $9.88 an hour. Most received over half of their earnings as wages; the rest of their income was a share of the proceeds from tip pools.

Median hourly earnings of hosts and hostesses were $7.52 in May 2004. The middle 50 percent earned between $6.48 and $8.63. The lowest 10 percent earned less than $5.77, and the highest 10 percent earned more than $10.49 an hour. Wages comprised the majority of their earnings. In some cases, wages were supplemented by proceeds from tip pools.

Median hourly earnings of combined food preparation and serving workers, including fast food, were $7.06 in May 2004. The middle 50 percent earned between $6.18 and $8.25. The lowest 10 percent earned less than $5.65, and the highest 10 percent earned more than $9.85 an hour. Although some combined food preparation and serving workers receive a part of their earnings as tips, fast-food workers usually do not.

Median hourly earnings of counter attendants in cafeterias, food concessions, and coffee shops (including tips) were $7.53 in May 2004. The middle 50 percent earned between $6.50 and $8.59 an hour. The lowest 10 percent earned less than $5.80, and the highest 10 percent earned more than $10.38 an hour.

Median hourly earnings of dishwashers were $7.35 in May 2004. The middle 50 percent earned between $6.41 and $8.37. The lowest 10 percent earned less than $5.76, and the highest 10 percent earned more than $9.81 an hour.

Median hourly earnings of nonrestaurant food servers were $7.95 in May 2004. The middle 50 percent earned between $6.64 and $9.98. The lowest 10 percent earned less than $5.86, and the highest 10 percent earned more than $12.53 an hour.

Many beginning or inexperienced workers start earning the Federal minimum wage of $5.15 an hour. However, a few States set minimum wages higher than the Federal minimum. Also, various minimum wage exceptions apply under specific circumstances to disabled workers, full-time students, youth under age 20 in their first 90 days of employment, tipped employees, and student-learners. Tipped employees are those who customarily and regularly receive more than $30 a month in tips. The employer may consider tips as part of wages, but the employer must pay at least $2.13 an hour in direct wages. Employers also are permitted to deduct from wages the cost, or fair value, of any meals or lodging provided. Many employers, however, provide free meals and furnish uniforms. Food and beverage service workers who work full time often receive typical benefits, while part-time workers usually do not.

In some large restaurants and hotels, food and beverage serving and related workers belong to unions—principally the Hotel Employees and Restaurant Employees International Union and the Service Employees International Union.

MAINTAINING PRODUCT QUALITY AND SAFETY

It is a fact that food product quality rarely improves with increased storage time. In most cases, the quality of ingredients you buy is at its peak when the product you ordered is delivered to you. From then on, the products can only decline in freshness, quality, and nutrition. The only exception to this might be the gourmet restaurant that elects to age some of its own products. The general case, however, is that your storeroom clerk must make every effort to maintain food quality in all of your storage areas, since food quality tends to diminish during the storage process. The primary method for ensuring product quality while in storage is through proper product rotation and high standards of storeroom sanitation. Storage areas are excellent breeding grounds for insects, some bacteria, and also rodents.

To protect against these potentially damaging hazards, you should insist on a regular cleaning of all storage areas. Compressor units on refrigerators and frozen-food holding units should be checked regularly for the buildup of dust and dirt. Interior storage racks should be kept free of spills and soil. Refrigerators and frozen-food holding units remove significant amounts of stored product moisture, causing shrinkage in meats and produce and freezer burn in poorly wrapped or stored items kept at freezing temperatures.

Unless they are built in, refrigerators and frozen-food holding units should be high enough off the ground to allow for easy cleaning around and under them to prevent cockroaches and other insects from living beneath them. Both refrigerators and frozen-food holding units should be kept 6 to 10 inches from walls to allow for the free circulation of air around, and efficient operation of, the units.

Drainage systems in refrigerators should be checked at least weekly. Ideally, frozen-food holding units and refrigerators should have *externally visible* internal thermometers, whether they are read as a digital display or in the more traditional temperature scale. In larger storage areas, hallways should be kept clear and empty of storage materials or boxes. This helps both in finding items in the storage area and in reducing the number of hiding places for insects and rodents.

Maintaining Product Security

Food products are the same as money to you. In fact, you should think of food inventory items in exactly that way. The apple in a produce walk-in is not just an apple. It represents, at a selling price of $2.00, that amount in revenue to the airport foodservice director, who hopes to sell a crisp, fresh apple to a weary traveler. If the apple disappears, revenue of $2.00 will disappear also. When you think of inventory items in terms of their sales value, it becomes clear why product security is of the utmost importance. As such, systems must be in place to reduce employee, vendor, and guest theft to the lowest possible level.

All foodservice establishments will experience some amount of theft, in its strictest sense. The reason is very simple. Some employee theft is impossible to detect. Even the most sophisticated, computerized control system is not able to determine if an employee or vendor's employee walked into the produce walk-in and ate one green grape. Similarly, an employee who takes home two sugar packets per night will likely go undetected for a great length of time. In neither of these cases, however, is the amount of loss significant, and certainly not enough to install security cameras in the walk-in or to frisk your employees as they leave for home at the end of their shifts.

What you do want to do, however, is to make it difficult to remove significant amounts of food from storage without authorization, so that you can know when that food has been removed. Good cost control systems must be in place if you are to achieve this goal.

It is amazing how large the impact of theft can be on profitability. Consider the following example. Jesse is the receiving clerk at the Irish Voice sports bar. On a daily basis, Jesse takes home $2.00 worth of food products. How much, then, does Jesse cost the bar in one year? The answer is a surprising $14,600 in sales revenue! If Jesse steals $2.00 per day for 365 days, the total theft amount is $730 (365 days _ $2.00 per day _ $730). If the bar makes an after-tax profit of 5% on each dollar of food products sold, the operation must sell _ $730 _ $14,600 to recover the lost $730.

In order to recover the dollar amount of Jesse's theft, the sports bar must sell $14,600 of food per year and make 5 cents per dollar sold on these sales. In the case of a smaller bar, $14,600 may well represent several days' sales revenue. Clearly, small thefts can add up to large dollar losses! Most foodservice operators attempt to control access to the location of stored products. This may be done, in some areas, by a process as simple as keeping the dry-storage area locked and requiring employees to "get the keys" from the manager or supervisor. In other situations, cameras may be mounted in both storage areas and employee exit areas.

While the physical layout of the foodservice operation may prevent management from being able to effectively lock and secure all storage areas, too much traffic is sure to cause theft problems. This is not because employees are basically dishonest. Most are not. Theft problems develop because of the few employees who either feel that management will not miss a few of whatever is being stolen or feel that they "deserve" to take a few things because they work so hard and are paid so little!

It is your responsibility to see to it that the storeroom clerk maintains good habits in securing product inventory. As a general rule, if storerooms are to be locked, only one individual should have the key during any shift. The temptation sometimes exists for management to hang the key by the door, that is, to have the storeroom locked, but give the key to any employee who says that he or she needs it.

This obviously defeats the purpose of the locked system. In reality, it is simply not possible to keep all inventory items under lock and key. Some items must be received and immediately sent to the kitchen for processing or use. Also, what would happen if you or another designated "key holder" were gone from the operation for a few minutes? Most operators find that it is impossible to operate under a system where all food products are locked away from the employees. Storage areas should, however, not be accessible to guests or vendor employees. Unlocked storage areas near exits are extremely tempting to the dishonest individual. If proper control procedures are in place, employees will know that you can determine if theft has occurred. Without such control, employees are aware that theft can go undetected. This must, and can, be avoided.

Determining Inventory Value

The inventory you have on hand should be maintained in a way that makes it easy to issue (place into production), as well as to count and to determine its monetary value. This is because you must be able to answer this fundamental question: "What is the value of the products I currently have on hand?" The answer to this question is critical because it is simply not possible to know your actual food expense without an accurate inventory. In fact, the mathematical formula used to determine the cost of food sold (food expense) is driven primarily by knowing the dollar value of all food products in inventory. The process of determining inventory value is quite simple, even if the actual task can be very time consuming. Valuing, or establishing a dollar value for your entire inventory, is done by using the following inventory valuation formula: Item Amount _ Item Value _ Item Inventory Value

Item Amount

Item amount may be determined by counting the item, as in the case of cans, or by weighing items, as in the case of meats. Volume, that is, gallons, quarts, and the like, is another method of establishing product amounts. If an item is purchased by the pound, it is generally weighed to determine item amount.

If it is purchased by the piece or case, the appropriate unit to determine the item amount may be either pieces or cases. If, for example, canned pears are purchased by the case, with six cans per case, management might decide to consider the item either as case or as can. That is, three cases of the canned pears might be considered as three items (by the case) or as 18 items (by the can). Any method you use to accurately establish the amount of product you have on hand is acceptable. If product is undercounted, your expenses will appear higher than they actually are. If, on the other hand, you erroneously (or on purpose) compute overstated, or padded inventory, costs will appear artificially low until the proper inventory values are determined.

Item Value

An item's actual value can be more complicated to determine than its amount. This is because the price you pay for an item may vary slightly each time you buy it. Assume, for example, that you bought curly endive for $2.20 per pound on Monday, but the same item was $2.50 per pound on Wednesday. On Friday, you see that you have one pound of the curly endive in your refrigerated walk-in. Is the value of the item $2.20 or $2.50? Item value is, generally speaking, determined by using either the LIFO or the FIFO method.

When the LIFO method is in use, the item's value is said to be the price paid for the least recent (oldest) addition to item amount. If the FIFO method is in use, the item value is said to be the price paid for the most recent (newest) product on hand. In the hospitality industry, most operators value inventory at its most recently known value; thus, FIFO is the more common method. A simple illustration may help. Peggy purchased grapes on Monday and paid $30.00 per lug. On Friday, she again purchased grapes, but paid $40.00 per lug. On Saturday morning, she took inventory and found that she had 1_1 2 _ lugs of grapes.

What is their inventory value? The LIFO system says that Peggy's grapes have an inventory value of $45.00 ($30.00 LIFO price _ 1.5 lugs _ $45.00). The FIFO method places a value of $60.00 on the grapes ($40.00 FIFO price _ 1.5 lugs _ $60.00). Because it is closest to the actual replacement cost of the inventory item, choosing to value inventory at the most recently paid price (FIFO) is the best method for establishing item value for the majority of hospitality operators.

This inventory valuation sheet has a place for all inventory items, the quantity on hand, and the unit value of each item. There is also a place for the date the inventory was taken, a spot for the name of the person who counted the product, and another space for the person who extended or established the value of the inventory. It is recommended that these two be different individuals to reduce the risk of inventory valuation fraud. The inventory valuation sheet should be completed each time the inventory is counted. It can be preprinted from a computerized list of items, a process that saves much in the way of staff time and effort. Regardless of the form used, the item's inventory value is determined as described earlier.

Thus, if we have five cases of fresh beets in our inventory, and each case has a value of $20.00, the inventory value of our beets is value of the item by the number of units on hand. The process becomes more difficult when one realizes that the average foodservice operation has hundreds of items in inventory. Thus, "taking the inventory" can be a very time-consuming task. A physical inventory, one in which the food products are actually counted, must, however, be taken to determine your actual food usage. Some operators take this inventory monthly, others weekly or even daily! Some, unfortunately, feel that there is no need to ever take inventory. These operators cannot effectively control their costs because they do not know what their costs are.

DETERMINING ACTUAL FOOD EXPENSE

Assume that you own and manage a small ice cream store that makes its own products. You have reviewed your records for the past month and found the following:

You have determined your revenue figure from the sales history you maintained. You have determined your food expense by adding the dollar value of all the properly corrected delivery invoices that you accumulated for the month. That is, you totaled the value of all food purchased and delivered between the first day of the month and the last. Would it be correct to say that your food expense for the month of January is $39,000? The answer is No.

Why not? Because you may have more, or less, of the food products required to make your ice cream in inventory on the last day of January than you had on the first day. If you have more food products in inventory on January 31 than you had on January 1, your food expense is less than $39,000. If you have fewer products in inventory on January 31 than you had on January 1, your food expense is higher than $39,000. To understand why this is so, you must understand the formula for computing your actual food expense.

Beginning Inventory

Beginning inventory is the dollar value of all food on hand at the beginning of the accounting period. It is determined by completing an actual count and valuation of the products on hand.

Purchases

Purchases are the sum cost of all food purchased during the accounting period. It is determined by adding all properly tabulated invoices for the accounting period.

Goods Available for Sale

Goods available for sale is the sum of the beginning inventory and purchases. It represents the value of all food that was available for sale during the accounting period.

Ending Inventory

Ending inventory refers to the dollar value of all food on hand at the end of the accounting period. It also is determined by completing a physical inventory.

Cost of Food Consumed

The cost of food consumed is the actual dollar value of all food used, or consumed, by the operation. Again, it is important to note that this is not merely the value of all food sold, but rather the value of all food no longer in the establishment and includes the value of any meals eaten by employees.

Employee Meals

Employee meal cost is a Labour-related, not food-related cost. Free or reduced-cost employee meals are a benefit much in the same manner as medical insurance or paid vacation. Therefore, the value of this benefit, if provided, should be transferred and charged not as a cost of food but as a cost of employee benefits. The dollar value of food eaten by employees is subtracted from the cost of food consumed to yield the cost of food sold.

Cost of Food Sold

As stated earlier, the cost of food sold is the actual dollar value of all food expense incurred by the operation except for those related to employee meals. It is not possible to determine this number unless a beginning inventory has been taken at the start of the month, followed by another inventory taken at the end of the month. Without these two numbers, it is impossible to accurately determine the cost of food sold. In the ice cream store example, had you completed such a form, you would have known your actual cost of food sold. Every manager should, on a regular basis, compute the actual cost of food sold because it is not possible to improve your cost picture unless you first know what your costs are.

VARIATIONS ON THE BASIC COST OF FOOD SOLD FORMULA

Unit to Another

This is the case when, for example, an operator seeks to compute one cost of food sold figure for a bar and another for the bar's companion restaurant. In this situation, it is likely that fruits, juices, vegetables, and similar items are taken from the kitchen for use in the bar, while wine, sherry, and similar items may be taken from the bar for use in the kitchen. The formula for cost of food sold in this situation would be as

follows:

Accounting Period: ____________ to ____________

Unit Name: ____________________________________

Beginning Inventory$

PLUS

Purchases $

Goods Available for Sale $

LESS

Ending Inventory$

Cost of Food Consumed $

LESS

Employee Meals $

Cost of Food Sold $

It is important for you to know exactly which formula or variation is in use when analyzing cost of food sold. The variations, while slight, can make big differences in the interpretation of your cost information. In all cases, it is critical that accurate beginning and ending inventory figures be maintained if accurate cost data are to be computed. In the following example, both beginning inventory and ending inventory figures are known, thus enabling you to determine your actual cost of food sold.

It is important to note that ending inventory for one accounting period becomes the beginning inventory figure for the next period. For example, in the case of your ice cream store, the January 31 ending inventory figure of $27,500 will become the February 1 beginning inventory figure. In this manner, it is clear that physical inventory need only be taken one time per accounting period, not twice. Again, while the physical inventory process can be time consuming, it must be performed in order to determine actual food expense. While there is no reliable method for replacing the actual counting of inventory items on hand, there are many computer programs on the market programmed to allow an individual to scan the bar codes on products using a handheld scanning device and, thus, perform both the counting and the price extension process necessary to develop actual inventory valuations. Using technology in this manner can make a time-consuming task much less tedious and more efficient.

Food Cost Percentage

Food expense is often expressed as a percentage of total revenue or sales. Since you can now determine your actual cost of food sold, you can also learn to compute and evaluate your operation's food cost percentage. Again, this is both the traditional way of looking at food expense and generally the method used by most operators when preparing the profit and loss statement. Food cost % represents that portion of food sales that was spent on food expenses. In the case of the ice cream store discussed previously, you know that the cost of food sold equals $33,275.

Estimating Daily Cost of Food Sold

Many operators would like to know their food usage on a much more regular basis than once per month. When this is the case, the physical inventory may be taken as often as desired. Again, however, physical inventories are time consuming.

It would be convenient if you could have a close estimate of your food usage on a weekly or daily basis without the effort of a daily inventory count. Fortunately, such an approximation exists. A six-column form that you can use for a variety of purposes.

One of them is to estimate food cost % on a daily or weekly basis. As an example, assume that you own an Italian restaurant that serves no liquor and caters to a family-oriented clientele. You would like to monitor your food cost percentage on a more regular basis than once a month, which is your regular accounting period.

You have decided to use a sixcolumn form to estimate your food cost percentage. Since you keep track of both daily sales and purchases, you can easily do so. In the space above the first two columns, write the word Sales. Above the middle two columns, write Purchases, and above the last two columns, enter the term Cost %. You then proceed each day to enter your daily sales revenue in the column labeled Sales Today. Your invoices for food deliveries are totaled daily and entered in the column titled Purchases Today. Dividing the Purchases Today column by the Sales Today column yields the figure that is placed in the Cost % Today column. Purchases to Date (the cumulative purchases amount) is divided by Sales to Date (the cumulative sales amount) to yield the Cost % to Date figure.

As can be seen, you buy most of your food at the beginning of the week, while sales are strongest in the later part of the week. This is a common occurrence at many foodservice establishments. As can also be seen, your daily cost percentage ranges from a high of 130% (Monday) to a low of 0% (Sunday), when no deliveries are made. In the Cost % to Date column, however, the range is only from a high of 130% (Monday) to a low of 39.20% (Sunday).

What is your best estimate about what your food cost % actually is as of Sunday? The answer is that it will be slightly less than 39.20%. Why? Let us go back to the formula for cost of food sold. Before we do, we must make one important assumption: "For any time period we are evaluating, the beginning inventory and ending inventory amounts are the same." In other words, over any given time period, you will have approximately the same amount of food on hand at all times. If this assumption is correct, the six-column food cost estimate is, in fact, a good indicator of your food usage. The reason is very simple.

The formula for cost of food sold asks you to add beginning inventory and then later subtract ending inventory. If these two numbers are assumed to be the same, they can be ignored, since adding and subtracting the same number to any other number will result in no effect at all. For example, if we start with $10, add $50, and subtract $10, we are left with $50. In terms of the cost of food sold formula, when beginning inventory and ending inventory are assumed to be the same figure, it is the mathematical equivalent of adding a zero and subtracting a zero. To continue our example, if we start with $0, add $50, and subtract $0, we are left, again, with $50.

Therefore, as stated earlier, if you assume that your inventory is constant, your cost of food sold for the one-week period is a little less than $4,034.21, or 39.20% of sales. Why a little less? Because we must still subtract the value of employee meals, if any are provided, since they are an employee benefit and not a food expense. How accurate is the six-column form? For most operators, it is quite accurate and has the following advantages:

1. It is very simple to compute, requiring 10 minutes or less per day for most operations.
2. It records both sales history and purchasing patterns.
3. It identifies problems before the end of the monthly accounting period.

4. By the ninth or tenth day, the degree of accuracy in the To Date column is very high.
5. It is a daily reminder to both management and employees that there is a very definite relationship between sales and expenses. The use of a six-column food cost estimator is highly recommended for the operator who elects to conduct a physical inventory less often than every two weeks.

The control of food expense is critical to all foodservice operations. From the purchase of the raw ingredient to its receiving and storage, the effective foodservice operator strives to have the proper quality and quantity of product on hand at all times. Food represents a large part of your overall expense budget. Protecting this product and accounting for its usage are extremely important in helping to manage overall costs.

Apply What You Have Learned

Tonya Johnson is the Regional Manager of Old Town Buffets. Each of the five units she supervises is in a different town. Produce for each unit is purchased locally by each buffet manager. One day, Tonya gets a call from Danny Trevino, one of the buffet managers reporting to her. Danny states that one of the local produce suppliers he uses has offered Danny the use of season tickets to the local university football games. Danny likes football and would like to accept them.

1. Would you allow Danny to accept the tickets? Why or why not?
2. Would you allow your managers to accept a gift of any kind (including holiday gifts) from a vendor?
3. Draft a "gifts" policy that you would implement in your region. Would you be subject to the same policy?

FOOD AND BEVERAGE COST TECHNIQUES

This portion presents the professional techniques and methods used to effectively purchase, receive, and store food products. It teaches the formulas used to compute the true cost of the food you provide your guests, as well as a process for estimating the value of food you have used on a daily or weekly basis, by applying the food cost percentage method, which is the standard in the hospitality industry.

The U.S. Bureau of Labour Statistics consumer expenditure surveys reported that sales of food consumed away from home grew an average of 5% per year in the 1990s, with annual increases expected to be even higher in the 2000s. According to the National Restaurant Association's current forecasts, continued economic growth, gains in consumers' real disposable income, and changes in the lifestyles of today's busy American families are all spurring the sustained rise in the number of meals served away from home. This is good news for your career as a hospitality manager. All this growth, activity, and consumer demand, however, will also create challenges for you. Consider the situation you would encounter if you used sales histories to project 300 guests for lunch today at the restaurant you manage. Your restaurant serves only three entrée items: roast chicken, roast pork, and roast beef. The question you would face is this, "How many servings of each item should we produce so that we do not run out of any one item?" If you were to run out of one of your three menu items, guests who wanted that item would undoubtedly become upset. Producing too much of any one item would, on the other hand, cause costs to rise to unacceptable levels unless these items could be sold for their full price at a later time.

Clearly, in this situation, it would be unwise to produce 300 portions of each item. While you would never run out of any one item, that is, each of your 300 estimated guests could order the same item and you would still have enough, you would also have 600 leftovers at the end of your lunch period. What you would like to do, of course, is instruct your staff to make the "right" amount of each menu item.

The right amount would be the number of servings that minimize your chances of running out of an item before lunch is over, while also minimizing your chance of having excessive leftovers. The answer to the question of how many servings of roast chicken, pork, and beef you should prepare lies in accurate menu forecasting. Let us return to the example cited previously. This time, however, assume that you were wise enough to have recorded last week's menu item sales on a form.

An estimate of 300 guests for next Monday makes sense because the weekly sales total last week of 1,500 guests served averages 300 guests per day (1,500/5 days _ 300/day). You also know that, on an average day, you sold 73 roast chicken (365 sold/5 days _ 73/day), 115 roast pork (573 sold/5 days _ 115/day), and 112 roast beef (562 sold/5 days _ 112/day).

Once you know the average number of people selecting a given menu item, and you know the total number of guests who made the selections, you can compute the popularity index, which is defined as the percentage of total guests choosing a given menu item from a list of alternatives. In this example, you can improve your "guess" about the quantity of each item to prepare if you use the sales history to help guide your decision. If you assume that future guests will select menu items much as past guests have done, given that the list of menu items remains the same, that information can be used to improve your predictions.

If we know, even in a general way, what we can expect our guests to select, we are better prepared to make good decisions about the quantity of each item that should be produced. In this example, your best guess of what your 300 guests are likely to order when they arrive. The basic formula for individual menu item forecasting, based on an item's individual sales history. The predicted number to be sold is simply the quantity of a specific menu item likely to be sold given an estimate of the total number of guests expected. Once you know what your guests are likely to select, you can determine how many of each menu item your production staff should be instructed to prepare. It is important to note that foodservice managers face a great deal of uncertainty when attempting to estimate the number of guests who will arrive on a given day because a variety of factors influence that number. Among these are the following:

1. Competition
2. Weather
3. Special events in your area
4. Facility occupancy (hospitals, dormitories, hotels, etc.)
5. Your own promotions
6. Your competitor's promotions
7. Quality of service
8. Operational consistency

These, as well as other factors that affect sales volume, makes accurate guest count prediction very difficult. In addition, remember that sales histories track only the general trends of an operation. They are not able to estimate *precisely* the number of guests who may arrive on any given day. Sales histories, then, are a guide to what can be expected.

In our example, last week's guest counts range from a low of 280 (Monday) to a high of 320 (Tuesday). In addition, the percentage of people selecting each menu item changes somewhat on a daily basis. As a professional foodservice manager, you must take into account possible increases or decreases in guest count and possible fluctuations in your predicted number to be sold computations when planning how many of each menu item you should prepare.

Forecasting can involve estimating the number of guests you expect, the dollar amount of sales you expect, or even what those guests may want to purchase. This forecasting is crucial if you are to effectively manage your food expenses. In addition, consistency in food production and guest service will greatly influence your overall success.

STANDARDIZED RECIPES

While it is the menu that determines what is to be sold and at what price, the standardized recipe controls both the quantity and the quality of what your kitchen will produce.

A standardized recipe consists of the procedures to be used in preparing and serving each of your menu items. The standardized recipe ensures that each time a guest orders an item from your menu, he or she receives exactly what you intended the guest to receive.

Critical factors in a standardized recipe, such as cooking times and serving size, must remain constant so the menu items produced are always consistent. Guests expect to get what they pay for. The standardized recipe helps you make sure that they do.

Inconsistency is the enemy of any quality foodservice operation. It will make little difference to the unhappy guest, for instance, if you tell him or her that while the menu item he or she purchased today is not up to your normal standard, it will be tomorrow, or that it was the last time the guest visited your operation.

Good standardized recipes contain the following information:

1. Menu item name
2. Total yield (number of servings)
3. Portion size
4. Ingredient list
5. Preparation/method section
6. Cooking time and temperature
7. Special instructions, if necessary
8. Recipe cost (optional)

Interestingly, despite their tremendous advantages, many managers refuse to take the time to develop standardized recipes. The excuses used are many, but the following list contains arguments often used against standardized recipes:

1. They take too long to use.
2. My people don't need recipes; they know how we do things here.
3. My chef refuses to reveal his or her secrets.
4. They take too long to write up.
5. We tried them but lost some, so we stopped using them.
6. They are too hard to read, or many of my employees cannot read English.

Of the preceding arguments, only the last one, staff's inability to read English, has any validity. The effective operator should have the standardized recipes printed in the language of his or her production employees. Standardized recipes have far more advantages than disadvantages. Reasons for incorporating a system of standardized recipes include:

1. Accurate purchasing is impossible without the existence and use of standardized recipes.
2. Dietary concerns require some foodservice operators to know exactly the kinds of ingredients and the correct amount of nutrients in each serving of a menu item.

3. Accuracy in menu laws require that foodservice operators be able to tell guests about the type and amount of ingredients in their recipes.
4. Accurate recipe costing and menu pricing is impossible without standardized recipes.
5. Matching food used to cash sales is impossible to do without standardized recipes.
6. New employees can be better trained with standardized recipes.
7. The computerization of a foodservice operation is impossible unless the elements of standardized recipes are in place; thus, the advantages of advanced technological tools available to the operation are restricted or even eliminated.

In fact, standardized recipes are so important that they are the cornerstones of any serious effort to produce consistent, high-quality food products at an established cost. Without them, cost control efforts become nothing more than raising selling prices, reducing portion sizes, or lessening quality. This is not effective cost management. It is hardly management at all. Without established standardized recipes, however, this happens all too frequently.

Any recipe can be standardized. The process can sometimes be complicated, however, especially in the areas of baking and sauce production. It is always best to begin with a recipe of proven quality. Frequently, you may have a recipe designed to serve 10 guests, but you want to expand it to serve 100 people. In cases like this, it may not be possible to simply multiply each ingredient used by 10. A great deal has been written regarding various techniques used to expand recipes. Computer software designed for that purpose is now on the market. As a general rule, however, any item that can be produced in quantity can be standardized in recipe form and can be adjusted, up or down, in quantity.

When adjusting recipes, it is important that measurement standards be consistent. Weighing with a pound or an ounce scale is the most accurate method of measuring any ingredients. The food item to be measured must be recipe ready. That is, it must be cleaned, trimmed, cooked, and generally completed, save for its addition to the recipe. For liquid items, measurement of volume (i.e., cup, quart, or gallon, etc.) may be preferred. Some operators like to weigh all ingredients, even liquids, for improved accuracy.

Percentage Method

The percentage method deals with recipe weight, rather than with a conversion factor. It is sometimes more accurate than using a conversion factor alone. Essentially, the percentage method involves weighing all ingredients and then computing the percentage weight of each recipe ingredient in relation to the total weight of all ingredients. To facilitate the computation, many operators convert pounds to ounces prior to making their percentage calculations. These are converted back to standard pounds and ounces when the conversion is completed.

To illustrate the use of the percentage method, let us assume that you have a recipe with a total weight of 10 pounds and 8 ounces, or 168 ounces. If the portion size is 4 ounces, the total recipe yield would be 168/4, or 42, servings. If you want your kitchen to prepare 75 servings, you would need to supply it with a standardized recipe consisting of the following total recipe weight:

When adjusting recipes for quantity (total yield), two general methods may be employed. They are:

1. Factor method
2. Percentage technique

Factor Method

When using the factor method, you must use the following formula to arrive at a recipe conversion factor:

You now have all the information necessary to use the percentage method of recipe conversion.

Note that % of total is computed as ingredient weight/total recipe weight. The proper conversion of weights and measures is important in recipe expansion or reduction. The judgment of the recipe writer is critical, however, since such factors as cooking time, temperature, and utensil selection may vary as recipe sizes are increased or decreased. In addition, some recipe ingredients, such as spices or flavorings, may not respond well to mathematical conversions. In the final analysis, it is your assessment of product taste that should ultimately determine ingredient ratios in standardized recipes. All recipes should be standardized and used as written. It is your responsibility to see that this is done.

Inventory Control

With a knowledge of what is likely to be purchased by your guests (sales forecast) and a firm idea of the ingredients necessary to produce these items (standardized recipes), you must make decisions about desired inventory levels. A desired inventory level is simply the answer to the question, "How much of each needed ingredient should I have on hand at any one time?"

It is clear that this question can only be properly answered if your sales forecast is of good quality and your standardized recipes are in place so you do not "forget" to stock a necessary recipe ingredient. Inventory management seeks to provide appropriate working stock, which is the amount of an ingredient you anticipate using before purchasing that item again, and a minimal safety stock, the extra amount of that ingredient you decide to keep on hand to meet higher than anticipated demand. Demand for a given menu item can fluctuate greatly between deliveries periods, even when the delivery occurs daily. With too little inventory, you may run out of products and therefore reduce guest satisfaction. With too much inventory, waste, theft, and spoilage can become excessive. The ability to effectively manage the inventory process is one of the best skills a foodservice manager can acquire.

Determining Inventory Levels

Inventory levels are determined by a variety of factors. Some of the most important ones are as follows:

1. Storage capacity
2. Item perishability
3. Vendor delivery schedule
4. Potential savings from increased purchase size
5. Operating calendar
6. Relative importance of stock outages
7. Value of inventory dollars to the operator

Storage Capacity: Inventory items must be purchased in quantities that can be adequately stored and secured. Many times, kitchens lack adequate storage facilities. This may mean more frequent deliveries and holding less of each product on hand than would otherwise be desired. When storage space is too great, however, the tendency by some managers is to fill the space. It is important that this not be done, as increased inventory of items generally leads to greater spoilage and loss due to theft. Moreover, large quantities of goods on the shelf tend to send a message to employees that there is "plenty" of everything. This may result in the careless use of valuable and expensive products. It is also unwise to overload refrigerators or freezers. This not only can result in difficulty in finding items quickly, but also may cause carryovers (those items produced for a meal period but not sold) to be "lost" in the storage process.

Item Perishability: If all food products had the same shelf life, that is, the amount of time a food item retains its maximum freshness, flavor, and quality while in storage, you would have less difficulty in determining the quantity of each item you should keep on hand. Unfortunately, the shelf life of food products varies greatly. Because food items have varying shelf lives, you must balance the need for a particular product with the optimal shelf life of that product.

Serving items that are "too old" is a sure way to develop guest complaints. In fact, one of the quickest ways to determine the overall effectiveness of a foodservice manager is to "walk the boxes." This means to take a tour of a facility's storage area. If many products, particularly in the refrigerated area, are moldy, soft, overripe, or rotten, it is a good indication of a foodservice operation that does not have a feel for proper inventory levels based on the shelf lives of the items kept in inventory. It is also a sign that sales forecasting methods either are not in place or are not working well.

Vendor Delivery Schedule

It is the fortunate foodservice operator who lives in a large city with many vendors, some of whom may offer the same service and all of whom would like to have the operator's business. In many cases, however, you will not have the luxury of daily delivery. Your operation may be too small to warrant such frequent stops by a vendor, or the operation may be in such a remote location that daily delivery is simply not possible. Consider, for a moment, the difficulty you would face if you were the manager of a foodservice operation located on an offshore oil rig. Clearly, in a case like that, a vendor willing to provide daily dough nut delivery is going to be hard to find! In all cases, it is important to remember that the cost to the vendor for frequent deliveries will be reflected in the cost of the goods to you.

Table: Shelf Life

Item	Storage	Shelf Life
Milk	Refrigerator	5–7 days
Butter	Refrigerator	14 days
Ground Beef	Refrigerator	2–3 days
Steaks (fresh)	Refrigerator	14 days
Bacon	Refrigerator	30 days
Canned Vegetables	Dry Storeroom	12 months
Flour	Dry Storeroom	3 months
Sugar	Dry Storeroom	3 months
Lettuce	Refrigerator	3–5 days
Tomatoes	Refrigerator	5–7 days
Potatoes	Dry Storeroom	14–21 days

Table: Recommended Freezer Storage Period Maximums

Food at_10 to 0°F (_2.23 to _17.7°C)	**Maximum Storage Period**
Meat	
Beef, ground and stewing	3–4 months
Beef, roasts and steaks	6 months
Lamb, ground	3–5 months
Lamb, roasts and chops	6–8 months
Pork, ground	1–3 months
Pork, roasts and chops	4–8 months
Veal	8–12 months

Variety meats (liver, tongue)	3–4 months
Ham, frankfurters, bacon, luncheon meats	2 weeks (freezing not recommended)
Leftover cooked meats	2–3 months
Gravy, broth	2–3 months
Sandwiches with meat filling	1–2 months
Poultry	
Whole chicken, turkey, duck, goose	12 months
Giblets	3 months
Cut-up cooked poultry	4 months
Fish	
Fatty fish (mackerel, salmon)	3 months
Other fish	6 months
Shellfish	3–4 months
Baked Goods	
Cakes, prebaked	4–9 months
Cake batters	3–4 months
Cookies	6–12 months
Fruit pies, baked or unbaked	3–4 months
Pie shells, baked or unbaked	1 to 11D 2–2 months
Yeast breads and rolls, prebaked	3–9 months
Yeast breads and rolls, dough	1D 2 month
Other	
French-fried potatoes	2–6 months
Fruit	8–12 months
Fruit juice	8–12 months
Precooked combination dishes	2–6 months
Vegetables	8 months

Vendors will readily let you know what their delivery schedule to a certain area or location can be. It is up to you to use this information to make good decisions regarding the quantity of that vendor's product you must buy to have both working stock and safety stock.

Relative Importance of Stock Outages

In many foodservice operations, not having enough of a single food ingredient or menu item is simply not that important. In other operations, the shortage of even one menu item might spell disaster. While it may be all right for the local French restaurant to run out of one of the specials on Saturday night, it is not difficult to imagine the problem of the McDonald's restaurant manager who runs out of French fried potatoes on that same Saturday night! For the small operator, a mistake in the inventory level of a minor ingredient that results in an outage can often be corrected by a quick run to the grocery store. For the larger facility, such an outage may well represent a substantial loss of sales or guest goodwill. Whether the operator is large or small, being out of a key ingredient or menu item is to be avoided, and planning inventory levels properly helps prevent it. In the restaurant industry, when an item is no longer available on the menu, you "86" the item, a reference to restaurant slang originating in the early 1920s (86 rhymed with "nix," a Cockney term meaning "to eliminate"). If you, as a manager, "86" too many items on any given night, the reputation of your restaurant as well as your ability to manage it will suffer.

A strong awareness and knowledge of how critical this outage factor is help determine the appropriate inventory level. A word of caution is, however, necessary. The foodservice operator who is determined never to run out of anything must be careful not to set inventory levels so high as to actually end up costing the operation more than if realistic levels were maintained.

Potential Savings from Increased Purchase Size

Sometimes, you will find that you can realize substantial savings by purchasing needed items in large quantities. This certainly makes sense if the total savings actually outweigh the added costs of receiving and storing the larger quantity. For the large foodservice operator, who once a year buys canned green beans by the railroad car, the savings are real. For the smaller operator, who hopes to reduce costs by ordering two cases of green beans rather than one, the savings may be negligible. Generally, however, reduced packaging and shipping costs result in lower per unit costs when larger bags, boxes, or cartons of ingredients are purchased.

Remember, too, that there are costs associated with extraordinarily large purchases. These may include storage costs, spoilage, deterioration, insect or rodent infestation, or theft. As a general rule, you should determine your ideal product inventory levels and then maintain your stock within that need range. Only when the advantages of placing an extraordinarily large order are very clear should such a purchase be undertaken.

Operating Calendar

When an operation is involved in serving meals seven days a week to a relatively stable number of guests, the operating calendar makes little difference to inventory level decision making. If, however, the operation opens on Monday and closes on Friday for two days, as is the case in many school foodservice accounts, the operating calendar plays a large part in determining desired inventory levels. In general, it can be said that an operator who is closing down either for a weekend (as in school foodservice or a corporate dining situation) or for a season (as in the operation of a summer camp or seasonal hotel) should attempt to reduce overall inventory levels as the closing period approaches. This is expecially true when it comes to perishable items. Many operators actually plan menus to steer clear of highly perishable items near their closing periods.

They prefer to work highly perishable items, such as fresh seafood and some meat items, into the early or middle part of their operating calendar. This allows them to minimize the amount of perishable product that must be carried through the close-down period.

Value of Inventory Dollars to the Operator

In some cases, operators elect to remove dollars from their bank accounts and convert them to product inventory. When this is done, the operator is making the decision to value product more than dollars. When it is expected that the value of the inventory will rise faster than the value of the banked dollar, this is a good strategy. All too often, however, operators overbuy or "stockpile" inventory, causing too many dollars to be tied up in non-interest-bearing food products. When this is done, managers incur opportunity costs.

An opportunity cost is the cost of foregoing the next best alternative when making a decision. For example, suppose you have two choices, A and B, both having potential benefits or returns for you. If you choose A, then you lose the potential benefits from choosing B (opportunity cost). In other words, you could choose to use your money to buy food inventory that will sit in your storeroom until it is sold, or you could choose not to stockpile food inventory and invest the money. If you stockpile the inventory, then the opportunity cost is the amount of money you would have made if you had invested rather than holding the excess inventory.

If the dollars used to purchase inventory must be borrowed from the bank, rather than being available from operating revenue, an even greater cost to carry the inventory is incurred since interest must be paid on the borrowed funds. In addition, a foodservice company of many units that invests too much of its money in inventory may find that funds for acquisition, renovation, or marketing are not readily available. In contrast, a state institution that is given its entire annual budget at the start of its fiscal year (a year that is 12 months long but may not follow the calendar year) may find it advantageous to use its purchasing power to acquire large amounts of inventory at the beginning of the year and at very low prices.

Setting the Purchase Point

A purchase point, as it relates to inventory levels, is that point in time when an item should be reordered. This point is typically designated by one of two methods:

1. As needed (just in time)
2. Par level

As Needed When you elect to use the as-needed, or just-in-time, method of determining inventory level, you are basically purchasing food based on your prediction of unit sales and the sum of the ingredients (from standardized recipes) necessary to produce those sales. Then, no more than the absolute minimum of needed inventory level is secured from the vendor. When this system is used, the buyer compiles a list of needed ingredients and submits it to management for approval to purchase.

For example, in a hotel foodservice operation, the demand for 500 servings of a raspberries and cream torte dessert, to be served to a group in the hotel next week, would cause the responsible person to check the standardized recipe for this item and, thus, determine the amount of raspberries that should be ordered. Then that amount, and no more, would be ordered from the vendor.

Par Level

Foodservice operators may set predetermined purchase points, called par levels, for some items. In the case of the raspberries and cream torte dessert referred to previously, it is likely that the torte will require vanilla extract. It does not make sense, however, to expect your food production manager to order vanilla extract by the tablespoon! In fact, you are likely to find that you are restricted in the quantity you could buy due to the vendor's delivery minimum, namely, bottle or case, or the manufacturer's packaging methods. In cases such as this, or when demand for a product is relatively constant, you may decide to set needed inventory levels for some items by determining purchase points based on appropriate par levels.

When determining par levels, you must establish both minimum and maximum amounts required. Many foodservice managers establish a minimum par level by computing working stock, then adding 25 to 50% more for safety stock.

Then, an appropriate purchase point, or point at which additional stock is purchased, is determined. If, for example, you have decided that the inventory level for coffee should be based on a par system, the decision may be made that the minimum (given your usage) amount that should be on hand at all times is four cases. This would be the minimum par level. Assume that you set the maximum par level at ten cases. While the inventory level in this situation would vary from a low of four cases to a high of ten cases, you would be assured that you would never have too little or too much of this particular menu item.

If cases of coffee were to be ordered under this system, you would always attempt to keep the number of cases between the minimum par level (four cases) and the maximum par level (ten cases). The purchase point in this example might be six cases; that is, when your operation had six cases of coffee on hand, an order would be placed with the coffee vendor. The intention would be to get the total stock up to ten cases before your supply got below four cases. Since delivery might take one or two days, six cases might be an appropriate purchase point.

Whether we use the as-needed or the par level method, or, as in the case of most operators, a combination of the two, each ingredient or menu item should have a management-designated inventory level. As a rule, highly perishable items should be ordered on an as-needed basis, while items with a longer shelf life can often have their inventory levels set using a par level system. The answer to the question "How much of each ingredient should I have on hand at any point in time?" must come from you. Many factors will impact this decision. The decision, however, must be made and compliance monitored on a regular basis.

Purchasing

Regardless of the method used to determine inventory levels, once the quantity needed on hand has been determined, you must then turn your attention to the extremely important area of purchasing. Purchasing is essentially a matter of determining the following:

1. What should be purchased?
2. What is the best price to pay?
3. How can a steady supply be assured?

What Should Be Purchased?

Just as it is not possible to determine inventory levels or items to be purchased without standardized recipes, it is not possible to manage costs where purchasing is concerned without the use of product specifications, or "specs."

A product spec is simply a detailed description of an ingredient or menu item. A spec is a way for you to communicate in a very precise way with a vendor so that your operation receives the *exact* item requested every time. A foodservice specification generally consists of the following information:

1. Product name or specification number
2. Pricing unit
3. Standard or grade
4. Weight range/size
5. Processing and/or packaging
6. Container size
7. Intended use
8. Other information such as product yield

It is very important to note that the product specification determines neither the "best" product nor the product that costs the least. It is the product that you have determined to be the *most appropriate* product for its intended use in terms of both quality and cost.

A product specification that is written too loosely can be a problem because the needed level of item quality may not be delivered. On the other hand, if your product specifications are too tight, that is, if they are overly and unnecessarily specific, too few vendors may be able to supply the product, resulting in your paying excessively high costs for that item. The necessity of specifications will become clear if we listen in on a telephone call made by Louie, a manager who is about to place an order for bread with a new vendor, Sam's Uptown Bakery:

Louie: *"Sam, I need bread for sandwiches."*
Sam: *"Louie, you know I have the best bread in town!"*
Louie: *"Well, send me 50 loaves as soon as possible."*
Sam: *"No problem, Louie. We will deliver this afternoon!"*

Little does Louie know that Sam's definition of bread for sandwiches is *quite* different from his own. Louie is expecting 1pound, white, split, thin-sliced, 45-slices-to-the-bag bread. From Sam's exotic shop, however, he may well receive a 2-pound, thick-sliced, sesame seed–topped Italian loaf. Thus, even for a product as common as bread, a specification must be developed. Fortunately, the process is relatively simple because it depends mainly on your own view of appropriate product quality.

Each menu item or ingredient should have its own spec. In fact, management should make it a habit to ensure that only telephone conversations such as the following take place:

Louie: *"Sam, I need 50 loaves of my spec #617 as soon as possible."*
Sam: *"Spec #617? Let's see, I've got it right here. That's your* white bread for sandwiches spec, right?"
Louie: *"That's right, Sam."*
Sam: *"No problem, Louie. We will deliver this afternoon!"*

Product Name

This may seem self-explanatory, but, in reality, it is not. Mangos are a fruit to those in the southwestern United States, but the word may mean a bell pepper to those in the Midwest. Bell peppers do not come only in green, their most common color, but can also be purchased in yellow and red forms. Thus, the product name must be specific enough to clearly and precisely identify the item you wish to buy.

Many canned hams are pear shaped, but a Pullman canned ham is square. You may be requesting 100% maple syrup when you place a syrup order, but your vendor could assume maple-"flavored" syrup is the item you desire. Purchasing food becomes even more difficult when you realize that, especially in the area of meats and seafood, different regions in the country may have different names for the same product. When developing the product specification, you may find it helpful to assign a number to the item as well as its name. This can be useful when, for example, many forms of the same ingredient or menu item may be purchased.

A deli-restaurant may use 10 to 20 different types of bread, depending on the intended use of the bread; thus, in our product specification example, bacon, which this operation uses in many forms, has both a name and a number assigned to the specification. The same may be true with a number of items such as cheese, which may come in a brick, sliced, shredded, or a variety of other forms, as well as several types (Colby, cheddar, Swiss, etc.).

Pricing Unit

A pricing unit may be established in terms of pounds, quarts, gallons, cases, or any other commonly used unit. Parsley, for example, is typically sold in the United States by the bunch. Thus, it is also priced by the bunch. How much is a bunch? You must know. Grapes are sold by the "lug." Unless you are familiar with the term, you may not be able to buy that product in an effective way. Again, knowledge of the pricing unit, whether it is a gallon, pound, case, bunch, or lug, is critical when developing a product specification. You should insist that your vendor supply you with definitions of each pricing unit upon which that vendor bases his or her selling price.

Standard or Grade

Many food items are sold with varying degrees of quality or desirability. Because that is true, the U.S. Department of Agriculture, Bureau of Fisheries, and the Food and Drug Administration have developed standards for many food items. In addition, grading programs are in place for many commonly used foodservice items. Trade groups such as the National Association of Meat Purveyors publish item descriptions for many of these products. Consumers also are aware of many of these distinctions. Prime beef, in the consumer's mind, may be superior to choice beef. In a similar manner, you may wish to purchase and serve Coca-Cola rather than a lower cost generic fountain soda. When developing a specification, a specific brand name or product source (A-1 Steak Sauce, Maine lobster) may be included in this section. You should be cautious, however, about specifying a brand name unless it is actually critical to your operation. Unless several vendors are able to supply you with a product you need, the price you may pay to the vendor who does have the item may be too high.

Weight Range/Size

Weight range or size is important when referring to meats, fish, poultry, and some vegetables. In our standardized recipe example of roast chicken, the quarters were to have come from chickens in the 3- to 3_ pound range. This will make them very different than if they came from chickens in the 4- to 4_pound range. In the case of products requiring specific trim or maximum fat covering, that should be designated also, such as 10-ounce strip steak, maximum tail 1 inch, fat covering half inch. Four-ounce hamburger patties, 16-ounce T-bones, and one by fourth pound hot dogs are additional examples of items of the type that require, not a weight range, but an exact size. It is important to note that while the operator may specify such a specific weight, it is likely that he or she will pay a premium for such accuracy, especially in items such as steaks, where the supplier's ability to perfectly control product weight is somewhat limited.

Count, in the hospitality industry, is a term that is used to designate size. For example, 16- to 20-count shrimp refers to the fact that, for this size shrimp, 16 to 20 of the individual shrimp would be required to make 1 pound. In a like manner, 30- to 40-count shrimp means that it takes 30 to 40 of this size shrimp to make a pound. Many fruits and vegetables are also sold by count. For example, a 48-count avocado means that 48 individual avocados will fit in a standard case. In general, the larger the count, the smaller the size of the individual food items.

Processing and/or Packaging

Processing and packaging refers to the product's state when you buy it. Apples, for example, may be purchased fresh, canned, or frozen. Each form will carry a price appropriate for its processed or packaged state. It is important to note that the term "fresh" is one with varying degrees of meaning. Fish that has been frozen and then thawed should be identified as such.

Packaging is also extremely important when determining product yield. For example, 3 pounds of canned corn will not yield the same number of 3-ounce servings as 3 pounds of fresh ear corn. Fresh fruits and vegetables may be of excellent quality and low in cost per pound, but the effective foo dservice operator must consider actual usable product when computing the price per pound.

Also, the Labour cost of washing, trimming, and otherwise preparing fresh products must be considered when comparing their price to that of a canned or frozen product.

The U.S. food supply is one of great variety and quality. Food can come packed in a large number of forms and styles, including slab packed, layered cell packed, fiberboard divided, shrink packed, individually wrapped, and bulk packed. While it is beyond the scope of this text to detail all of the many varieties of food processing and packing styles, it is important for you to know about them. Your vendors will be pleased to help explain to you all the types of item processing and packaging they offer.

Container Size

This term refers to the can size, number of cans per case, or weight of the container in which the product is delivered. Most operators know that a 50-

pound bag of flour should contain 50 pounds. Some may not be sure, however, what the appropriate weight for a "lug" of tomatoes would be.

Intended Use

Different types of the same item are often used in the same foodservice operation, but in a variety of ways. Consider, for example, the operator who uses strawberries in a variety of ways. Obviously, perfect, large berries are best for chocolate-dipped strawberries served on a buffet table. Less-than-perfect berries, however, may cost less and be a perfectly acceptable form for sliced strawberries on strawberry shortcake. Frozen berries may make a good choice for a baked strawberry pie and would be much more cost effective. Breads, milk products, apples, and other fruits are additional examples of foods that come in a variety of forms; this requires you to know that the "best" form of a food product is not necessarily the most expensive.

Other Information Such as Product Yield

Additional information may be included in a specification if it helps the vendor understand exactly what you have in mind when your order is placed. An example is product yield. Product yield is simply the amount of product that you will have remaining after cooking, trimming, portioning, or cleaning. Product yield will help you and your vendor determine how much product you will have to purchase in order to have the desired product quantity after waste is removed.

How Can a Steady Supply Be Assured?

Unfortunately, very little has been written in the field of foodservice about managing costs through cooperation with vendors. Your food salesperson can be one of your most important allies in controlling costs. Operators who determine their supplier only on the basis of cost will find that they receive only the product they have purchased, whereas their competitors are buying more than just food! Or, as one food salesperson said when asked why he should be selected as the primary food vendor, "With my products, you also get me!" And so it is; just as good foodservice operators know that guests respond to both products and personal service levels, so, too, do effective food suppliers. Assuring a steady supply of quality products at a fair price is extremely important to the long-term success of a foodservice operator, yet many operators treat their suppliers as if they were the enemy. In fact, suppliers can be of immense value in assuring a steady supply of quality products at a fair price if you remember the following points.

Suppliers Have Many Prices, Not Just One

Unlike the restaurant business, which tends to hold its prices steady between menu reprints and generally charges the same price to all who come in the door, suppliers have a variety of prices based on the customer to whom they are quoting them. Therefore, when an operator gets a quote on a case of lettuce, the telephone conversation may sound like this:

Foodservice manager: *"Hello, is this Ready Boy Produce?"*
Ready boy: *"Yes, how can I help you?"*
Foodservice operator: *"What is your price on lettuce today?"*
Ready boy: *"$28.50 per case."*
This conversation should really be interpreted, as follows:
Foodservice operator: *"Hello, is this Ready Boy Produce?"*
Ready boy: *"Yes, how can I help you?"*
Foodservice operator: *"What is my price on lettuce today?"*
Ready boy: *"Based on our relationship, it is $28.50 per case."*

Suppliers Reward Volume Customers

It is simply in the best interest of a supplier to give a better price to a high-volume customer. The cost of delivering a $1,000 order is not that much different from the cost of delivering a $100 order. It still takes one truck and one driver. Those operators who decide to concentrate their business in the hands of fewer suppliers will, as a general rule, pay a lower price. Of course, the volume of products you must buy from a vendor to meet his or her minimum delivery requirement will vary. In addition, larger foodservice units certainly have a greater degree of flexibility in selecting multiple vendors because managers of these large units can more easily meet supplier requirements while still minimizing overall costs.

Cherry Pickers Are Serviced Last

Cherry pickers is the term used by suppliers to describe the customer who gets bids from multiple vendors, then buys only those items each vendor has "on sale" or for the lowest price. If an operator buys only a vendor's low-end item, the vendor will usually respond by providing limited service. It is a natural reaction to the foodservice operator's failure to take into account varying service levels, long-term relationships, dependability, or any other vendor characteristic, except cheapest price. It is important to remember, however, that a foodservice manager who meets minimum delivery requirements and buys regularly from the same vendor is not seen as a cherry picker just because he or she buys each item from the vendor with the lowest price. The key concept here is to develop a history of regular buying and cooperation with your vendor.

Slow Pay Means High Pay

Those operators who do not pay their bills in a timely manner would be surprised to know what their competitors are paying for similar products. In most cases, operators who are slow to pay will find that the vendor has decided to add the extra cost of carrying their account to the price the operator pays for his or her products.

Vendors Can Help Reduce Costs

Vendors have a knowledge of the products they sell that exceeds that of the average foodservice operator. This skill can be used to help the competition, or it can be harnessed for your own good use. Vendors can be a great source of information related to new products, cooking techniques, trends, and alternative product usage.

What Is the Best Price to Pay?

Once purchase specifications have been developed and quantities to be purchased have been established, your next step is to determine how to buy these items at the best price. Some would say that determining the best price should be a simple matter of finding who has the lowest cost product and placing an order with that person. In fact, that is almost always a sure sign of a manager who lacks understanding of the way vendors operate. The best price, in fact, is more accurately stated as the lowest price that meets the long-term goals of both the foodservice operation and its vendor.

When you have a choice of vendors, each supplying the same product (your specification), it is possible to engage in comparison shopping. The vehicle used to do this is called the bid sheet. The bid sheet includes vendor information, buyer information, and item description, unit of bid, bid price, salesperson's signature, and date. It also includes the dates that the bid prices will be "fixed," which means the dates that the supplier agrees to keep the bid price in effect. The bid sheet would be sent to all meat vendors each week on Friday to be returned Monday for the weekly bid prices. Then you would compare the item prices to see which vendor you would buy.

After you have received bids from your suppliers, you can compare those bids on a price comparison sheet. A price comparison sheet typically has a place to list the category being bid on, namely, produce, dairy products, meats, and so on, the name of the vendors available to bid, bid date, item description, unit of purchase, best bid price, best company quote, and last price paid. This information may then be used to select a vendor, based on the best price. Once the best price is determined for each item, then a purchase order using the best prices can be developed for each vendor.

Bid sheets and price comparison sheets may be used to determine the specific vendor who can supply the *lowest* price, but they do not give enough information to determine the *best* price. This makes sense when you realize that your own guests do not necessarily go to the lowest-priced restaurants for all of their meals. If they did, there would be no hope of success for the operator who tried to provide a better food product, in a better environment, with better service. In fact, most foodservice operators would resent guests who came into their operation and claimed they could get the exact same item for a lower price down the street.

It is a truism that any product can be sold a little cheaper if quality is allowed to vary. Even with the use of product specifications, vendor dependability, quality of vendor service, and accuracy in delivery can be determining factors when attempting to determine the "best price." Bill's Produce may be the preferred vendor for these items if price alone is the issue. If, however, Bill's Produce is frequently late in delivery, has questionable sanitary habits, and frequently is short or unable to deliver the promised product, the lower price may be no bargain. Davis Foods, on the other hand, may have a reputation for quality products and service that make it the vendor of choice. Any foodservice operator who uses price as the only criterion when shopping will find it very difficult to develop any meaningful relationship with a supplier.

For the smaller operation, the manager may be interested in comparing the *total* price from each supplier, rather than the price of individual items. That is, each ordering day, the manager would multiply the quantity of an item needed by the best price. An approach such as this is used when buying strictly from the price comparison sheet may result in orders too small to meet a supplier's minimum order requirement, that is, the smallest order that can be placed with a vendor who delivers. If the minimum order requirement cannot be met using the lowest prices, then the manager may have to choose the supplier with the next highest price to fill a complete order.

In some cases, the vendor to be used by the foodservice operator has been determined in advance. This is often true in a large corporate organization or in a franchise situation. Contracts to provide goods may be established by the central purchasing department of these organizations. When that happens, the designated vendor may have a national or a long-term contract to supply, at a predetermined price, items that meet the operation's specifications.

One Vendor versus Many Vendors

Every operator is faced with the decision of whether to buy from one vendor or many vendors. In general, the more vendors there are, the more time must be spent in ordering, receiving, and paying invoices. Many operators, however, fear that if they give all their business to one supplier, their costs may rise because of a lack of competition. In reality, the likelihood of this occurring is extremely small.

Just as foodservice operators are unlikely to take advantage of their best guests (and, in fact, would tend to offer additional services not available to the occasional guest), so, too, does the vendor tend to behave in a manner that is preferential to the operator who does most of his or her buying from that vendor. In fact, it makes good business sense for the vendor to do so. It is never advisable, however, to be at the mercy of a particular vendor. A good business relationship can only occur among equals; thus, many operators strive to maintain both a primary and a secondary supplier of most products.

Using one or two vendors tends to bring the average delivery size up and should result in a lower per item price. On the other hand, giving one vendor all of the operation's business can be dangerous and costly if the items to be purchased vary widely in quality and price. Staples and nonperishables are best purchased in bulk from one vendor. Orders for meats, produce, and some bakery products are best split among several vendors, perhaps with a primary and a secondary vendor in each category so that you have a second alternative should the need arise. If you are using bid buying as a purchasing method, having three vendors is advisable so that you have an adequate choice of prices and services.

Purchasing Ethics

Purchasing food products is an area that can test the ethics of even the most conscientious manager. Ethics have been defined as the choices of proper conduct made by an individual in his or her relationships with others. Ethics come into play in purchasing products because of the tendency for some suppliers to seek an unfair advantage over the competition by providing "personal" Favours to the buyer. These Favours can range from small holiday gifts given in appreciation for another year's partnership to outright offers of cash "bribes"/kickbacks to the buyer in exchange for volume purchases. Some suppliers have been known to offer buyers computers, monthly cash payments, trips to Hawaii, and other such "big ticket" items to guarantee business.

Although you, as a buyer, might personally benefit from these items, the foodservice operation, your employer, will ultimately "pay" for these kickbacks through higher product prices. Should you get caught accepting these items, it is possible that you will be fired. It is the wise manager who knows the boundaries of appropriate behaviour with suppliers. Some large foodservice organizations have formal codes of conduct for their buyers. When these are in place, they should, of course, be carefully reviewed and followed. If your organization does not have a formal set of ethical guidelines for buying, the following self-tests can be helpful in determining whether a considered course of action with your supplier is indeed ethical.

Ethical Guidelines

1. Is it legal?

   Any course of action that violates written law or company policy and procedure is wrong.

2. Does it hurt anyone?

   Are benefits accruing to the buyer that rightfully belong to the owner of the business? Discounts, rebates, and free products are the property of the business, not the buyer.

3. Am I being honest?

   Is the activity one that you can comfortably say reflects well on your integrity as a professional, or will the activity actually diminish your reputation with other suppliers?

4. Would I care if it happened to me?

   If you owned the business, would you be in Favour of your buyer behaving in the manner you are considering? If you owned multiple units, would it be good for the business if all of your buyers followed the considered course of action?

5. Would I publicize my action?

   A quick way to review the ethical merit of a situation is to consider whom you would tell about it. If you are comfortable telling your boss and your other suppliers about the considered course of action, it is likely ethical. If you would prefer that your actions go undetected, you are probably on shaky ethical ground.

Daily Inventory Sheet

Before you can place an order, you will need to find out what you need! The process is much like going through your house and making a shopping list of all items before you go to the store. Some managers say that they intuitively "know" what they need without looking at their storage areas. If you have ever gone grocery shopping without a list, however, you know that you will inevitably miss a few items. We have all been in a situation in which we went to the store, purchased what we thought we needed, only to find that we forgot an important item!

You, as a foodservice manager, will want to have a detailed look at your inventory before you place an order. A good way to make sure that you have checked all your items in your storage areas is to use a daily inventory sheet. A daily inventory sheet will have the items listed in your storage areas, the unit of purchase, and the par value preprinted on the sheet. In addition, the form will have the following columns: on hand, special order, and order amount.

A preprinted list of all your items in storage and unit of purchase is important so that you will not have to write down the items every time you check the inventory. The list should be in the same order that you store the items so that you can quickly and easily locate your products. The par value is listed so that you know how much inventory you should have in storage at any given time. You may also want to list the purchase point, if appropriate. To use the daily inventory sheet, you would physically walk through your storage areas to determine what items (and amounts) you should order for the following day. Under the "On Hand" column, you would list how many of each item you have on hand, that is, sitting on the shelf. You also need to list any "Special Order" amounts needed above the par level. An example of this would be extra cases of perishables, such as strawberries, ordered for a banquet.

Preparing the Purchase Order

Some items will be purchased daily, others weekly, and some, perhaps, monthly. In addition, you may be able to choose from a variety of ways to communicate with your supplier. Of course, much purchasing is done face-to-face, but the technology available for placing orders today is significant and includes the fax machine, telephone keypad, e-mail, and direct access to the vendor's order system via modem on software supplied to you by that vendor.

Some vendors will also come to your business and place orders for you on their laptop computers and then transfer your order electronically. In addition, more and more vendors are posting current prices on their Web pages, thus ensuring a rapid transfer of information to their customers.

Regardless of your communication method, however, it is critical that you prepare a written purchase order, or record of what you have decided to buy. The purchase order (PO) should be made out in triplicate (three copies). One copy goes to the receiving area for use by the receiving clerk. One copy is retained by management for the bookkeeping area. The original is, of course, sent to the vendor. If the purchase order is developed by telephone, management retains the original copy, with a notation in the Comments section, stating that the vendor has not seen the PO. In all cases, however, it is important to place all orders using a purchase order form. If this is not done, the receiving clerk will have no record of what is coming in on the delivery.

Purchase order preparation can be simple or complex, but, in all cases, the written purchase order form should contain space for the following information:

Purchase Order Information

1. Item name
2. Spec number, if appropriate
3. Quantity ordered
4. Quoted price
5. Extension price
6. Total price of order
7. Vendor information

8. Purchase order number
9. Date ordered
10. Delivery date
11. Ordered by ________
12. Received by ________
13. Delivery instructions
14. Comments

Each order you place should result in the preparation of a PO. This is true even if the vendor is delivering a standing order on a daily basis. The advantages of a written purchase order are many and include the following:

1. Written verification of quoted price
2. Written verification of quantity ordered
3. Written verification of the receipt of all goods ordered
4. Written and special instructions to the receiving clerk, as needed
5. Written verification of conformance to product specification
6. Written authorization to prepare vendor invoice for payment

The chef has used a sales forecast to determine the quantity of products needed for next Thursday's delivery. A check of the produce walk-in lets the chef know what is on hand and the quantity of each product required. This information allows for the accurate preparation of the PO. In this case, the order is then faxed to Scooter's Produce. The receiving clerk at the Ardmoor is now prepared with the information necessary to effectively receive the product from Scooter's.

Receiving

Once the PO has been prepared by the purchasing agent, it is time to prepare for the acceptance or receiving of the goods. This function is performed by the receiving clerk in a large operation or may be performed in a smaller operation by you, as the manager, or by a staff member you designate. In all cases, however, it is wise for you to establish the purchasing and receiving functions so that one individual places the order, while another individual is responsible for verifying delivery and acceptance of the product. When this is not done, the potential for fraud or theft is substantial.

Auditors, those individuals responsible for reviewing and evaluating proper operational procedures, have frequently found that the purchasing agent in an operation ordered a product, signed for its acceptance, and thus authorized invoice payment when, in fact, no product was ever delivered! In this case, the purchasing agent could be getting cash payment from the purveyor or supplier without the manager's knowledge. This could happen unless there are additional individuals in the purchasing chain. If it is not possible to have more than one person involved in the buying process, the work of the purchasing agent/receiving clerk must be carefully monitored by management to prevent fraud.

There is probably no area of the foodservice establishment more ignored than the area in which receiving takes place. This is truly unfortunate, since this is the area where we are ensuring we receive the quality of products we ordered. Proper receiving includes all of the following features:

1. Proper location
2. Proper tools and equipment
3. Proper delivery schedules
4. Proper training

Proper Location

The "back door," which is usually reserved for receiving, is often no more than that—just an entrance to the kitchen. In fact, the receiving area must be adequate to handle the job of receiving, or product loss and inconsistency will result.

First, the receiving area must be large enough to allow for checking products delivered against both the invoice, which is the supplier's record of products delivered and price charged, and the PO, which is the operation's record of the same thing. In addition to space required to allow for counting and weighing, accessibility to equipment required to move products to their proper storage area and to dispose of excess packaging is important.

A location near refrigerated areas is helpful in maintaining refrigerated and frozen products at their desired temperatures. You should make sure the area stays free of trash and clutter, as these make it too easy to hide delivered food items that may be taken home at the end of the dishonest employee's shift. It is important to remember that the delivery person is also a potential thief. While most suppliers are extremely careful to screen their delivery personnel for honesty, it is a fact that a delivery person has access to products and has a truck available to *remove* as well as deliver goods. For this reason, it is important that the receiving clerk work in an area that has a clear view of both delivery personnel and their vehicles.

The receiving area should be kept extremely clean, since you do not want to contaminate incoming food, or provide a carrying vehicle for pests. Often, suppliers themselves are responsible for delivering goods that can harbor roach eggs or other insects. A clean receiving area makes it easier to both prevent and detect this type of problem. The area should be well lit and properly ventilated. Excessive heat in the receiving area can quickly damage delivered goods, especially if they are either refrigerated or frozen products. Too little light may cause product defects to go unnoticed; therefore, the receiving area should be well lit. Flooring should be light in color and of a type that is easily cleaned. In colder climates, it is important that the receiving area be warm enough to allow the receiving clerk to carefully inspect products. The outside dock area in February, if the temperature is below freezing, is no place for an employee to conduct a thorough inspection of incoming products!

Proper Tools and Equipment

While the tools and equipment needed for effective receiving vary by type and size of operation, some items are standard in any receiving operation. These include the following:

Scales

Scales should be of two types: those accurate to the fraction of a pound (for large items) and those accurate to the fraction of an ounce (for smaller items and pre-portioned meats). Scales should be calibrated regularly to ensure accuracy.

Wheeled Equipment

These items, whether hand trucks or carts, should be available so that goods can be moved quickly and efficiently to their proper storage areas.

Box Cutter

This item, properly maintained and used, allows the receiving clerk to quickly remove excess packaging and thus accurately verify the quality of delivered products. Of course, care must be taken when using this tool, so proper training is essential.

Thermometer

Foods must be delivered at their proper storage temperatures. You must establish the range of temperatures you deem acceptable for product delivery. For many operators, those temperatures would be the following:

Item Acceptable Temperature Range
°F °C
Frozen Foods 10°F or less _12°C or less
Refrigerated Foods 30–45°F _1–7°C

Calculator

Vendor calculations should always be checked, especially when the invoice has been prepared by hand. It is especially useful if the calculator has a physical tape that can be used by the receiving clerk when needed. The calculator should also be available in case the original invoice is either increased or decreased in amount due to incorrect vendor pricing or because of items that were listed on the invoice but not delivered. In addition, invoice totals will change when all or a portion of the delivery was rejected because the items were of substandard quality.

Records Area

This area should, in the best of cases, include a desk, telephone, computer/ fax, copy machine, file cabinet, and ample office supplies such as pens, pencils, and a stapler. Obviously, larger operations are more likely to have such an area. In a smaller operation, however, the need for basic equipment still exists. In all cases, the records area should include a copy of all product specifications so there is no confusion about whether a delivered food or supply item meets the spec and, thus, should be accepted or rejected.

Proper Training

Receiving clerks should be properly trained to verify the following product characteristics:

1. Weight
2. Quantity
3. Quality
4. Price

Weight

One of the most important items to verify when receiving food products is, of course, their weight. It is simply true that 14 pounds of ground beef in a box looks exactly like 15 pounds. There is no way to tell the difference without putting the product on the scale. Receiving clerks should be required to weigh all meat, fish, and poultry delivered. The only exception to this rule would be unopened Cryovac (sealed) packages containing items such as hot dogs, bacon, and the like. In this situation, the entire case should be weighed to detect shortages in content. Often, meat deliveries consist of several items, all of which are packaged together.

When the receiving clerk or supplier is very busy, the temptation exists to weigh all of the products together. The following example shows why it is important to weigh each item rather than the entire group of items as a whole. Assume that you ordered 40 pounds of product from Bruno's Meats. When the Bruno's delivery person arrived, all three items were in one box and the deliverer was in a hurry. He, therefore, suggested that your receiving clerk simply weigh the entire box. Your receiving clerk did just that and found that the contents weighed 40_1 2 _ pounds. Since the box itself weighed about _1 2 _ pound, she signed for delivery.

If you called the supplier to complain about the overcharge ($248.50 total price _ $232.75 actual value _ $15.75 overcharge), you would likely be told that the misdelivery was simply a mistake caused by human error. It may well have been, but the lesson here is to always instruct your receiving personnel to weigh delivered items individually, even if they are in a hurry.

When an item is ordered by weight, its delivery should be verified by weight. It is up to the operator to train the receiving clerk to *always* verify that the operation is charged only for the product weight delivered. Excess packaging, ice, or water in the case of produce can all serve to increase the delivered weight. The effective receiving clerk must be aware of and be on guard against deceptive delivery practices as far as the delivery of the agreed-upon product is concerned.

Quantity

The counting of products is as important as weighing them. It is a fact that suppliers make more mistakes in not delivering products than they do in excessive delivery. Products delivered but not charged for cost the supplier money. Products *not* delivered but charged for cost you money. If you order five cases of green beans, then, of course, you want to receive and pay for five cases. This is important for two reasons. First, you only want to pay for products that have been delivered. Second and just as important, if you have prepared your purchase order correctly, you truly need five cases of green beans. If only three are delivered, you may not be able to prepare the menu items that are necessary to service your guests.

If this means you will run out of an item or have to make a substitute, you may be forced to deal with unhappy diners. Shorting is the term used in the industry to indicate that an ordered item has not been delivered as promised. When a vendor shorts the delivery of an item you ordered, that item may or may not appear on the invoice. If it does not appear, note must be taken so that management knows that the item is missing and appropriate action can be taken. If the item is listed on the invoice, the delivery driver should sign a credit memo. The credit memo should be filled out in triplicate (three copies).

One copy goes to the receiving area to be filed. One copy is retained by management for the bookkeeping area. The original is, of course, sent to the vendor. Note that the credit memo has a place for the signature of a representative from your operation, as well as that of the vendor. It must be signed by both. The credit memo is simply a formal way of notifying the vendor that an item listed on the original invoice is missing, and, thus, the value of that item should be deducted from the invoice total. If a supplier consistently shorts your operation, that supplier is suspect in terms of both honesty and lack of concern for your operation's long-term success.

The counting of boxes, cases, sacks, barrels, and the like must be routine behaviour for the receiving clerk. Counting items, such as the number of lemons or oranges in a box, should be done on a periodic basis, but the value of counting items such as these on a regular basis is questionable. While an unscrupulous supplier might be able to remove one or two lemons from each box delivered, the time it would take for an employee to detect such behaviour is hardly worth the effort expended. It is preferable to do a periodic check and to work with reputable vendors.

The direct delivery of products to a foodservice operator's storeroom or holding area is another cause for concern. The delivery person may deliver some items, such as bread, milk, and soda, directly to the storage area, thus bypassing the receiving clerk. This should not be allowed. After such an activity, it simply may be impossible to verify the accurate quantity of items delivered. If this process must be used, product dates on each item can help assure that all products listed on the invoice were indeed delivered.

Quality

No area of your operation should be of greater concern to you than that of the appropriate quality of product delivered. If you go to the trouble of developing product specifications, but then accept delivery of products that do not match these specifications, you are simply wasting time and effort. Without product specifications, verification of quality is difficult because management itself is unsure of the quality level that is desired.

Some foodservice operators think that all food items are basically alike. Nothing could be further from the truth. Suppliers know their products. They also know their customers. Some customers will accept only those items they have specified. Others will accept anything that comes in the back door because they do not take the time to verify a product's quality when it is delivered. If you were a supplier and you had a sack of onions that was getting a bit old, which customer would you deliver it to?

Unscrupulous suppliers can cost your operation guests because of both overcharging and shortchanging. Imagine, for example, a restaurant manager who requests a ¼-inch fat cover on all New York strip steaks ordered. Instead, the meat company delivers steaks with a ½-inch fat cover. The operation will, of course, pay too much for the product, since steaks with a ¼-inch fat covering sell at a higher price per pound than those with a ½-inch covering.

Guests, however, will hold the operator responsible for steaks that suddenly seem to be a little "fatter" than they used to be. Coincidentally, the guests who eat the fatter steaks may tend to be a bit fatter themselves in the future! Checking for quality means checking the entire shipment for conformance to specifications. If only the top row of tomatoes in the box conforms to spec, it is up to the receiving clerk or manager to point that out to the vendor. If the balance of the box does not meet the specification, it should be refused. The credit memo can then be used to reduce the total on the invoice to the proper amount.

Sometimes, quality deficiencies are not discovered until after a delivery driver has left your establishment. When that is the case, you should notify the vendor that a thorough inspection has uncovered substandard product.

The vendor is then instructed to pick up the nonconforming items. Many managers use the same "Additional Information" section of the credit memo to record this requested pickup. When the product is picked up, the pickup information is recorded. Alternatively, a separate memo to the vendor requesting a product pickup could be produced. It is best, however, to keep the number of cost control forms to a minimum whenever possible, especially when minor modifications of one form will allow that form to serve two purposes.

Vendors are sometimes out of a product, just as you may sometimes run out of a menu item. In cases such as these, the receiving clerk must know whether it is management's preference to accept a product of higher quality, lower quality, or no product at all, as a substitute. If this information is not known, one can expect that suppliers will be able to downgrade quality simply by saying that they were "out" of the requested product and did not want the operator to be "shorted" on the delivery.

Training your receiving clerk to assess and evaluate quality products is a continuous process. The effective receiving clerk should develop a keen eye for quality. This is done not merely to protect the operation and ensure that it gets what it pays for, but also to ensure that guests get what they pay for. The receiving clerk might accept a lower quality. Your guests, however, may not. In fact, accepting a lower-quality substitute merely because it costs less is almost always a sure sign that management is unclear about the concept of establishing quality standards and sticking to them.

Price

In the area of training for price, two major concerns are to be addressed. *They are:*

1. Matching PO unit price to invoice unit price
2. Verifying price extensions and total

Matching Purchase Order Unit Price to Invoice Unit Price

When the person responsible for purchasing food for the operation places an order, the confirmed quoted price should be written on the purchase order because it is never safe to assume that the delivered price will match the price on the purchase order. While most suppliers are honest, it is amazing how often the price quoted on the telephone or in person ends up being lower than the price the operation is charged at delivery time.

Often, this variation is said to be "computer error" or a "clerical mistake." It is interesting to note, however, that the errors most often result in the foodservice operator being overcharged and rarely result in an undercharge. As an ethical manager, you should not be happy with either an overcharge or an undercharge for a purchased product. Just as you would hope that a guest would inform you if a waiter forgot to add the price of a bottle of wine to the dinner check, a good receiving clerk works with the supplier to ensure that the operation is fairly charged for all items delivered. The proper acceptance of products puts the integrity of both supplier and operator on the line. Honesty and fair play must govern the actions of both parties.

If the receiving clerk has a copy of the purchase order, it is a simple matter to verify the quoted price and the delivered price. If these two do not match, management should be notified immediately. If management notification is not possible, both the driver and the receiving clerk should initial the "Comments" section of the purchase order, showing the difference in the two prices, and a credit memo should be prepared. Obviously, if the receiving clerk has no record of the quoted price, from either a purchase order or an equivalent document, price verification of this type is not possible. An inability to verify the quoted price and the delivered price *at the time of delivery* is a sure indication that all is not well in the food cost control system.

Some operators deal with suppliers in such a way that a contract price is established. A contract price is simply an agreement between buyer and seller to hold the price of a product constant over a defined period of time. For example, Bernardo uses Dairy O Milk. Dairy O agrees to supply Bernardo with milk at the price of $2.55 per gallon for three months from January 1 through March 31. Bernardo is free to buy as much or as little as he needs. The milk will always be billed at $2.55 per gallon; $2.55, then, is the contract price.

The advantage to Bernardo is that he knows exactly what his per-gallon milk cost will be for the three-month period. The advantage to Dairy O is that it can offer a lower price in the hope of securing all of Bernardo's milk business. Even in the case of a contract price, however, the receiving clerk must verify the invoice delivery price against the established contract price.

Verifying Price Extensions and Total

Price extension is just as important for you to monitor as is the ordered/delivered price. Price extension is the process by which you compute extended price. Extended price is simply the unit price multiplied by the number of units delivered.

Extended price verification is extremely important. It is critical that the receiving clerk verify: Unit prices Number of units delivered Extended price computations (unit price _ number of units delivered) Invoice totals There seem to be two major reasons why operators do not always insist that the receiving clerk verify the extended prices and invoice totals. The most common reason is the belief that there is not enough time to do so.

The driver may be in a hurry and the operation may be very busy. If that is the case, the process of verifying the extended price can be moved to a slower time. Why? Because there is a written record provided by the vendor of both the unit price and the number of units delivered. Remember that verification of price extensions is a part of the receiving verification process that need not be done at the time of delivery. Extension errors are vendor errors, in the vendor's own handwriting! Or, more accurately, today they are in the vendor's own computer. The second reason operators sometimes ignore price extensions is related to these same computers. Some operators believe that if an invoice is computer generated, the mathematics of price extension must be correct. Nothing could be further from the truth.

Anyone familiar with the process of using computers knows that there are many possible entry errors that can result in extension errors. Once all extensions have been verified, it is always a good idea to check the invoice total against the sum of the individual, correct price extensions. Managers must ensure that delivery clerks verify both extension prices and invoice totals. If this cannot be done at the time of delivery, it must be done as soon thereafter as possible. Errors are made, and they can cost your operation greatly if they go undetected.

Proper Delivery Schedules

In an ideal world, you would accept delivery of products only during designated hours. These times would be scheduled during your slow periods, when there would be plenty of time for a thorough checking of the products delivered. In fact, some operators are able to demand that deliveries be made only at certain times, say between 9:00 A.M. and 10:30 A.M. These are called acceptance hours. In a case such as this, the operation may refuse to accept delivery at any other time. Some large operations prefer to establish times in which they will *not* accept deliveries, say between 11:00 A.M. and 1:00 P.M. These are called refusal hours. Since a busy lunchtime may make it inconvenient to accept deliveries at this time, some operators will simply not take deliveries then. In both cases, however, the assumption is that the operator is either a large enough or a good enough customer to make demands such as these.

You may find yourself in a situation, however, where the supplier will determine when goods are delivered. While this may seem inconvenient (and often is), remember that all foodservice units would like to have their deliveries made during the slow periods, between peak meal times. In many cases, it is simply not possible for the supplier to stop his or her trucks for several hours to wait for a good delivery time. In fact, in a remote location, some foodservice operators will be told only the day a delivery will be made, not a specific time!

The key to establishing a successful delivery schedule with suppliers is, quite simply, to work with them. If an operator is seen as especially difficult or costly to do business with, the supplier will pass those costs on, in the form of higher prices. On the other hand, the foodservice operator must make the supplier understand that there are certain times of the day when it is just not possible to accept delivery. While every relationship between operator and supplier is somewhat different, both sides, working together, can generally come to an acceptable solution on delivery hours. If you do decide to post either acceptance hours or refusal hours, these should be equally enforced with all vendors.

Receiving Record or Daily Receiving Sheet

Some large operations use a receiving record when receiving food. This method, while taking administrative time both to prepare and to monitor, does have some advantages. A receiving record generally contains the following information:

1. Name of supplier
2. Invoice number
3. Item description
4. Unit price
5. Number of units delivered
6. Total cost
7. Storage area (unit distribution)
8. Date of activity

Note that some items are placed directly into production areas (direct use), while others may be used in specific units or sent to the storeroom. Sundry items, such as paper products, ashtrays, matches, and cleaning supplies, may be stored in specific nonfood areas.

Note also that subtotals for storage areas can be determined in terms of both units or dollars, as the operator prefers. In all cases, the sums for each distribution area should equal the total for all items received during the day. Receiving reports can be useful to management if it is important to record where items are to be delivered or where they have been delivered. While some foodservice operators will find the receiving report useful, many will not, since most of the information it contains is also included in the receiving clerk's copy of the purchase order.

Storage

The ideal situation for you and your operation would be for you to store only the food you will use between the time of a vendor's delivery and the time of that vendor's next delivery. This is true because storage costs money, both in terms of providing the storage space for inventory items and in terms of money that is tied up in inventory items and, thus, unavailable for use elsewhere. It is always best, whenever possible, to order only the products that are absolutely needed by the operation. In that way, the vendor's storeroom actually becomes your storeroom. The vendor then absorbs the costs of storing your needed products. In all cases, however, you must have an adequate supply of products on hand to service your guests. They are your main concern. If you are doing your job well, you will have many guests and will need many items in storage!

Once the receiving clerk has properly accepted the food products you have purchased, the next step in the control of food costs is that of storing those items. The storage process, in most foodservice establishments, consists of essentially four main parts:

1. Placing products in storage
2. Maintaining product quality and safety
3. Maintaining product security
4. Determining inventory value

Placing Products in Storage

Food products are highly perishable items. As such, they must be moved quickly from your receiving area to the area selected for storage. This is especially true for refrigerated and frozen items. An item such as ice cream, for example, can deteriorate substantially if it is at room temperature for only a few minutes. Most often, in foodservice, this high perishability dictates that the same individual responsible for receiving the items is the individual responsible for their storage.

Consider the situation of Kathryn, the receiving clerk at the Fairview Estates, an extended care facility with 400 residents. She has just taken delivery of seven loaves of bread. They were delivered in accordance with the purchase order and now must be put away. While Kathryn stores these items, she must know whether management requires her to use the LIFO (last in, first out) or FIFO (first in, first out) method of product rotation.

LIFO System

When using the LIFO storage system, the storeroom operator intends to use the most recently delivered product (last in) before he or she uses any part of that same product previously on hand. If Kathryn decides, for example, to use the new bread first, she would be using the LIFO system. In all cases, you must strive to maintain a consistent product standard. In the case of *some* bread, pastry, dairy, fruit, and vegetable items, the storeroom clerk could practice the LIFO system, if these items have been designed as LIFO items by management. With LIFO, you will need to take great care to order only the quantity of product needed between deliveries. If too much product is ordered, loss rates will be very high. Costs can rise dramatically when LIFO items must eventually be discarded or used in a way that reduces their revenue-producing ability. For most items you will buy, the best storage system to use is the FIFO system.

FIFO System

First in, first out (FIFO) means that you intend to rotate your stock in such a way that product already on hand is sold prior to the sale of more recently delivered product. If this is the case, the storeroom clerk must take great care to place new stock behind or at the bottom of old stock. It is the tendency of employees not to do this. Consider, for example, the storeroom clerk who must put away six cases of tomato sauce. The cases weigh about 40 pounds. The FIFO method dictates that these six cases be placed *under* the five cases already in the storeroom. Will the clerk place the six newly delivered cases underneath the five older cases? In many instances, the answer is no. Unless management strictly enforces the FIFO rule, employees may be tempted to take the easy way out.

FIFO is the preferred storage technique for most perishable and nonperishable items. This is because it is generally a good idea to sell the oldest stock first. Failure to implement a FIFO system of storage management can result in excessive product loss due to spoilage, shrinkage, and deterioration of quality. All of these must be avoided if you are to effectively manage food expenses. Decisions about storing food items according to the LIFO or FIFO method are your decisions. Once these decisions have been made, they should be communicated to the storeroom clerk and monitored on a regular basis to ensure compliance. To ensure that this is so, some foodservice managers require the storeroom clerk to mark or tag each delivered item with the date of delivery.

These markings provide a visual aid in determining which product should be used first. This is especially critical in the area of highly perishable and greater-cost items such as fresh meats and seafood. Special meat and seafood date tags will be available from your vendor. These tags contain a space for writing in the item name, quantity, and delivery date. The use of these tags or an alternative date tracking system is strongly recommended. If the supplier has computerized his or her delivery, the box or case may already bear a strip identifying both the product and the delivery date. When this is not the case, however, the storeroom clerk should assume this function.

Storage Areas

The food and related products you buy will generally be placed in one of the following three major storage areas within your facility:

1. Dry storage
2. Refrigerated storage
3. Frozen storage

Dry Storage

Dry-storage areas should generally be maintained at a temperature ranging between 65°F (18°C) and 75°F (24°C). Temperatures lower than those recommended can be harmful to food products. More often, however, dry-storage temperatures can get very high, exceeding by far the upper limit of temperature acceptability.

This is because storage areas are frequently in poorly ventilated closed-in areas of the building. Excessive temperatures damage dry-storage products. Many dry-storage areas are not air conditioned, so it may be necessary to monitor the temperature of these areas with a thermometer. Shelving in dry-storage areas must be easily cleaned and sturdy enough to hold the weight of dry products. Local health codes can vary, but shelving should generally be placed at least 6 inches above the ground to allow for proper cleaning beneath the shelving and to ensure proper ventilation.

Dry-goods products should never be stored directly on the ground, and it is a violation of all local health codes to do so. Slotted shelving is generally preferred over solid shelving when storing food, because slotted shelving allows better air circulation around the product. Can labels should face out for easy identification.

For those bulk items stored in bins or large containers, wheels on these containers should be used whenever possible so that heavy lifting and resulting employee injuries can be avoided. Most important, dry-storage space must be sufficient in size to handle your operation's needs. Cramped and cluttered dry-storage areas tend to increase costs because inventory cannot be easily rotated, maintained, and counted. Theft can go undetected, and you may find yourself accidentally using the FIST (first in, still there!) method of inventory storage because products get "lost" in the storeroom.

Refrigerated Storage

Refrigerator temperatures should generally be maintained between 32°F (0°C) and 36°F (2°C). In fact, the refrigerator itself will vary as much as four degrees (F) between its coldest spot (near the bottom) and its warmest spot. The bottom tends to be coldest in a refrigerator because warm air rises and cold air falls. Refrigerators actually work by removing heat from the contents, rather than "making" food cold.

This is an important point to remember when refrigerating food. Foods that are boiling hot should be precooled to 160°F (71°C) before placing them in the refrigerator. This results in lower operating costs for the refrigerator, but is still well above the potentially hazardous food danger zone, which most food experts place at 40°F to 140°F (4°C to 60°C).

Refrigerators should have easily cleaned shelving units that are at least 6 inches off the floor and are slotted to allow for good air circulation. They should be properly cleaned on a regular basis and should be opened and closed quickly, both to lower operational costs and to ensure that the items in the refrigerator stay at their peak of freshness. Carryover items should be properly labeled, wrapped, and rotated so that items can be found easily, resulting in both greater employee efficiency and reduced energy costs because refrigerator doors will be opened for shorter periods of time. Many managers find that requiring foods to be stored in clear plastic containers also helps in this regard.

Freezer Storage

Freezer temperatures should be maintained between 0°F and _10°F (_18°C and _23°C). What is usually called a freezer, however, is more properly a "frozen-food storage unit." The distinction is an important one. To be frozen at its peak of freshness, a food item must be frozen very quickly. This involves temperatures of _20°F (_29°C) or lower. Freezer units in a foodservice operation do not generally operate at these temperatures; thus, they really are best at "holding" foods that are already frozen, rather than freezing food. Frozen foods comprise an increasingly large portion of the foods you are likely to buy.

Therefore, the conversion of dry or refrigerated space to frozen-food storage is highly recommended. Most foodservice operators also find that their carryover items will, in many cases, have a longer shelf life when held frozen rather than in refrigeration. Frozen foods should be wrapped securely to reduce moisture loss, and newly delivered products should be carefully checked with a thermometer when received to ensure that they are at the proper temperature. In addition, these items should be carefully inspected to ensure that they have not been thawed and refrozen.

Frozen-food holding units must be regularly maintained, a process that includes cleaning inside and out and constant temperature monitoring to detect possible improper operation. A thermometer permanently placed in the unit or read from outside the unit, as is the case with digital displays, is required in most areas. It is also a good idea to periodically check that gaskets on freezers, as well as refrigerators, tightly seal the food cabinet. This will not only reduce operating costs, but will also maintain food quality for a longer period of time.

Storage Basics

Regardless of the storage type, food and related products should be stored neatly in some logical order. This makes them easier to find and to count when the need arises. You may decide, for example, to arrange your stored products on the basis of how often your staff uses them. That is, frequently used items are placed near the front of the storage area. When a few items constitute a majority of the sales volume in your unit, this can be an effective storage technique.

No matter what type of storage system you choose, make sure your inventory sheet matches the physical order of items in storage. This saves time in taking inventory, and it results in fewer errors. It is also important to note that the objective of a neat storage area is both to maximize storage space and to minimize the time it takes to locate the item in storage. When possible, the storage area should be in close proximity to the area in which the product will be used. This reduces unnecessary time lost in traveling to remote storage areas to secure needed products.

In this regard, proper storage techniques, while assisting in lowering the cost of food products, also help in reducing costs associated with Labour. It is sometimes amazing how long it can take an employee to go to the storeroom for a can of beans! In an improperly maintained storage area, employees can claim that it took a long time to "find" the desired product. When a storage area is well located, properly labeled, kept clean, and monitored regularly, problems such as this will not occur.

7

Tourism Trends and Career Prospects

The World Tourism Organization forecasts that international tourism will continue growing at the average annual rate of 4 per cent. By 2020 Europe will remain the most popular destination, but its share will drop from 60 per cent in 1995 to 46 per cent. Long-haul will grow slightly faster than intraregional travel and by 2020 its share will increase from 18 per cent in 1995 to 24 per cent.

Since e-commerce has taken off on the internet, tourism products have become one of the most traded items on the net. Tourism products and services have been made available on the net at bargain prices through intermediaries. In recent time, tourism providers (hotels, airlines, etc.) have started to sell their services through the internet.

This has put pressure on intermediaries from both the virtual and the traditional brick and mortar stores. Space tourism is expected to "take off" in the first quarter of the 21st century, although compared with traditional destinations the number of tourists in orbit will remain low until technlogies such as a space elevator make space travel cheap.

Technological improvement is likely to make possible air-ship hotels, based either on solar-powered airplanes or large dirigibles. Underwater hotels, such as Hydropolis, expected to open in Dubai in 2006, will be built. On the ocean tourists will be welcomed by ever larger cruise ships and perhaps floating cities. Some futurists expect that movable hotel "pods" will be created that could be temporarily erected anywhere on the planet, where building a permanent resort would be unacceptable politically, economically or environmentally.

BENEFITS OF TOURISM

Tourism is now the world's largest industry. The World Tourism Council estimates that travel and tourism provides employment for more than 100 million people world wide (that's one in sixteen workers) and is responsible for over 7% of world wide capital investment. In the year ended June 2003, there were 1,261,818 visitors to the Fraser Coast. Of these 67% were intrastate visitors (849,000), 17% were interstate visitors (214,000) and 16% were international visitors (198,818). In the same period 5,223,187 visitor nights were spent in the region. Domestic and International tourism contributed in net terms approximately $6 billion to the Queensland economy. Tourism generates $2.4 billion annually as an export earner, accounting for 11% of total Queensland exports overseas, second only to coal exports.

ECONOMIC TRENDS AND BYPRODUCTS IN MAINSTREAM TOURISM

Because of the growing awareness of tourism as an activity, an industry, and a catalyst for economic growth and development, competition for the tourist and for tourism expenditures has been significant in recent decades. One result has been market segmentation and a considerable broadening of the perceived and actual opportunities available for potential tourists. Thus tourists can choose from "sun and sand" holidays, "adventure travel," "theater tours," "shopping sprees," summer or winter sports vacations, cultural immersion, historic re-enactments, and various other tourism experiences.

An interesting illustration of product identification and market segmentation is offered by two of the fastest growing tourism destinations in the United States: Orlando, Florida and Las Vegas, Nevada.

Both of these tourist-dominated cities offer predominantly artificially created tourism experiences: Orlando with the presence of Disney World, Epcot Centre, and MGM and Universal Studio "Hollywood"-themed parks; and Las Vegas with its variety of themed "must see" casino-hotel resorts such as The Mirage, Caesars Palace, and Excalibur, along with high-technology showroom extravaganzas and unparalleled convention facilities, all framing a wide variety of gambling opportunities.

Both Orlando and Las Vegas offer escapism and fantasy in highly artificial environments and have been tremendously successful in doing so. It is no accident that Las Vegas is often referred to as providing an "adult Disneyland" for its visitors, whereas Orlando provides the "real" Disney experience. With the exception of the slot machines and gambling tables, there are strong similarities between these two rapidly growing tourism destination cities. Indeed, it may not be so farfetched to call Orlando, with all of its thrilling but nonetheless artificial attractions, an "adolescent's Las Vegas."

It is worth noting that the economic success of both Las Vegas and Orlando has led to many recent attempts to emulate them; legalization or attempted legalization of casino-style gambling has been widespread in the United States, Canada, and Australia over the past fifteen years, and Mickey Mouse has gone abroad to France and Tokyo to found new Disney Worlds to conquer.

However, in spite of the many forms it has taken, not all tourism industries in the developed or the developing world have been beneficial. Success in attracting tourists and tourism-related investments has sometimes led to over-exploitation of tourism resources, which has deteriorated the tourism experience for visitors and hosts alike.

Conflicts have arisen between natural and constructed tourism resources as governments and entrepreneurs have cooperated in competition with those of other locations to attract the economic benefits and prestige that popular destination resorts could bring. Sheer numbers of tourists have altered the "pristine" or "natural" experience that some regions initially offered.

The development of high volume tourism facilities, such as high-rise hotels and tourist-oriented strip retail centers, with inadequate attention paid to traffic patterns, urban planning, infrastructure needs, or aesthetic considerations, has created more than a few "tourism disasters." It is clear in retrospect that, in many cases, the benefits linked to tourism development were quickly dissipated, either due to inadequate or inept planning or because of short-term, shortsighted exploitation.

Disillusionment with mainstream or mass tourism is reflected in the retrospective disappointment of many locals and tourists alike with the ultimate results of tourism developments. An interesting illustration is provided by the case study of Maui, Hawaii, written by Farrell in this volume. For the locals — the hosts — the concerns may be of promises unfulfilled, destruction of an older and simpler way of life, inadequacy of employment opportunities, or dissatisfaction with other economic changes which came with tourism development.

For tourists the view is often summarized with statements such as "This used to be a nice place, but now it is ruined" because of overcrowding, overcommercialization, or overdevelopment. The "mass tourism," the tackiness, and the variety of problems experienced in such places as Niagara Falls, Waikiki, Spain's Costa Brava, and Australia's Gold Coast have too often created eyesores alongside beautiful natural settings; herded large numbers of tourists as if they were so many cattle; disrupted traditional cultures and occupational patterns by creating a pervasive tourism industry characterized by low-paying service jobs and manipulative values; and ignored the needs of local citizens and the community values that were inconsistent with pragmatic economic requirements of the tourism industry.

The decade of the 1990s has been predicted to become the "Decade of Eco-Tourism," and the travel industry is becoming sensitized to mounting global concern about the social costs and environmental damage created by too much tourism. In the past, planners in the private and public sectors have relied heavily on short and intermediate term economic and investment criteria for decision making and for resource allocation considerations regarding tourism projects.

This has often led to problems of overdevelopment accompanied by rapid decline in a destination's general appeal to more upscale tourists. Select coastlines in Florida, Spain, and Mexico provide a variety of examples of this pattern of development. One reason for this short-sightedness is that the market pricing mechanism and other economic processes do not always provide a full and complete accounting of all costs and benefits associated with tourist developments. In instances where important resources are held as the property of "all the people," or where individual property rights are poorly defined, externalities — defined as costs (or benefits) resulting from transactions undertaken between buyers and sellers but falling on otherwise uninvolved third parties — can and frequently do arise.

Pristine beaches and alpine settings, for example, are usually perceived as complementary resources for tourism development projects. Yet the attempt of too many projects to capture the common benefits from such shared resources can lead to congestion, pollution, and a general degradation of the value of such resources for tourism purposes.

Thus local residents at tourist destinations, as well as the general public, often bear the costs of overdevelopment through diminished aesthetic or use value of the resources; by paying for mitigation, abatement, or clean-up efforts through private endeavors or increased taxes; or with lower wealth through foregone opportunities, diminished incomes, or depressed property values.

There is also the socially destabilizing issue of redistribution of income and wealth that invariably follows rapid economic change. Tourism development creates "winners" and "losers" among the local residents, often without a common acceptance as to the equity of such redistribution.

Alternatively, many of the "winners" might be outsiders who are then viewed as exploiters of the native population and rapists of the land. Furthermore, the changes in income and wealth are often viewed in light of the long term depletion of an area's resource base; the ability of such destinations to capitalize fully on their tourist resources in the future may become permanently impaired because of rapid tourism development.

Good decision making procedures should take all such externalities and their costs fully into account in planning for tourism development and in directing the evolution of existing tourist industries. Private market forces by themselves cannot rectify such external costs and often ignore altogether — or treat amorally — the income and wealth redistribution issues. When such situations occur, policy makers should structure government intervention to stimulate more desirable outcomes. Regrettably, such enlightened planning is often not realized in practice.

Awareness of such resource and social conflicts, however, and their relationship to the health of a tourism industry is growing. Antonio Savignac, Secretary-General of the World Tourism Organization, was the keynote speaker at the International Travel Industry Expo 1990, held in Chicago. Among his comments delivered to some 3,000 travel agents and 400 industry suppliers were: "if the destination deteriorates, so do the profits."

This conference dealt with "green tourism," or tourism in the context of man's stewardship with nature, with the development of rural tourism, and with the need to develop responsible tourism policies. It was emphasized that industry and tourism planners need to establish criteria which would determine carrying capacities, both physical and social, for many tourist destinations.

Those criteria then require implementation to insure a more enjoyable and lasting experience for the guest and an economically and psychologically more rewarding environment for the hosts. This volume's article by Bryan Farrell provides discussion and a case study of the aspects and pitfalls of this process. In short, the direction of tourism planning in the 1990s should be toward enlightened self-interest and the value of preserving the quality and stability of both natural and human resources in tourism destinations.

PROFILES OF CONCEPTUALIZATION

We may approach the problem in two ways. There is a difference between the emergence of a practical concept and the construction of a scientific concept. The analysis must go further than surveying the various meanings and denouncing the confusion, even in order to clarify them. Listing the different uses of the term and coming up with an approximate definition is easy but insufficient.

Using the methods of structural linguistics, we analyse the structure of meanings underlying the discourse of Alternative Tourism — the discourse of the tourists, professionals, politicians, scientists. We deconstruct this discourse in order to lay bare the conceptual operations from which it derives its power of persuasion. This is only a much needed preliminary step.

The expression Alternative Tourism can be baffling; to one businessman interviewed in the French Alps it meant "that the roads, the hotels, the whole place, is periodically filled and emptied!" The word "alternative," taken literally, engenders such images as ebb and flow, going and returning, leaving and arriving! But to the initiated, "alternative" (as in Alternative Tourism) is a special kind of qualifier. The whole phrase is an "autonomous syntagm"; the words are bound together like a single noun.

Using the methods of structural analysis, we look at the opposing pairs in which Alternative Tourism is used in speech. We find that Alternative Tourism always has an antithesis: commercial, conventional, mass tourism. It arises as the contrary to whatever is seen as negative or bad about conventional tourism, so it is always a semantic inversion, found at all levels of discourse.

For instance, some tourists are motivated to think that Alternative Tourism is individualized or selective, expressing their good taste, as opposed to mass tourism, which is seen as plebeian, organized, gregarious, and allowing little individual choice.

As lodging, Alternative Tourism refers to human scale, small and medium sized local, family, or community enterprises, well integrated into the area. Anything other than the usual concrete tourist establishments qualifies.

Alternative Tourism connotes local artisanship, with wood and fine materials and typical local architecture.

As a tourist product, Alternative Tourism is expensive, sold by travel agents to a wealthy clientele or social leaders. "Cultural tourism" is the key word. Paradoxically, it also claims to be free of commercial circuits and capitalist profits. It appeals to advocates of "social tourism" and independent tourists alike.

As activity, it favors physical well-being acquired by good health habits, competitive sports, or strenuous outings. It implies intellectual and aesthetic attitudes, trips to far regions with unexplored cultural or natural treasures appealing to the socially mobile. It opposes mass tourism for its comfort and repetition of the "four S's" (sun, sand, ski, sex) of the average middle classes.

Finally, as planning, Alternative Tourism appears to express local wishes to bring together tourists and host communities and thereby enters into endogenous development policies concerned with local interests. Some claim that this "new model" of tourism will replace mass tourism as "old fashioned" or out of date. Thus for some, "alternative" is not just another kind of tourism, but aspires to become *the* tourism in the promotion of a new order.

THE PRINCIPLE OF THE ALTERNATIVE

In logic, an alternative is based on a judgment that there are only two possibilities. Two contemporaneous terms are placed in mutual exclusion, with an "excluded middle," that is, no other possible course is open. It is either one or the other. Thus the promotion of Alternative Tourism relies on a series of value-laden judgments: devaluation/valuation, negation/affirmation, neutralization/idealization.

Emerging from such a series of discriminating processes between"reference tourism" and Alternative Tourism, logically Alternative Tourism becomes *the* tourism.

After analyzing many texts referring to tourism, an unending repetition of these mental processes can be noted. We idealize what we promote and reject what we disapprove of.

TRAVEL PROFESSIONALS

In the context of socio-economic and cultural change discussed earlier coupled with the associated growth of the new middle classes, there have been two notable processes at work. First, professions have become relatively more open following the educational 'revolution' of the 1960s, and the aura (medicine, law, the City and so on) with which they had been traditionally conceived has, at least in part, been dismantled.

Second, however, with still relatively limited access to the established professions, the new middle classes have been busy legitimising new licences and certificates: a classic process of establishing new professions (with professional education and qualification periods, codes of ethics and accrediting bodies or institutes), or professionalisation as Bourdieu notes (1984).

This dual process may indicate that the infallibility of professional distinction is beginning to falter and surprisingly little analytical consideration appears to have been focused on a logical extension (or migration) of the struggle for distinction through professionalisation, into consumption practices.

Professionalism is a key characteristic assigned to company tour leaders, who in many cases are introduced personally: 'dedicated professionalism' as one brochure says indicating that a tour manager not only has a 'deep love of and insight into the areas visited', but also has 'academic credentials and expertise in a specialised field'.

This citation of 'experience' and academic qualifications is commonplace. The following pages cite and quote many tour company brochures dating from 1992 to 2000. In many cases the quoted passages are repeated from year to year.

In tour companies specialising in overland trucking and travelling for ego-tourists, this also means that tour leaders are 'experienced international travellers in their own right'. At Journey Latin America even the reservation staff are 'South American experts' and have 'travelled extensively in Latin America'; the tour leaders are all graduates (some in Latin American Studies), a portfolio similar to Trailfinders. Tour leaders in these companies also embody, and are ambassadors of, new middle-class lifestyles, testify.

In addition, the spirit of professional dedication is also widely cited, where work in this part of the tourism industry is more akin to a vocation. Encounter Overland refer to their trips as 'projects' and talk of their leaders in glowing terms: 'ordinary men and women - often previous trip members - who have elected to put promising careers on hold and devote half a dozen years or more to what they like doing best'.

And, of course, with greater flexibility in the service sector a higher proportion of new middle-class employees are able to take longer periods off between jobs or contracts, or are able to negotiate relatively long periods of absence. All in all a more dedicated, professional, and avaricious tourist class has emerged.

The point we anticipated earlier is that 'travelling' has emerged as an important informal qualification, with the number and range of stamps in a passport acting, so to speak, as a professional certificate; a record of achievement and experience. Not only is travel a professional pre-requisite for employment in parts of the tourism industry, but it is an important attribute in many new professions, such as overseas development work; it has become a rite of passage into certain occupations. There are also indications that professionals working in other disciplines have begun to diversify into travel.

Many of the occasional tour leaders, for instance, are professionals in other fields. For example, the two directors of Papyrus Tours, a company established in 1984 with an aim to provide tours to East Africa, who were supportive of conservation efforts are also a senior officer in a large local authority and a self-employed professional landscape architect, respectively.

Of course, we should also note that Third World tourism has created a huge range of job opportunities for the new middle classes in the First World. It is not just operators in the industry but consultants, journalists, tourism commentators, academics and charities focusing on tourism issues; take The International Ecotourism Society (TIES), for example, whose founder and president, Megan Epler Wood, explains that: 'It was decided that The Ecotourism Society should be an organisation for professionals.

It was clear in 1991 that a broad array of professionals from a variety of disciplines was needed to make ecotourism a genuine tool for conservation and sustainable development'. And more recently, TIES website describes the organisation as 'Representing a worldwide network of 1,700 members from 55 professions and 65 countries ... We'd like to invite you to the growing ranks of ecotourism professionals who are working with TIES'.

It is these professionals who are the opinion formers, the teachers, the advisers, even the ones who take decisions, and a number of publications have sought to prescribe 'technical information on how to do ecotourism "right"'. But the degree to which these 'benevolent' organisations are somehow value free is questionable. It is clear who these professionals are: in the TIES's case, middle-class Americans, many of whom represent other powerful NGO interests (WWF, Conservation International, IUCN and so on - see listing of board of directors and advisers). We must ask what vision of the world they are pursuing and the degree to which such visions are imposed from the First World on the Third World, a question considered in the context of the activities of these organisations.

The commencement of professionalisation processes in consumption is also detectable. As noted earlier, consumption has become more skilled. First, there are clear signals that the distinctions between occupational professionalism, and consumption and leisure, are beginning to blur. Illustrative of this is the growth of outdoor management and 'team' building exercises, especially popular among the new middle classes.

High Places, for example, which offer mountain holidays in a number of Third World countries, also offer 'another type of HOLIDAY! ... training programmes for people at work in industry, commerce and the public sector'. This is an operation appropriately called 'HIGH PROFILE', an experience for people like 'YOU, the sort of people who come on our holidays', described elsewhere as 'intelligent and discerning people who wish to retain a taste of independent travel'. Second, and more significant, tourists themselves are attempting to professionalise travel, a process encouraged, it would appear, by tour operators and environmental organisations. While the emergence of a formal travel qualification, such as the need to support an application for a Himalayan Kingdom expedition 'with your climbing CV', remains the exception rather than the rule for the time being, the number of tourist codes addressing the ethics and conduct of travel have exploded.

A tourist 'Code of Conduct' established by the ECTWT, has been reproduced in many places, especially by the network of organisations concerned with the effects of tourism, but also, for example, among travel agency associations and tour operators who have formulated their own versions. Area-specific codes with emphasis on ecological and cultural issues such as the 'Himalayan Tourist Code' formulated by Tourism Concern (in the UK) have also appeared.

Organisations such as these have attracted increasing support from members of the new middle classes and from new independent tour operators like High Places, which reproduces the Himalayan Code in full and which claims to strive to 'adhere to the ethics' of Tourism Concern. It is the emergence of an ethical, if not professional, approach to tourism reminiscent of Kutay's observed 'Peace Corps-type travellers looking for a more meaningful vacation'.

These codes of ethics form the backbone of a hegemony of travel (or ecotravel as it is now known in North America), which is advanced by the new middle classes, the small independent tour operators and the vanguard of this hegemony, tourism organisations.

Together they begin to represent a new tourism social movement with organisations such as Tourism Concern, the Campaign for Environmentally Responsible Tourism (CERT) and the US-based International Ecotourism Society, emerging as symbolic 'institutes of travel'.

These institutes now provide ethical yardsticks against which the activities of operators and tourists can be measured and classified. With an overwhelming concern for environmental ethics (such as the US National Audubon Society's 'Travel Ethic for Environmentally Responsible Travel'), it is in the ecological and indigenous heartlands of the Third World that these hegemonic struggles are most readily detected and played out.

AUTHENTICITY IN TOURISM AND MEANING IN DEVELOPMENT

The idea of Alternative Tourism as centering on the search for authenticity would appear not to have an equivalent in Alternative Development. Authenticity as a characteristic of Alternative Tourism is wholly focused on the tourist; it concerns his or her perceptions of the reality encountered in the tourist experience.

Cohen's recent paper deals with this issue brilliantly and in detail, his main point being that authenticity does not have an "objective quality," but is attributed by moderns to the world "out there" and thus is a socially constructed concept with a connotation that is not given but "negotiable". In spite of all the nuances brought to the discussion, authenticity remains an issue of importance only to the tourists, or to the hosts insofar as they want to please the tourists; the questions it raises lie outside the realm where Alternative Development provides the pointers for comparison.

Nevertheless, there is an area of overlap, because authenticity deals with meaning, and meaning — for the subjects of development — is an important issue in Alternative Development also. As Dudley Seers noted more than twenty years ago, the question of meaning in development addresses the issue of values often disregarded in the development discourse.

"The starting-point is that we cannot avoid what the positivists disparagingly refer to as 'value judgements.'...Development is inevitably a normative concept, almost a synonym for improvement". And however crucial it remains to the poor to have greater access to material goods, this does not define exhaustively what people regard as "improvement" nor what meaning they can discover in development.

Mainstream development is a child of Western civilization. With the growth of science and technology over the past four centuries, the manipulation and mastering of nature has become the driving force of material "progress." "Development," as it is now understood in mainstream Western thinking, translates this instrumental rationalism into action, constantly "transforming" and "improving" the world. Beyond science and technology, economics dominates the social and human sciences. The mainstream theories of development focus mostly on the economic processes in that material transformation (economics as the science of the management of scarce resources) and devote less attention to the ecological, cultural, and sociopolitical context within which the economy operates.

This has contributed to the dominance of economic policies in the political arena, with governments often paying scant attention to the impact of such policies on culture or nature or to issues arising in these spheres in the first place. Innovation in production and the stimulation of an everchanging demand for the latest in consumption became the final hallmarks of Western "consumer society"; these have provided the meaning of development for "Westerners" and those influenced by them.

Nature, culture, and community have been at the forefront of people's concerns in many non-Western societies. It is clear that in modern society these have moved backstage; they no longer provide the prime motivations for people's actions.

Proponents of Alternative Development want to change that and thereby give a new meaning to development. For even when their language is that of analysis and interpretation, the underlying thrust is political, ideological, and moral. "People-centredness" or "humancentredness" implies small scale institutions, a relocation of decision making, and a rearrangement of the locus of power. Yet Alternative Development enjoins people to relinquish the meaning they have given to everyday life through the products of the consumer society.

They are called to reorient their *Weltanschauung* to the fulfillment of basic human needs, not only for themselves — the simplest life — but for all their fellow human beings (distributive justice) and their posterity (intergenerational justice). Included therein is a concern to achieve harmony with nature and its creatures. This ideological or moral streak in Alternative Development — and Alternative Tourism — has been prominent.

THE SENSE OF OUTRAGE

There are three areas in which this ideological concern has focused in regard to both Alternative Tourism and Alternative Development: nature, materialism, and culture. As long ago as 1971 the Founex Report, prepared for the Stockholm Conference, characterized environmental problems as the "effluence of affluence" and the "pollution of poverty"; this evocative terminology encapsulated a battle cry for action.

From the same decade came the predictions of doom from the Club of Rome with *The Limits to Growth*. In spite of the torrent of scientific criticism unleashed, these are still being used in ecological arguments to portray economic growth as a cancer eating away at the earth's resources. Bandyopadhyay and Shiva accuse transnational companies, operating in the global market economy which has no built-in mechanisms to ensure ecological rehabilitation, of being in the forefront of this misuse of nature; once a mining company has exhausted the mine, or agribusiness has destroyed the grazing lands and forests, it will move elsewhere to maintain its profits.

They argue that mainstream development, in encouraging the use of hitherto unexploited resources, fails to take account of the ecological interrelatedness of the world and the way in which scarce natural resources have competing uses; often damage is done not only to nature as such and to the future productive base, but directly to people. Protests may occur against the disregard for these basic interests, as in India with the so-called ecological movements.

Movements by those directly affected are spreading in other countries, too, as are more generalized protest groups to highlight the costs of present day attitudes to the environment (Greenpeace, Friends of the Earth, etc.).

The alleged disregard for the environment by conventional tourism development also yields expressions of outrage. Hong expresses that mood:

Having ruined their own environment, having either used up or destroyed all that is natural, people from the advanced consumer societies are compelled to look for natural wildlife, cleaner air, lush greenery and golden beaches elsewhere. In other words, they look for other environments to consume. Thus armed with their bags, tourists proceed to consume the environment in the countries of the Third World — that last "unspoiled corner of earth." Protest movements also arise around tourism development, witnessed by the recent impassioned call for international support by the Federation of Ecological Societies of the Dominican Republic to deal with the "extremely delicate situation" that has arisen as a result of ecologically destructive tourism development, involving massive damage to such elements as forests, mangroves, marine life. Such protests have helped place these matters on the agenda of analysts and policy makers.

Materialism has also brought its own hegemony. The emergence of "modernity" and consumer society as the twin pillars of mainstream development has already been commented upon. Neo-liberals believe that the market should provide the basic organizing principles of economic activity and that the role of the state in this area should be drastically reduced.

The market as it operates in reality, however, is far from "perfect." On the one hand, small numbers of powerful producers can influence market choice in their favour; on the other, large numbers of consumers are left with decreasing areas of choice and often with insufficient resources to operate in the market to their advantage. Individual acquisitiveness is at a premium; intervention by the state, notably to promote distributive justice, is limited domestically and virtually absent internationally.

This kind of development is seen as being narrowly focused on economic growth and expansion of the market; it leads to the growth of consumerism and is founded on short term commercial criteria. Many have applied similar arguments to tourism. A recently published Swiss doctoral dissertation can speak for them all:

The thesis is put forward that the chief beneficiaries of tourism development in the Third World are foreign capitalists and, secondly, the local economic and political elite. Tourists from abroad benefit from comparatively low prices in Third World tourist destinations, while the local population is left with modest employment opportunities, the loss of economic and political decision-making, and predominantly negative socio-cultural effects from institutionalized tourism.

This, as Krippendorf puts it, is because in "industrial *society*, values of being have been crowded out by values of having; possession, property, wealth, consumption, egoism are ranked above community, tolerance, contentment, modesty, meaning, honesty." The economy dominates and "man and the environment are at the service of the economy".

Krippendorf and Bachmann also extend their censure to the sociocultural effects of tourism and the "loss of culture," and in this they echo the more general anguish about the effects of modernity and industrialism as cultural homogenizers. The keynote address of the Jordanian Crown Prince to a conference in Morocco picks up many of the doubts about development as modernization and Westernization.

"Progress" has come to be identified with improvement in quantitative indicators; these concern mainly economic processes, seldom social, hardly ever cultural — and if they do, then it is simply to "measure" such matters as the number of museums operating or books published. As Prince Hassan pointed out, however, culture is more: a system of values and norms which give order and meaning to a society. Planners, however, simply cannot deal with what people want out of "development" and even less with why they want it (the meaning of development, again).

And as the planners treat "our peoples as simple numbers, they respond as numbers, multiply like numbers, increase their consumption like numbers" (author's translation). Others have examined this cultural impact of mainstream development on Less Developed Countries through the lens of dependency theory.

Erisman, for example, argues in a discussion of the West Indies that cultural dependency exists when those values, norms, and rules are conditioned by or reflect those in an external culture, leading to a relationship of domination and subordination between the cultural centre and the cultural periphery.

Cultural dependency results in the "incorporation of exogenous norms and values into a nation's socialization process, which can then be said to be penetrated," so that eventually the main stimuli for cultural development come from the outside and people lose their desire to maintain a cultural identity separate from that of the dominant nation.

In a more ideological and outraged vein Nyoni writes that ideas coming from outside the community are expressions of "imposed universalism" which "destroy local initiatives and self-reliance" through "self-colonization and elitism" of local elites, which "are heavily influenced and dominated by foreign and unworkable ideas".

Loss of culture is also explored with respect to the commoditization of relationships, when things and activities that were hitherto outside it are brought into the sphere of market transactions through exchange values. This is often said to be the result of tourism, but in fact it usually arises primarily out of those broader processes promoted by mainstream development.

The already mentioned debates over authenticity are also relevant. Though these have been pursued above all in relation to tourism development, those opposing mainstream development may also allude to these questions.

Thus we read in an already quoted article in IFDA Dossier, one of the main outlets for *engagé* discussions of Alternative Development is that the market economy defines people as poor who do not participate very much in the market and do not consume the products of consumer society — that is, if they eat "self-grown nutritious millets" instead of junk food or if they wear "indigenously designed handmade garments of natural fibre" rather than clothes made of manmade fibers. "The culturally conceived poverty based on non-western modes of consumption is often mistaken to be misery".

This quote represents the polar opposite to the often thoughtless sense of social and cultural superiority of those who stand for mainstream development because in its anger with cultural domination it appears to play down the very real poverty of hundreds of millions in the Third World. These neither eat their insufficient diet of "selfgrown nutritious millets" nor own just one set of simple "indigenously designed [?!] handmade garments of natural fibre" out of their own volition, and they would gladly exchange these for basic needs of the modern variety if they were available. There are, however, signs that more balanced approaches are winning adherents both in the scientific community and in the political arena.

TOURISTIC RESTORATION/APPROPRIATION

In the analysis of the creation of "tourist attractions," cultural heritage is exploited as a "mineable resource." It must be "put to good use" by changing its purpose, and hence its meaning. It is restored along rational lines for commercial promotion and may end up looking like one in a series of reproductions rather than its own historic self.

In Europe, for example, historic landmarks and properties were often preserved by philanthropy derived from a sense of community pride. Now, however, every city restores its historic ramparts, church, or castle to attract tourists, and funding is solicited from art dealers, from cultural sponsors, and from the tourist arms of the state.

Tourism promotion is allied with marketing, and uses the quick functional "cultural engineering" perfected in the United States. Heritage, transformed into productive capital, is renovated and the profit used to repay the cost rather than for safeguarding. Tourism therefore ensures renewal.

Goaded by European unification in 1992 and the prospect of additional millions of tourists, France is now turning itself into a vast "theme park." Compared with the new EuroDisneyland near Paris, other cities and villages will appear authentic!

Castles, cathedrals, old villages, prehistoric sites, and public gardens appeal increasingly to the public. The new ecomuseums have also met with great success, as they look to older people to explain the activities and tools displayed. In disused factories, on canal towpaths, or in historic urban areas we might just meet the last person who has the skill for these obsolete phenomena or the last memories of their working past.

RESURRECTION CREATION OUT OF NOTHING

Much time and money is now devoted to the "remaking of memory" (Jeudy 1986) to create new marketable identities. Thus we restore, regenerate, conserve, and preserve works and events as identities for a touristic society. Things long resigned to decrepitude are resuscitated as heritage or "collectibles." The obsolescent and the obsolete once more become profitable. We extract the old from fragments of collective memory or, better still, from rare survivals still found in daily life. Anything can become a tourist product as long as it can be given value. We invent new deposits to be mined: forgotten folklore, buildings in ruin, the sites of ancient cities. We move monuments from one place to another, change their meanings, and make new springs gush. Thus even the "natural" regional distribution of tourist attractions may become obsolete.

NEW CONSECRATION

MacCannell (1976) first analyzed the process of the transformation of things into tourist products. In order to become an attraction, the phenomenon must be "baptized"; it must be named and become associated with a recognizable sign or "marker" bringing it to the attention of the tourist, guaranteeing its "uniqueness," and making it worth seeing.

To display this object, we frame it, elevate it, light it up, mount it like a jewel, and mark it off from ordinary objects. Detached from the ordinary world, it becomes "sacred" within the ritual of tourism. Its old meaning as heritage is stripped, and it is given a new one appropriate to its role within the tourist system. Thus marked, it becomes a signifier of the identity of the society for foreign visitors.

THE NEW SETTING

The requirements of commercialism join with the moral goals of international organizations: to use tourism for the promotion of mutual understanding and to maintain, preserve and respect cultural identities. This accords with modern humanistic ecumenical and universalist ideals whereby each culture is supposed to make a special contribution to "universal culture."

Through the will of these organizations, patrimony and the extant traditions of archaic societies are placed in new relationships and come to constitute a common cultural foundation for all humanity. The chosen markers represent the identity of the place and its rank within the panoply of world heritage. Thus we can see that international tourism acts as a powerful force in the universalization of culture and society.

THE DILEMMA OF TOURISM

The modern concept of tourism as a factor in economic development is pivotal and is the only way to understand the contradiction between the economic and the cultural. Though first aimed at the Developing Nations, this doctrine has recently been adopted by nearly all countries in response to internal challenges. The key document is Kurt Krapf's paper, presented to the Association Internationale d'Experts Scientifiques du Tourisme (AIEST) in 1961.

TREATED AS AN INFANT

In bringing together developing nations and consumer societies in one global vision, Krapf embraced Rostow's theory of development, by which societies are classified into five stages: (1) traditional; (2) pre-take-off; (3) take-off; (4) push to maturity; and (5) mass consumer. This theory of economic growth has encouraged rich countries to aid poor ones. It imitates child development theory and, though naive, provides criteria for the distribution of aid according to what economists call "the coefficient of capital."

Using this vocabulary, developing nations are "still in their infancy" and need to be pushed to maturity where citizens are assured a "stable consumption economy." The "immature" countries are labeled by their inability and have to accept the paternalistic aid of scientific experts in tourism. They are shown that it is "tourism or nothing." But nothing is not just nothing in this case, it is "the image of death appearing on the horizon".

ECONOMIC DEVELOPMENT

Krapf's argument conceals a paradox: "No one needs imagination to know that a developing country presents the characteristics of an economic take-off." In the terms described above countries have attained stage (2) or (3). As for "traditional society," Rostow's first stage, it is, according to Krapf "doomed to disappear." The economists' death sentence provokes us, for they assert that without tourism a society turns its back on development. In this theory, the gap is accentuated between those developing societies veering toward modernization and isolated traditional societies sliding back into decline.

Yet "traditional society" keeps haunting the imagination. Put aside in the economic order it is stored in the symbolic order, and tomorrow it may reemerge, promoted as a touristic product. Threatened with "imminent death," "traditional society" must be conserved, as a haven of tradition and infancy, in order to sustain the argument for development. Tourism promotion often concentrates on destinations that are virgin, intact, and distant in space.

THE IMAGE OF DEATH

Let us recall some of the debate of the 1960s about the ruinous effects of tourism on culture and environment.

Davydd Greenwood, a U.S. anthropologist studying agriculture in the community of Fuentarrabia in the Spanish Basque country in 1968-69, turned his attention to the Alarde, a lively local festival that drew many tourists. It was a Basque ceremony to celebrate the victory of their ancestors over the French in 1638.

To attract more tourists, the municipality decided to perform the Alarde twice in the same day. The inhabitants not only refused to cooperate with this commercial masquerade but lost their will to participate in the event. For Greenwood "tourism killed the Alarde."

Many similar cases probably exist. Just as the economic benefits emerge, tourism is discredited by the transformation of culture into market value, desecration of ceremonies, debasement of culture and the arts, falsification of traditions, and the loss of identity. The opposition of the economic and the cultural is revealed; here we are faced with the "dilemma of tourism."

In logic, a dilemma is reasoning where the major premise contains an alternative and the minor premises lead to the same conclusion. In practice a dilemma occurs when there are two contradictory possibilities, yet the subject making the choice finds that either way leads to the same consequences.

The discourse of tourism decision making and management is rife with this figure of speech. Actors, whose interests should converge but are in fact opposed, face a dilemma: to develop or contain tourism, to restore culture or celebrate it, leads to the same result. To reject tourism is death, but to accept it is also death.

"The touristic dilemma is clear: to freeze or not to freeze, to maintain boundaries or to remove them...the sword cuts both ways".This double-edged sword underlines the break between tourism as seen by outside agents and by the local society, placing visitors and the visited in a reciprocal extermination.

For a developing nation not to choose tourism amounts to eventual death according to economists, but to choose tourism is also death according to anthropologists. To choose in favour of tourism is the outcome of a double bind, the requirement to make a choice between two impossibilities.

The figure of this dilemma is a leitmotif in the discourse on tourism: "blessing or blight," "trick or treat," "boom or doom," "panacea or a new slave trade," "mirage or strategy for the future." There is always the same disjunction between the economic and the cultural which governs the problematics, be they alternative or dominant. This is still the dilemma which underlies the argument for Alternative Tourism, wherein the word "Alternative" gains its force.

Three Examples:

1. The dilemma of tourism pertains to actual situations. The 1989 WTO Seminar on Alternative Tourism in Tamanrasset took place at a symbolically loaded site, which could have been the source of the love of Uranus and Gaia, in the heart of the Sahara Desert. Here at the gates of Ahaggar the difficulties are magnified because of the barrenness of the place. Yet decisions had become urgent; every year the tourists were coming in greater numbers. Algeria, which previously had no tourism policy, had decided on large scale projects, with perhaps 100,000 beds. Ahaggar was targeted as exemplifying the touristic image of the nation.

   But the desert is an extremely fragile environment, with diminishing ancient water sources. Vegetation is sparse but includes unique local species. Garbage is not degradable. The desert people, adapted to the severe environment, have become guides, serving the tourists but anxious about uncontrolled growth. The experts were conscious of the risks and felt the proximity of total destruction. The government was perplexed when some seminar participants prophesied the end Ahaggar within twenty years if mass tourism develops.

2. In Australia's Northern Territory, the management of the National Parks faced another classic dilemma. This is a special case applied to the Aborigines who at the turn of the century were seen as one of the most "primitive" groups on earth. Survivors of these "totemic societies" are scattered throughout the vast territory. The Australian Government has chosen the National Parks of this region as a "pole of growth," a plan also favored by the White residents of Darwin and the nearby mining camps. The area is highly valued by some for its nature resources and its primitive life. Here we must ask who speaks about the dilemma and whose dilemma it is.

   For the Aborigines, the policy gives them the poignant choice of "to be or not to be." Already decimated and chased away by military maneuvers, their numbers are greatly reduced. These lands, ceded to them in the early 1960s, were temporarily retracted by the regional government without extinguishing Aboriginal rights. For the state as well as for the industry, the Aborigines provoke ambivalent attitudes. On the one hand they are inconvenient inhabitants, an obstacle to the development of the parks; on the other, they are a positive presence, certifying the original character of the place and its preservation from the ravages of civilization. From this point of view, Aborigine society is valued precisely because it is near extinction. One can weigh the tensions between international tourism promotion and a "traditional society." It is not just for economic reasons that the Aborigines are valued; they also possess unique skills, especially in hunting and fishing.

   Thus we can see the dilemmas of both the parties involved. For the Aborigines to reject tourism is to remain welfare recipients. But to choose tourism and participate in it they would have to learn the industry's skills and become "servants," and thereby be evicted from their welfare status. They might be ready to say, "Anything other than Tourism!" In addition, the state risks making investments from which it would not reap a profit, as the land belongs to the Aborigines who, without spending any capital, might in twenty years become an economic power. Thus each of the participants might be tempted to reject the option of tourism. Do the problematics of the alternative find meaning in this kind of case?

3. The Statement on Responsible Tourism propounded by the 1989

Seminar on Alternative Tourism at Tamanrasset is fraught with paradoxes. It amounts to a paradoxical injunction when it supposes symmetrical behaviour between the partners involved, within the framework of relations defined as complementary. Proponents of Alternative Tourism favour the lodging of tourists in the houses of local people, some of whom respond: "When someone comes to my home because I have invited them, I receive them as a friend. But when they are imposed on me from the outside, they are an occupier!"

Yes, tourism produces many situations where the imperative of the double bind traps the recipients of the message of development. To escape, it is not enough to reverse the terms of the alternative; one must break away from the frame of reference.

MISLEADING ARGUMENT

In 1970 the American anthropologist P. F. McKean thought about the possible consequences of mass tourism in Bali, where it had not yet developed. The Indonesian government, following the usual plans of the World Bank, included a focus on tourism in Bali in its first Five Year Plan for Economic Development.

The experts invited by the government drew up a Master Plan for Balinese Tourism with a somber prognostication: Bali risked the destruction of its well conserved traditions which would be devastated by the advent of mass tourism; the very attractions of Bali, its artistic creations, were at greatest risk.

To these experts the Balinese were a poor and isolated agricultural population. It was a "traditional society" where temple festivals, shadow puppetry, and sacred dances were integrated with village life. The experts proposed that, for the protection of the Balinese, tourists should be restricted to enclaves on the southern coast, for ordinary seaside tourism.

But the Balinese adopted a contrary policy. They wanted tourists spread throughout the island so that all villages could benefit. They came up with their own idea of "cultural tourism" and wanted to offer the tourists their best. McKean agreed: "Far from destroying, ruining or spoiling the culture of Bali, I am arguing here that the advent and increase of tourists is likely to fortify and foster the arts."

CAREER IN TOURISM OPERATORS

Maximum benefit from community involvement for the tourism operator occurs when a tourism venture operates in harmony with the social and cultural aspirations of the local community. Involving the community in the development and subsequent operation of tourism projects will not only create greater local support for the operation, it also has the potential to:

- Increase business profits through improved word of mouth referral;

- Grow repeat business from improved experiences with the community; and
- Increase visitation through recognition of best practice standards.

Communities form the backdrop of any tourism product. They provide the support that tourism needs to survive and are often part of the reason visitors are attracted to a destination. Sustainable and responsible tourism is about ensuring a win-win for the community, economy and environment. The attitude, resources and strategic thinking of tourism operators is essential.

OUTLINE OF ADVANTAGES AND DISADVANTAGES

Advantage (depending upon implementation some of these can turn into disadvantages):

- Employment (1 emp/1000 tourist) (labour intensive, few administrative positions, little upward mobility.)
- Infrastructure development (roads, water, electricity, telecom and cybercom, but not necessarily local priorities.)
- Cultural preservation (economic incentives to preserve food, fashion, festivals and physical history, but these tend to be superficial elements of a culture.)
- Environmental protection (econ incentives to preserve nature, wildlife and urban cleanliness)
- Foreign exchange (generates resources to import food, pharmaceuticals, technology, consumer goods.)
- Development of health care services (those these aren't always available to local people.)

Disadvantages (depending upon implementation some of these can turn into advantages):

- Cultural destruction, (modernization (world mono-culture), freezes culture as performers, loss: language, religion, rituals, material culture.)
- Primary products (sun, sand, surf, safari, suds, ski, sex) (little value added, neo-colonialism)
- Environmental destruction (game drives, resorts: golf, ski, beach, desert, world as play ground, SUV.)
- Marginal employment (low skill, low wage, menial services, prostitution, drug trade, gambling, hustlers.)
- Low benefits (no job security, no health care, no organizing, no work safety rules or enviro standards.)
- Development of illegal and/or destructive economic activities (markets for drugs, endangered species, etc.)

- Outside hiring (skilled middle and senior management recruited out of the area and transferred in.)
- Concentration employment (walled resort enclaves.)
- Seasonal employment
- Outside decision making (decisions made outside of the area, corporate dollars corrupt government.)
- Unrealistic expectations (divert young people from school and brighter futures.)
- Anti-democratic collusion (industry support of repressive governments)
- Land controlled by the elite (people relocated, agriculture eliminated, prohibited from N.P.)
- Negative lifestyle's (STD's, substance abuse, begging, hustling)
- Diverted and concentrated development (airport, roads, water, electricity to tourist destinations, development not accessible to locals),
- Little forex stays in country (airplanes, vehicles, booze, hot air balloons, generally have foreign owners),
- Package programs
- Cruises (eat and sleep on board so the economic benefits to the ports-of-call is very thin and limited.)
- Unstable market (fickle, affected by local and world events, generally highly elastic)
- Health tourism (traveling to get medical procedure at lower cost) has it own set of unique challenges, which include: Determining the credential, skills and quality of the facility and personnel. Language communication challenges on topics requiring a lot of details, sometimes even when both parties seemingly speak the same language. Different cultural issues and expectations around health care and the body. Post-treatment complications, after the "tourist" has left the facility.

Solutions (for visitor):

- Act to support cultural diversity
- Engage in activities that add value to the community
- Don't do activities that deteriorate the environment
- Don't engage in illegal activities
- Act to disperse the benefits
- Patronize locally (community) owned enterprises.

Solutions (for the host):

- Support the traditional cultural legacy
- Training and education in local culture, history, natural science, etc.
- Select development and activities that draw from local traditions and add value to the community
- Don't promote activities that deteriorate the environment
- Don't engage in illegal activities
- Adopt a programme to disperse the benefits
- Patronize locally produced products and locally (community) owned enterprises.
- Make business and foreign exchange transactions transparent and efficient.

ECOTOURISM, RESPONSIBLE TOURISM AND E^3 TRAVEL PROGRAMS

IBF has long been uncomfortable with the terms eco-tour and ecotourism because there is no accountability and they have been used to embrace ANY travel that includes "nature" — getting out of a city — even when getting there is by a gas guzzling SUV (sport-utility vehicle or four-wheel drive); ripping up the savannah in the process, and regardless of its impact — that is not us. Other not uncommon characteristics of "eco-tourism" can be; energy-intensive accommodations, encouraging gluttonous amounts of eating (with no reference to dining room waste, how food was produced, or where — a reliance of imported foodstuff and drinks,) prodigious amounts of promotional materials that are paper intensive, and other wasteful and/or energy intensive practices, and little client education on impact of cultural behaviour on the environment.

Consequentially we rarely use the term ecotourism in any of our publicity. "Responsible travel" is facing the same deterioration. It should be "(original) eco-tourism plus". Too often it is defined and practiced with a diluted focuses on cultural responsibility and economic benefit, and a general neglect energy intensiveness (i.e. motorization) and other sustainability issues.

As an alternative we measure programs by a "E^3 Travel" standard (environment, economics and education). This is very similar to the triple bottom line concept of sustainable business (environment, social justice and fiscal), but we like to think of it as the top line for travel programs.

- Environmentally friendly (using primarily non-motorized transport, but reflecting all aspects of the projects including reducing printing and paper consumption, selection of energy efficient lodging, consuming local produced food and goods, and minimizing waste at all levels),
- Economic/equity benefits (supporting the decentralized, indigenous

economy, including local produced food, goods and services, and local employment generator) and

- Educational/enriching/engaging (training guides and helping participants to explore the diversity and complexity of the local natural and human ecology.)

If you draw these as a triangle, each element reinforces the others:

- The use of non-motorized transports virtually mandates patronizing local business. In many parts of the world it is often impossible to bicycle from tourist enclave to tourist enclave in a day. The increased exposure to the local culture, local cuisine, local economy, local interaction, and environment inherently leads to enhanced education and more enriching experiences. But environmental issues go beyond choosing the mode of travel. It is worth bringing your environmental consciousness/audit to every aspect of your travel project: If you use a travel provider, is the advertising and back office side of the "eco-tour" company as environmentally friendly as they would have you thing that their programme is? Can you steer away from energy intensive and import intensive hotels and over-sized everything and steer toward local produced services and goods? Vacation is a time to pamper yourself, and you can still indulge yourself in quality, but you may want to pass on providers of lavish (and wasteful) quantity.
- Aiming for an enriching and well rounded educational experience, is a natural to get more into the community and supporting local business. This argues for eliminating the barriers of glass, steel and speed that go with motor vehicles. Walking and bicycling are great modes for picking up information, engaging with the community and environment around you and supporting the most-local economy.
- Including as a goal equity and supporting local suppliers of goods and service dictates increased interaction with the cultural and enriching experiences. The use of non-motorized transport virtually assures that the benefits will be decentralized and widely beneficial. Sort through you choices is not always easy: There are foreign owned businesses with excellent environments practices and who provide their employees and the surrounding community with excellent compensation and benefits. And, there are local owned business that exploit their employees, do very little to share there good fortune with the surrounding community, are energy and resource intensive, and materially wasteful (make no attempt to reduce, reuse or recycle.) It is hard to make hard and fast rules here, but the small businessperson in the community is usually pretty equitable and a contributing member of the community. The

also likely to be fairly well interwoven in the culture and environmentally responsible.

Incidentally, in tourism E^3 product doesn't seem to be a gender thing: We have seen both male and female own travel specialist who were both good and bad. We have seen foreign owned, male and female, boutique hotel operators who were good and bad. And, we have seen locally owned, male and female service providers who were both good and bad on a E^3 audit.

Within the E^3 structure, an urban bike ride with a lecture on a historic district, a work project in a village and forest walk learning about ethno-botany and looking for primates all can come out on top, as we think they should. Traditional "S"-tourism" (sun, sand, sea, skiing, sailing, sitting, swimming, scuba, snorkel, safari, sitting, sleeping, sight-seeing) can be done in a E^3 way. It is not necessarily the location, the activity or the personnel, but it is how it fits together, the benefits and the costs. Help heal the world when you travel. Do the E^3 of defined activity guarantee sustainability? No, not if integral to getting to the activity is airplane travel by the participants.

Given current technology, even with carbon offsets, you are at best at a "second-best solution". The theory is that second-best solutions are never as good first-best, which in this case would forgoing the flying. A reasonable expectation of how people are going to get to the E^3 activity must be incorporated into the equation. The triple bottom line of responsible tourism is 3 E's: environmental sustainability, engaging in the local economic, and enriching your life from the culture. Actually, it is about the same for all life.

Tourism is the act of travel for the purpose of not only recreation, but also the provision of services for this act. It might occupy local services such as entertainment, accommodation and catering for tourists. It may seem, that tourism brings only benefits, but further consideration shows that it also has disadvantages. Firstly, many countries depend heavily upon travel expenditures by foreigners as a source of taxation and as a source of income for the enterprises. Therefore, the development of tourism is often a strategy to promote a particular region for the purpose of increasing commerce through exporting goods and services.

Secondly, it provides direct employment for the people associated with occupations in bars and hotels. Thanks to it, the average standard of living of people increases well and at the same time unemployment is on the decrease. However, tourists cause environmental damage through forest fires, destruction of sand dunes and pollution. Consequently this serves negatively as increased pollution disturbs local residents and also it may discourage tourists from further entering the country.

After this, tourism undermines culture by commercializing it and this is often connected with increasing litter, graffiti, vandalism and noise - tourists do not always respect traditional cultures, which is sad but true. In general, tourism is an extremely profitable process in loads of countries, especially those in which the process of development continue to depend on this industry because this industry does not require a lot of literacy and also it yields maximum profits with less investment.

There are a number of benefits of tourism for both the tourist and the host destination. On a large scale it offers a good alternative to some more destructive industries for generating income both on nationally and privately. The tourism industry encompasses many different areas, so it also creates jobs in many different areas. With tourism comes hotels, resturants, car rental agencies, tour companies, service stations, souvenier shops, sports equipment rentals, and much more. All of this creates many different levels of employment for people in a given community.

In many places the introduction and development of tourism allows local people an opportunity for economic and educational growth that would not otherwise be available. In addition, it allows both the tourist and the local community a chance to experience other cultures, which broadens understanding. If properly used, tourism generated income can be tremendously beneficial to the host country and it's local communities. Tourism generated income can be used on a national and local level to better education, improve infrastructure, to fund conservation efforts, and to promote more responsible tourism.

8

Hotel Management Courses in India

HIMACHAL PRADESH INSTITUTES

Institute of Hotel Management, Catering Technology and Nutrition is one of the most popular hotel management institutes in Himachal Pradesh. One can come across both degree and diploma courses in this institute. Candidates willing to pursue a career in this field may opt for the undergraduate programme in hospitality and hotel administration. Candidates who have qualified their 12th standard examination with English as a subject may apply for admission. The age limit specified by the institute is 22 years as on 1st July, of the academic year in which the student wishes to take admission. The diploma programme in food and beverage science offered is of one year six months duration. Craftsmanship course in food production provides the students in-depth knowledge about food products and its allied field. Moreover, students can also learn about bakery and patisserie.

Job Scope

The state being a major tourist destination houses some of the best hotels in India. Individuals are hired on a regular basis for the various departments of the hotels. Candidates after gaining required experience in this field can also seek for various job openings as senior executives and managers. Candidates with specialization in cookery do enjoy excellent career prospects in the hotel industry. Institute of Hotel Management, Catering & Nutrition Kufri, Shimla 171012 Himachal Pradesh.

Hotel Management After 10th

CMTES Institute of Hotel Management, Vijayawada offering 2 years Intermediate (Govt of A.P) in Hotel Management Intermediate in Hotel Operations - 02 years, Eligibility - 10th pass.

Students who have completed their 10th standard have a golden opportunity to undergo 2 years Intermediate in Hotel Operations and stand a very good chance of employment with handsome salary.

TRAVEL AND TOURISM - COURSES AND INSTITUTES

Travel and Tourism, one of the world's largest foreign exchange earner among industries, provides employment directly to millions of people worldwide and indirectly through many associated service industries. Tourism industry has achieved a fast growth rate to emerge as the major driving force of the global economy.

On the basis of growth rate, India has been ranked the second, with Montenegro and China on the first and third position respectively. Over the next ten years, India is all set to gain an annual growth rate of 8.8 per cent in the travel sales sector. This immense growth in travel and tourism industry has created plenty of job opportunities for hospitality and travel sales.

As the relative cost of air travel falls, and more and more people take to the skies for both business and pleasure, the sale of airline tickets and holiday packages has become a rapidly expanding business. New travel companies are springing up in towns and cities all over the world and the big tour operators are teaming up with the major airlines to offer ever better deals to an ever wider range of destinations.

A career in this industry is worth taking up because opportunities abound after successful completion of these courses in Travel and Tourism, you can be recruited in diverse job profiles related to this field in the travel agencies, Airlines and governmental organizations dealing with Tourism. After gaining relevant knowledge and expertise as a Travel professional, you can also choose to get self employed. Personality: Young people with drive and a capacity for hard work can rise to top positions very quickly in travel and tourism or even head their own agencies.

Courses in Travel and Tourism in India: With the expansion of travel and tourism industry in India, a career in this field has become lucrative leading to emergence of several courses in Travel and Tourism. Below mentioned are the various courses in Travel and Tourism available in India. Students many need to appear for All-India level or institute-specific entrance test for admission to a particular course. The eligibility criteria may differ from one tourism institute to another.

Basic/ Certificate Course:

- Airlines Management Course
- Basic Course in Air and Sea Cargo
- Service Management Basic course in Airline Travel, Fares & Ticketing Management
- Basic Course in Computer Application & Software Studies Basic course in Computerized Reservation System
- Basic course on Airlines Travel Agency & Tour Operation Management

- Certificate course in Airlines ticketing & Tour planning
- Course in Domestic, International Ticketing & Airlines with Computer
- Courses in Airlines, Tourism, Tours & Travel Management with Marketing & Ticketing Foundation & Consultant Course in International Tourism Language Training course

DIPLOMA COURSES

Diploma Course in Multimodal Transport & Logistics Management

Diploma Course in Rail Transport & Management Diploma course in Transport Economics & Management

Diploma in Hotel & Tourism Management

Diploma in Tourism & Destination Management

Diploma in Tourism & Travel Management

Diploma in Tourism Management (DTM)

Diploma in Travel & Tourism Industry Management

Bachelor Course:

Bachelor in Tourism Administration

Bachelor of Hotel & Tourism Management

Bachelors Degree in Tourism and Hospitality Management

Graduate Integrated Course in Tourism

Vocational Programme in Tourism & Travel Management

PG Diploma Courses:

PG Diploma in Airlines

PG Diploma in Business Administration (Tourism)

PG Diploma in Cargo Operation & Management

PG Diploma in Destination Management

PG Diploma in Guiding & Destination Management

PG Diploma in Travel & Tourism Management PG Diploma in Tourism & Hoteliering Management

PG Diploma in Tourism and Hotel Management

PG Diploma in Tourism Management

PG Diploma in Travel Management (PGDTM)

Master/ PG Courses:

Master of Tourism Administration (MTA)

Master of Tourism Management

Master of Travel & Tourism Management

Eligibility: The eligibility criteria for admission to Travel and Tourism courses at the undergraduate level is, higher secondary examination pass.

Institutes offering Courses in Travel and Tourism in India: There are several universities and institutes in India offering undergraduate, postgraduate and postgraduate diploma courses in tourism.

- National Institute Of Tourism & Hospitality Management (NITHM),Hyderabad:

It is a sector-specific management institute. Modeled on the lines of IITs and IIMs. Courses Offered: MBA (Tourism & Hospitality) 2 years MS (Tourism and Hospitality)-Integrated 5 year course

- Indian Institute for Travel and Tourism Management(IITM), Gwalior
- Sita Travel and Tourism Academy, New Delhi
- Kerela institute of tourism and travel studies (KITTS)

Courses Offered: MBA (tourism), it is a rare course in India:

- Anand Institute of Management Science (AIMS), Gujarat:

Courses Offered: MBA -Hospitality:

- College of vocational studies, Delhi:

Courses Offered: Diploma in Hotel & Tourism Management:

- College of Hospitality and Tourism (CHAT), Gurgaon, (Haryana):

Courses Offered: Masters of Hospitality and Tourism Management
B.Sc in Hotel Management & Tourism
AHLA Diploma.

DIPLOMA IN HOSPITALITY & TOURISM

PG in Hotel Management & Tourism

- Heritage Institute Of Hotel & Tourism, Agra, (Uttar Pradesh)

Courses Offered: Bachelor Degree in Hotel Management & Catering Technology (BHMCT) -3 years.

- Amro Tourism Academy, Nasik, (Maharashtra)

Courses Offered: Diploma in Hotel Management-3 years

- Amity Institute of Travel and Tourism (AITT), Noida

Courses Offered: Bachelor of Tourism Administration (BTA) 3 years, Fees per semester: Rs.42,000. Master of Tourism Administration (MTA) 2 years, Fees per semester: Rs.60,000.

Job prospects both in public and private sector's are bright. However, the best prospects for qualified tourism professionals are in the private sector with travel agencies, tour operators, airlines, hotels, transport and cargo companies etc. Jobs requiring a bachelor's degree, and which usually offer higher pay and benefits, will account for about 7.3 million job openings through 2010. Employment in occupations requiring at least a bachelor's degree is expected to grow 21.6 per cent.

Job sectors: A person willing to make a career in hospitality jobs should look for openings in the avenues such as Tourism Department, Travel Agencies, Hotels, Road and Airlines Transport, Tour Operators, Time Share Companies, Holiday Consultants and Banks. A very wide industry, it includes Government tourism departments, Immigration and customs services, travel agencies, airlines, tour operators, hotels etc and many associated service industries such as airline catering or laundry services, Guides, Interpreters,

Tourism promotion and sales etc. Jobs in the travel and tourism industry offer good remuneration and perquisites, which include free travel for employees and their families. Salaries can vary somewhat within the industry and are higher in foreign airlines and agencies. Pay scales can vary greatly depending on the company, the city, the kind of job, etc. since the travel and tourism industry is so far spread and competitive. Reputation of the company or firm or airline makes a difference as well. Some of the general pay scales for a agency or company dealing in travel/tourism are as follows: Position Pay Counter Clerk Rs. 1,700 - Rs. 2,000 Assistant Rs. 2,000 - Rs. 2,500 Junior Executive Rs. 3,000 - Rs. 3,500 Regional Manager Rs. 3,900 - Rs. 4,500 General Manager Rs. 5,000 - Rs. 6000.

Work in the travel and tourism industry is essentially concerned with providing services for people who are away from home, on business or holiday. Whether you're a travel agent, hotel concierge, or chef, your job is to provide the best possible service you can during a client's visit. So in addition to developing stronger problem solving skills, diplomacy, and communication your studies will focus on honing whatever applicable crafts and skills are involved.

A job in the industry gives good returns as well as perks including opportunity to see many locales at low prices. Like any other industry, there are usually perks that come along with the job. In the travel & tourism industry, some of those perks can be pretty substantial. You can expect to receive discount air tickets, hotel vouchers, free meals, and promo items on a fairly regular basis. Not to mention, you might also receive ample vacation time. What could be more perfect than that?

Intermediate - Vocational is just similar to normal Intermediate or 10+2 with focous on particular specializations. CMTES Vocational College offers specialization in Hotel Operations. This course is designed to provide Technical Skills to the students which will enable them to work in any of the Major Departments of the Hotel.Hence,emphasis is given more on practical to achieve these skills.

The students who pass out of Intermediate in Hotel Operations are the Hot Cakes for the Hospitality Industry. The On-The-Job training imparted during course work will provide them an Opportunity to earn while learning. Candidates after completing Vocational Intermediate in Hotel Operations are eligible to go for Higher Education.

Subjects tought:

- English,
- General Foundation,
- Food Production,Bakery & Pastry,
- Food & Beverage service,
- Room Division

COURSE STRUCTURE

There are 9 lessons as follows:

- Introduction: Scope and Nature of Hotel Management

The Hotel Industry, The Scope of the Industry, The Firm in the Hotel and Catering Industry, Hotel Management, Planning, Policy

- Organisation of the Hotel Workplace

Organisation, The Nature and Purpose of Organisation, The Mechanistic View of Organisation, The Human Relations View of Organisation, The Systems Approach to Organisation, Organisation Structure, The Informal Structure, Hotel Organisation

- Staff Management in Hotels

Work Charts, Communication and Coordination, Staff Management, Monitoring Workloads and Work Procedures, Authority/Chain of Command, Career Structure.

- Control Systems

Sources and Storage of Information, Creating and Maintaining Information, Creating and Maintaining Control Systems, Types of Control, Production Control, Quality Control, Sales Control, Labour Utilisation Control, Materials Control, Maintenance Control, Financial Control, Setting Standards and Corrective Action, Work Study, Organisation and Methods

- Front Desk Management (Reception)

The Functions of the Front Office, Customer Service, Dealing with Grievances & Complaints, Understanding Communication, Conversation Development, Using the Telephone, Business Letters, Promotions and Customer Relations, Client Interpersonal Skills, Self Esteem & Reinforcement, etc.

- Servicing Rooms and General Cleaning

Service Equipment, Direct Purchase of Hire of Equipment, Linen: Purchase or Hire, Choice of Fabrics, Structure and Properties of Fibres, Linen Room Organisation.

- Building and Facility Maintenance

Daily, Periodic and Planned Preventative Maintenance, Frequent Maintenance Problems, Safety, Furniture, Fittings, Managing Maintenance, Building Maintenance, Toilets and Locker Rooms.

- Activities Management

Tour desk, gymnasium, events (eg. Weddings, balls etc), In house Services, Recreation Facilities, Guest Information Services, Swimming Pools, Spa & Sauna Facilities, Activities Management, Tourism.

- Food Service

Types of Food Service (eg. Room Service, Bar, Restaurant, Coffee Shop etc), Kitchen Design & Equipment, Service Facilities, Food Service Management, Food Purchasing, Dealing with Complaints.

AIMS

On successful completion of the course you should be able to do the following:

- To understand the range of hotels in operation and their management policies
- To understand management structures and the way in which the workplace is organised.
- To draw a team of professional staff together to ensure quality delivery of these services requires a tremendous amount of skill and organisation.
- To gain an understanding of the complexity of hotel management consider the following areas of management:
- To understand the importance of maintaining an overall system of control within a hotel
- To develop knowledge of the complexities and management issues relating to front desk operations.
- To develop knowledge of equipment and understanding of linen available
- To implement facilities management systems
- To implement and manage an activities service
- To understand a range of food services offered in the hotel industry

What the Course Covers

Here are just some of the things you will be doing:

- Interview a manager or senior staff at a local hotel to enquire about their set up and structured policies.
- Find out about the organisational structure of either one department of the hotel, or the whole hotel.
- Observe how managers give direction/orders/requests to staff.
- Discuss the procedures which should be followed when creating and maintaining a budgetary control system.
- Observe and evaluate the Front Desk management of a selected hotel, commenting on the style of communication used, efficiency of the staff and your suggestions for improvement.
- Discuss room service and room standards (ie cleanliness, etc.) in hotels and other guest accommodation, with three different colleagues or friends to identify areas of concern.
- Visit a hotel in order to develop a checklist for conducting maintenance inspections.

- Compare guest services (including fitness and health services) fat two different hotels or chains in the same region
- Compare the different food services (including range/scope of services, times of service, types of food and beverage, prices, and quality of serviced) at three hotels in the same area.

Broad based, basic training to work in hospitality, accommodation, hotels, motels or resorts. A popular and substantial starting point for anyone in the hotel industry, this course is 100 hours duration.

HOTEL MANAGEMENT COLLEGES ANDHRA PRADESH

- BLOOMS COLLEGE OF HOTEL MANAGEMENT & CATERING TECHNOLOGY, 12, Om Nagar, Langar House, Hyderabad 500008 (Ph 040-23511948, 23522892, 55762208) (Affiliated to Osmania University) offers 3-year Degree in Hotel Management and Catering Technology. Eligibility: 10+2/Intermediate/Graduation/ PDC.
- NIRAJ COLLEGE OF HOTEL MANAGEMENT & CATERING TECHNOLOGY, 44, Uma Nagar, Kundan Bagh Area, Begumpet, Hyderabad 500016 (Affiliated to Osmania University) offers Bachelor's Degree in Hotel Managementd and Catering Technology (BHMCT). Eligibility: 10+2.
- REGENCY COLLEGE OF HOTEL MANAGEMENT AND CATERING TECHNOLOGY, 'Regency Place', 8-2-677, Road No. 12, Banjara Hills, Hyderabad 500034, offers 3-year degree in Hotel Management and Catering Technology Technology. Eligibility: Intermediate/10+2/equivalent in any group. Hostel facility is available. Notification: June.
- SHRI SHAKTI COLLEGE OF HOTEL MANAGEMENT, Venus Plaza, Adjacent to "The Manohar", Begumpet, Hyderabad 500016 (Ph 040-27908585/8787, 55316757 Fax 040-55316756 Email www.sschm-hyd@eth.net Website: www.sschm.com) offers Bachelor of Hotel Management and Catering Technology (Affiliated to Osmania Univ.). Eligibility: Intermediate exam (10+2) or equivalent.Age:22 years for SC/ST.There is provision for special concession in Tution fee for meritorious students.
- SIDDHARTHA INSTITUTE OF HOTEL MANAGEMENT & CATERING TECH, Siddhartha Nagar, Vijayawada, Krishna District 520 010 (Andhra Pradesh) offers Hotel Management & Catering Technology (Seats 60).
- SRI PADMAVATHI WOMEN'S POLYTECHNIC, Tirupati Chittoor Dist. 517502 (Pvt.) offers Diploma in Hotel Management & Catering Technology.

- SRI VENKATESWARA INSTITUTE OF HOTEL MANAGEMENT AND CATERING TECHNOLOGY, No 11-20, renigunta Road, Post Box No. 54 Tirupati 517501, offers 3-years Diploma in Hotel Management & Catering Technology. Eligibility: +2/P.D.C../ Intermediate exam. Last date: June. Course commences in: July.

HOTEL MANAGEMENT COLLEGES BIHAR

- INDIAN INSTITUTE OF BUSINESS MANAGEMENT, Buddha Marg, Patna 800001, offers 3-year diploma in Hotel Management & Catering Technology. Eligibility: Intermediate/10+2. Age: Not more than 22 years. Selection: All India Technical and Management Admission Test Comprising written test, followed by GD and personal interview. Hostel facilities are available for boys and girls. Last date July.
- SHANTI SEWA SAMITI'S INDIAN INSTITUTE OF HOTEL MANAGEMENT, 11, I.A.S. Colony, Kidwaipuri, Patna 800001 (Email iihmbkb@yahoo.com) offers 3-year Diploma in Hotel Management & Catering Technology. Eligibility: 10+2 pass/appeared and age within 22 years. Selection: Written test followed by a personal interview. Hostel facilities available for boys/girls separately. Last date: August.

HOTEL MANAGEMENT COLLEGES DELHI

- BHARATIYA VIDYA BHAWAN, 1, Kasturba Gandhi Marg, New Delhi (Ph 233382002 Email:bhaviday@del2 Webiste www.bvbdelhi.org) offers 1-year Part-time Evening Job Oriented Course in Hotel Management (with Hospitality oriented German Language). Eligibility: 10+2/Graduates and working people. Age: No Bar.
- DELHI INSTITUTE OF HOTEL MANAGEMENT & CATERING TECHNOLOGY (An Autonomous Body under Govt. of NCT, Delhi), Behind Lady Shri Ram College, Lajpat Nagar-IV, New Delhi 110024, offers one and half year Trade Diploma Courses in: (i) cookery (ii) Bakery & Confectionery, (ii) Hotel Keeping, (iv) Hotel Reception & Booking Keeping (iv) Restaurant & Counter Service (24 Seats for each course). Eligibility: 10TH or 12th of 10+2 pattern or its equivalent from any frecognised Board with minimum 50% aggregate marks and having passed in English as compulsory subject. There is a provision for relaxation of 10% in minimum aggregate marks for SC/ST candidates. Age: Maximum 25 years as on 1st August of the year of admission. Reservation of seats as per Govt. of Delhi norms. Last date: June.

- EIKON ACADEMY, KLJ Complex 1, 70/B-39, Nasafgarh Road, Opp. Moti Nagar Police station, New Delhi 110015 (Ph 41427070, 41427712-15, 17, 19 Email admissions@eikonacademy.com Website www.eikonacademy.com) offers Professional Courses in Hotel Management, Catering and Tourism.
- FHRAI INSTITUTE OF HOSTPITALITY MANAGEMENT, B-82, 8th Floor, Himalaya House, 23, Kasturba Gandhi Marg, New Delhi 110001 (Ph 23318781-82 offers the following courses (i) 4-years International Hospitality Administration (ii) 4-years International Culinary Administration (with academic Certification from Ecole hoteliere de Lausanne, Switzerland). Further details can be had from Plot No. 45, Knowledge Park II, Greater noida 201306, Phone 0120-2231801-04 E mail info@fhraiinstitute.com Website www.fhraiinstitute.com.
- GURU GOBIND SINGH INDRAPRASTHA UNIVERSITY, Kashmere Gate, Delhi 110006 (Website www.ipu.ac.in) conducts a Common Entrance Test (CET) for admission to 4-year Bachelor of Hotel Management & Catering Technology (BHMCT).
- BANARSIDAS CHANDIWALA INSTITUTE OF HOTEL MANAGEMENT & CATERING TECHNOLOGY, Chandiwala Estate, Maa Anandamayee Ashram Marg, Kalkaji, New Delhi 110019 (Ph 26382276 Fax 26382278 Email: hm@chandiwalaestate.com Website: www.chandiwalaestate.com). Seats: 60. Eligibility: 12th class of 10+2 pattern or equivalent with a minimum of 50 % marks in aggregate with English as a compulsory subject. Category/ Reservation: There is categorization of free seats, payment seats, regionwise allocation, reservation for SC/ST, Physically Handicapped, Children/wards of defence personnel as well as some seats earmarked for NRI/NRI sponsored/Industry sponsored/foreign candidates as detailed in the information bulletin. Last date: April.
- INSTITUTE OF HOTEL MANAGEMENT, CATERING & NUTRITION, Library Avenue, Pusa Complex, New Delhi 1100012 (Ph 25842429, 25843177 Telefax 25843177 Email ihmpusa@rediffmail.com Website www.ihmpusa.net) offers the following courses: Diploma in Food and Beverage Service (DFBS) Eligibility: Class XII of 10+2 system or equivalent with English as a compulsory subject. Age: 22 yrs. Last date: June. Diploma in Bakery and Confectionery (DBC). Eligibility: Class XII of 10+2 system or equivalent with English as a Compulsory subject. Age: 22 yrs. Last Date: June. Craftsmanship Course in Food Production (CCFP). Eligibility: Class X of 10+2 System or equivalent.Age:22Years. Last Date: June. Reservation: For Scheduled Castes: 15%, Scheduled Tribe:

7% and Physically Handicapped: 3%. Medium of Instruction: English or Hindi. Last date: December.

- INTERNATIONAL INSTITUTE OF CULINARY ARTS, 39, Daracharya, Hauz Khas Village, Near Village Bistro Restaurant, New Delhi 110016 (Mob. 981199918, 9811999620 Email chefiica.com Website www.chefiica.com) offers the following courses:
  - In India: Level I- Preparing and serving of food
  - Level II- Food Preparation & Cooking during their studies in India.
  - In UK: Level III-Food Preparation & Cooking Basic Food & Hygiene Course. Eligibility: 10+2. Selection is made on the basis of interview and assessment of Personal Skills and Qualification.
- LAKSHYA BHARTEE INSTITUTE OF INTERNATIONAL HOTEL MANAGEMENT, B-98, Pushpanjali Enclave, Outer Ring Road, Pitampura, Delhi 110034 (Ph/Fax 55155115, 27011495 Mob. 9810820369, 9818119156 Email info@lbiihm.com Website www.lbiihm.com) (Authorized Academic Centre of IASE- Deemed University & Affiliated to EI-AHLA, USA) offers the following courses:
- 3-year B.Sc in Hotel Management & Tourism Eligibility: 12th STd.
- 2-year Postgraduate Diploma in International Hotel Management (Equivalent to MBA Hospitality). Eligibility: Graduation. Selection is made on the basis of Personal Interview.
- Facilities:
- Intensive on the job-training in leading 5 star Hotel.
- Highly Experienced & Dedicated faculty
- Assistance provided for Bank Loans
- Placement Assistance in India & Abroad

Member of:

- The Fedration of Hotel & Restaurant Association of India(FHRAI)
- Hotel & Restaurant Association of Northern India (HRANI)
- Chhatisgarh Hostelliers Association, Raipur (CHA)

Detailed information about the courses and Application Form for admission is mentioned in the Prospectus, which can be obtained by sending DD/MO in favour of Lakshya Bhartee Institute of International Hotel Management payable at Delhi for Rs. 300/- by post at the address given above, or on cash payment of Rs. 250/- from the Insitute's Office.

- NEW DELHI YMCA, Institute for Career Studies, Jai Singh Road, New Delhi 110001 (Ph 23360501, 23361915 Extn. 128/123) (Co-education) offers one and half year Certificate in Hotel & Catering Management.

- OBEROI SCHOOL OF HOTEL MANAGEMENT, Oberoi Centre for Learning & Development, 7, Sham Nath Marg Delhi (Ph 23890505 Website: www.careerstheoberoigroup.com) offers 3-year Bachelor of Hotel and Tourism Management Course. The course conducted at athe Institute consists of two Modules: (1) Kitchen Operation Management and (2) Hotel Operation Management (internally called STEP Programme.). The degree is awarded by IGNOU, New Delhi.
- R. M. INSTITUTE OF HOTEL MANAGEMENT, N-13 Sainik Farms New Delhi (Ph 26867827, 26966073) offers 3-year Diploma in hotel Management. Eligibility: 10+2 with English as a compulsory subject. Selection: Written Test, Individual and Group Interviews. Notification: April
- SOUTH DELHI POLYTECHNIC FOR WOMEN, Lajpat Nagar IV, Amar Colony, Behind Lady Shri Ram College, New Delhi 110024 (Ph 26294833, 26464917 Fax 011-26474425 Email polytech@nda.vsnl.net.in Website polytechnic-sdpw.com) offers Certificate courses in Hotel Catering & Hospitality.

HOTEL MANAGEMENT COLLEGES GOA

- ACADEMY OF CULINARY EDUCATION, Cidade de Goa Beach Resort, Vainguinim Beach, Goa 403004 offers 3-year course in Hotel Management.
- ANN INSTITUTE OF HOTEL MANAGEMENT, Nova Cidade Commerical Complex, S-1 Building, 2nd Floor, Near Chodankar Hospital, Porvorim Bardez, Goa (Ph 0832-2411350, 3114919 Website www.annhmctgoa.com) offers 3-year Degree in Hotel Management and Catering, 2-year Diploma in International Hospitality Management. Eligibility: 12th pass. Also offers 1-year Diploma in Hotel Management and Catering Eligibility: SSC.
- IAM – The Hotel School. Gaurvaddo, Holiday Street, Calangute, Bardez 403516 (Goa) (Ph 0832-2282774, 2281880 Website www.iam-cal.net) (Approved by AICTE) offers 3-year integrated Degree courses in Hotel and Hospitality Management. (Degree is awarded by Queen Margaret University, UK). The curriculum ensures that the students undergo a 22 weeks supervised workplace experience at 5-star Hotels in India, UK, Dubai, Singapore and other exciting distinations. Eligibility: 10+2 passed or appeared. Selection is made on the basis of Admission Test, Group Discussion and Interview held at all major citites in India and online Admission TESt (CHAT) Age: Age of the candidate should be below 22 years. Application

Form and Prospectus can be had from specified branches of UTI Bank or can be downloaded from the website of the Institute given above.

- I.I.A.S., Pooja building, Miramar Tonca Road, Miramar, P.O. Caranzalem, Goa 403002 (Ph 0832-2462469/2464204 Email: iiassancharnet.in Website www.iiasindia.com) (Approved by AICTE.) offers Hotel Management and Catering Tecnology course. Eligibility: 10+2. Selection is made on the basis of written test and Personal Interview. Hostel Facilities are available for girls and boys separately. Placement: facilities available. Further details can be had from the Institue.

HOTEL MANAGEMENT COLLEGES GUJARAT

- VIVEKANAND INSTITUTE OF HOTEL & TOURISM MANAGEMENT, Rajkot (Gujarat) (Ph 0281-84384, Telefax 0281-84474 Email vihtm2001@rediffmail.com Website www.vihtm.com) offers 4-year Degree in Hotel Management & Tourism Management (Apporved by the Gove. Of Gujarat). Eligibility: PUC/Class (10+2) or equivalent with minimum 50% marks (45% for SC/ST Candidates) in aggregate with Science, Commerce or Arts subjects with English as a compulsory subject form India/abroad or a pass in degree exam in any discipline. Last date: July.

HOTEL MANAGEMENT COLLEGES HARYANA

- INSTITUTE OF HOTEL MANAGEMENT, CATERING AND NUTRITION, Department of Tourism, Panipat, offers one and half year Craftsmanship curses in: (1) Bakery & Confectionery, (2) Food and Beverage Service, (3) Food Production. Eligibility: 10+2 or equivalent with English as a compulsory subject.
- INTERNATIONAL INSTITUTE OR HOTEL MANAGEMENT, Institutional Area, Plot No. 38, Sector 32, Gurgaon (Har.) (Ph 0124-4104708, 09899746100 Email gurgaon@ iihm.ac.in. Website www.iihm.ac.in) offers, 3-year Full-time Diploma in Hotel & Catering Management (In collaboration with the Queen Margaret Univ. College, Edinhurgh, UK) BA Degree course in International Hospitality Mgmt. (of QMUC).

The Course includes 22-week of compulsory Industrial training in a reputed j5-star Hotel in India, Singapore, Dubai or at United Kingdom. The Students have the option of doing the third year of the course at QMUC, Edinburgh, UK or at any for the IIHM compuses in India. The Student can also choose to study the final year of the course at the Napier University or at the sprawling Mega Campus of the Thames Valley University, Landon.

Eligibility: Candidate must have passed or appeared in Class 12 level Board examination form a recognized Board and should possess good communication skills. Age: 22 years.

Selection: The Selection is made through online admission test- Common Hospitality Admission Test (CHAT). Selected candidates are required to appear for Group Discussion and Interview to be held at all major cities in India.

Application form and Prospectus can be obtained from the selected branches of Axis Bank/ Reliance Web World or may also be downloaded from IIHM Website

- KURUKSHETRA UNIVERSITY, in collaboration with Indian Tourism Development Corporation, Department of Tourism and Hotel Management, Kurukshetra 136119 (Ph 01744-238026, 238999 Website www.kuk.ernet.in, www.itdc.org) offer 4-year Bachelor's degree in International Hospitality Business Management.

Eligibility: 10+2 from any recognized Board or equivalent with English as one of the subjects.

Selection: Selection is made on the basis of Entrance Test held during June. Last date: June.

- M.M INSTITUE OF COMPUTER TECHNOLOGY & BUSINESS MANAGEMENT, M.M. Educational Complex, Mullana, Haryana-133203 offers Hotel Management course
- NORTH INDIA INSTITUTE OF HOTEL MANAGEMENT, North Park Complex, Near Ghagghar Bridge, Panchkula 134109 (Near Chandigarh) (E-mail npark@ch1.dot.net.in) offers 3-year Diploma course in hotel Management.
- VATEL-OBEROI & OBEROI, A23/21 DLF-I, Gurgaon 122002 (Email Vatel-oberoi@hotmail.com Website www.vatel.fr) offers 3-yer (sem. Pattern) course in Hotel Management.

The Programme: First Semester Food & Beverage Management is conducted at Gurgaon (Har.) followed by the remaining 5 semesters in France, with paid internship.

Eligibility: A warm and outgoing personality, candidates should have cleared their CBSE, ICSE or equivalent board in India or abroad

HOTEL MANAGEMENT COLLEGES HIMACHAL PRADESH

- INSTITUTE OF HOTEL MANAGEMENT, CATERING & NUTRITION, Kufri, Shimla 171012 offers 3-year diploma in Hotel Management (Affiliated to the NCHMCT, New Delhi).

HOTEL MANAGEMENT COLLEGES JHARKHAND

- BIRLA INSTITUTE OF TECHNOLOGY, Mesra, Ranchi 835215

(Website www.bitmesra.ac.in) offers 4-year Bachelor of Hotel Management & Catering Technology (BHMCT).

Eligibility: A pass in ISc./10+2 or equivalent with Physics, Chemistry and Mathematics/ Biology.

Age: Maximum 21 years as on 1st September of the year of admission (5 years relaxation for SC/ST candidates). Selection: Selection is made on the basis of written test held during June. Last date: April.

- INDIAN INSTITUTE OF SCIENCE & MANAGEMENT (IISM), Department of Hotel Management, IISM Campus, Institutional Area, Pundag, Ranchi 834004 (Ph 0651-2242062 Fax 0651-2240630 Email rch_iism@sancharnet.in Website www.iismr.org) offers 3-year Diploma in Hotel Management & Catering Technology.

Eligibility: 10+2 or its equivalent in any discipline. Appearing candidates can also apply.

- *Age:* Not more than 22 years on on 31st July of the year of admission (25 years for SC/ST candidates).
- *Selection:* Result of UGAT, Group Discussion and Personal Interview.
- Hostels facilities are available for boys and girls separately.
- *Last date:* June
- Also offers 1-year Certificate course in Food and Beverage Service and Food Production.
- *Eligibility:* 10+2. Appearing candidates may also apply.

HOTEL MANAGEMENT COLLEGES KARNATAKA

- AE & CS MARUTI COLLEGE OF HOTEL MANAGEMENT, 3rd Cross, Bangalore, Karnataka offers Hotel Management and Catering Technology Course.
- AMC COLLEGE, 30th Cross, 4th Block, Behind Police Station, Jayanagar, Bangalore 560011 (Ph 080-26638991/992 Mob. 9880215355 Fax 26638994 Campus: Banneraghatta Main Road, Bangalore 560083 (Email amceduacation@rediffmail.com) (Affiliated to Bangalore Univ.) offers BHM.

Hostel facilities are available for boys and girls separately:

- ACHARYA INSITITUTE OF HOTEL MANAGEMENT & CATERING TECHNOLOGY, 1st Stage, 1st Cross, Peenya Industrial Area, Bangalore 560058 (Ph 080-28376430, 28398699, 57679113, 51253496 Fax: 080-28378268 Email admission@acharyaims.ac.in. Website www.acharyaaims.ac.in) offers Bachelor of Hotel Management. Further details can be had from: 080-57679113.
- ADMINISTRATIVE MANAGEMENT COLLEGE, AMC Building,

30th Cross, 6th Main, 4th Block, Jaya Nagar, Bangalore 560011 (Ph 27828656 Email: gpuru@vsnl.net.in.

Website www.amcinstitutions.com) (Approved by AICTE and affiliated to Bangalore University) offers 3-year degree in Hotel Management.

Eligibility: Passed/appeared in 10+2 system of any recognized Board with 40% marks. Selection: An entrance test with personal interview held at various centres.

- AL-AMEEN ARTS SCIENCE & COMMERCE COLLEGE, Bangalore Offers Hotel Management and Catering Technology Course.
- ARMY INSTITUTE OF HOTEL MANAGEMENT AND CATERING TECHNOLOGY, c/O ASC Centre and College, PO Agram, Bangalore 560007 (Ph 25714338

  Email principal@aihmctbangalore.com Website www.aihmctbangalore.com) offers 3-year Bachelor of Hotel Management (BHM) (40 seats) at the following centres: Pune, Chennai, Secunderabad, Bangalore, Mumbai, Thiruvanathapuram, Ahmedabad, Jaipur, Kolkata, Shillong, Guwahati, Dimapur, Sukna, Delhi, Jalandhar Cantt. Ambala, Meerut, Bareilly, Mathura, Lucknow, Jabalpur, Dehradun, Mhow, Jammu, Pathankot, Srinagar.

Eligibility: Children of serving army personnel/regular army pensioners.

Educational Qualification: 10+2 equivalent examination from a recognized Board with English as compulsory subject. Candidates who have appeared for 10+2 exam and are awaiting results may also apply subject to producing the proof of passing the examination at the time of admission.

Age: Not less than 17 years and not more than 22 years as on 1st July of the year of admission. Prospectus: For further details, prospectus, along with application forms can be had on payment of requisite charges in cash/demand draft drawn in favour of Army Institute of Hotel Management and Catering Technology payable at SBI ASC Centre (South), Bangalore Code No. 4742 from Headquarter following commands and Headquarters ASC Centre (South), Bangalore 560007.

- Headquarters Nothern Command, Udhampur 182101
- Headquarters Eastern Command, Kolkata 700021
- Headquarters Western Command, Chandimandir 134107
- Headquarters Central Command, Lucknow 226001
- Headquarters Southern Command, Pune 411001
- Headquarters ASC Centre (South), Bangalore 560007
- Army Headquarters DDG (Welfare), AG's Branch, New Delhi 110011.

Applicants are advised to contact Colonel 'A' at above mentioned command Headquarters for any further information.

Sale of prospectus and application forms: May.

Written Admission Test (WAT): April.

Notification: November.

Last date: March.

- CHRIST COLLEGE OF HOTEL MANAGEMENT, Hosur Road, Bangalore 560029 (Ph 080-25536280 Email princi@christcollege.edu Website www.christcollege.edu) offers Bachelor's Degree in Hotel Management (BHM).
- COLLEGE OF HOTEL MANAGEMENT, A.B. Shetty Circle, Mangalore 575001 (Affiliated to Mangalore University) offers 4-year Bachelor of hotel & Restaurant Management.

Eligibility: Pass in PUC of Karnataka or equivalent exam. (10+2) of other Universities/ Board recognized by Mangalore University with 45% marks in aggregate.

Last date: June:

- GANGA KAVERI INSTITUTE OF SCIENCE AND MANAGEMENT, # 1699 (43/1), Dr. Rajkumar Road, III Stage, Rajajinagar, Bangalore 560010 (Ph 080-23429266, 23429917, 9845972721 Fax 23537245 Email keveris@vsnl.net Website www.gkism.com) offers Bachelor of Hospitality and Catering Science (BHCS)
- GARDEN CITY COLLEGE OF SCIENCE & HOTEL MANAGEMENT, 628/C, 1st Stage, Indira Nagar, Bangalore 560038 (Ph 080-25288831, 25271385, 22972754/3 9818702858, 9815251023 Fax 080-25291414 Campus: 16th Km, Old Madras Road, Bangalore 560049 (Email gcetrust@vsnl.com Website www.gardencitycollege.edu) offers Bachelor of Hotel Management.

Eligibility: 10+2/equivalent in any discipline. Students appearing for 10+2/ equivalent exam in April/May of the year of admission can also apply.

Hostel facilities are available for boys and girls separately. Further Details can be had from: Virgonagar, PO Bangalore 560029 (Ph 080-25288831)

- HINDUSTAN ACADEMY OF ENGINEERING & APPLIED SCIENCES, Adm. Office: No. 12,1st Floor, Service Road (Next to Hotel Shanti Sagar), Domlur, Bangalore 560071; Campus: P.B. No 3776, Chinnappanahalli, Marathahalli Post, Bangalore 560037 (Ph 25238650, 25232217 Fax 080-25290618 E-mail hindacademy@satyam.net.in Website www.hindustanacademy.com) (Affiliated to Bangalore University) offers 3-year Bachelor's Degree in Hotel Management (BHM).

Eligibility: Pass in 10+2 or equivalent in any group.

- INDIAN INSTITUTE OF HOTEL MANAGEMENT & CATERING

TECHNOLOGY, ASC Centre (south) Bangalore 560007, offers Bachelor of Hotel Management.

- INSTITUTE OF HOTEL MANAGEMENT, S.J. Polytechnic Campus, Seshadri Road, Bangalore 560001 (Email: ihm@vsnl.com) offers M.Sc Hospitality Administration.

Eligibility: (i) B.Sc in Hospitality and Hotel Administration from NCHMCT and IGNOU, or (ii) 3-year Diploma in Hotel Management from NCHMCT stream +B.A/B.Sc./ B.Com or equivalent qualification or (iii) 3-year Diploma in Hotel Management form NCHMCT or State Boards of Technical Education.

Such Candidates will additionally have to take up and pass Bridge course comprising TS-1, TS-3, TS-6 and TS-7 of IGNOU'S Programme in Tourism studies within two year duration of the M.Sc programme or (iv) Candidate possessing any of the above qualifications and possessing minimum 2-years of work experience either the Institute of Hotel Management or in Hotel and allied industry. Application form can be downloaded from the Website: www.nchmct.org org or on the payment or requisite charges from National Council of Hotel Management and Catering Technology, New Delhi and should reach the Director, Institute of Hotel Management, Bangalore. Last date: November.

- K.L.E. SOCIETY'S NIJALINGAPPA COLLEGE, 2nd Block, Rajajinagar, Bangalore 560010 (Ph 080-23325020, 23320910 Fax 080-23320902 Email infodesk@klesociety.org Website www.kle-college.edu) (Affiliated to Bangalore University) offers 4 year Bachelor of Hotel Management (BHM).

Eligibility: Candidates with a minimum of 40% aggregate marks in PUC II/Class XII in Arts, commerce or science. Candidates appearing for PUC II/ Class XII exam in April/ May may also apply.

Last date: April.

- KPHRA EDUCATION TRUST COLLEGE OF HOTEL, Kaveri Continental, Kannimgham Road, Bangalore offers Hotel Management and Catering Technology Course

- KADANDALE KRISHNA RAO MEMORIAL (WOODLANDS) COLLEGE OF HOTEL MANAGEMENT, Woodlands Hotel Complex, 5, Raja Rammohan Roy Road, Bangalore 560025 (Email-kkrmcollege@excit.com) (Affiliated to Bangalore University) offers 3-year Bachelor Degree in Hotel Management.

Eligibility: 10+2 or equivalent with 50% marks in aggregate in any discipline.

Selection: Entrance exam.

Age: Maximum 22 years.

Last date: June.

- KARAVALI COLLEGE, NH170, Karavali Hotel Complex, Near Kottara Chowki, Adl Udupi, Mangalore 575013 (Telefax 0824-2455656, 245658, 2452931 Mob 098450-82990 Email info@karavalicollege.ac.in Website www.karavalicollege.ac.in) offers Bachelor of Hotel Management.

Eligibility: Pass in 10+2 in any Steam or equivalent.

- KARNATAKA VALLEY COLLEGE OR HOTEL MANAGEMENT, Pipe Line Road, Bangalore 86. Offers Hotel Management and Catering Technology Course.
- LAXMI COLLEGE OF HOTEL MANAGEMENT, (Affiliated to Mangalore University) offers following courses:
- 3-year Bachelor's Degree in Hospitality Sciences (B.H, S.)
- 3-year Advanced Diploma in hospitality management & Catering Operations.Eligibility: Pass in 10+2/P.U.C. examination in any discipline.
- One and half year Diploma in Rooms Division Mgt, Housekeeping Mgt. Food & Service, Food Production Principles. Eligibility: 10th std.

Further details can be had from Laxmi Memorial Education Trust A.J. Towers Balmatta, Mangalore 675002 (Karnataka) (Website www.ajfoundation.com).

- M.S. RAMAIAH COLLEGE OF HOTEL MANAGEMENT, M.S. Ramaiah Road, M.S.E.I.T. Post, Bangalore 560054 (Ph 080-23601829 Fax 080-23601815 Email principal@msrchm.edu Website www.msrchm.edu) (Affiliated to Bangalore University) offers 4-year Bachelor's Degree in Hotel Management.

Eligibility: Pre-Univ. or 10+2 or any other equivalent exam.recognised by Banglore university.Students appearing for exams may also apply.

Classes commence in July.

Hostel facilities are available for boys and girls separately.

- MANIPAL ACADEMY OF HIGHER EDUCATION (Deemed University), Madhav Nagar, Manipal 576109 (Ph 0825-2571978 Fax 080-2571982 Email admission@manipal.edu Website www.manipal.edu) offers 4-year Bachelor's degree in Hotel Management (BHM).

Eligibility: Passed PUC/Class XII or equivalent in any discipline in the first attempt with 50% aggregate marks. Selection: Entrance examination & group discussion held during the month of March at Bangalore, Kolkata, Mumbai and Delhi and interview held at Manipal.

Last date: March.

- MAURYA INSTITUTE OF HOTEL MANAGEMENT, No. 9, Wheeler

Road, Frazer Town, Bangalore 560005 (Affiliated to Bangalore University) offers 3-year Bachelor's degree in Hotel Management.

Eligibility: P.U.C. or 10+2 or equivalent exam. From a recognized institution.

Hostel and bus facilities are available

- MOTI MAHAL COLLEGE OF HOTEL MANAGEMENT, Hotel Moti Mahal Annexe, Falnir Road, Mangalore 575001 (Ph 0824-2441411, 2428439 Ext. 674 Fax 0824-2441011 Email motimahalbhs@rediffmail.com Website motimahalchm.org) (Affiliated to Mangalore University) offers 4/3-year Advance Diploma in Hospitality Management and 3-year Specialised Diploma in Food & Beverage Management & Operation
- NRI INSTITUTE OF HOTEL MANAGEMENT, P R Pallaya, Bangalore 72 Offers Hotel Management and Catering Technology Course.
- PGP COLLEGE OF ARTS & SCIENCE, Pillaikalathoor, Bangalore 72 Offers Hotel Management and Catering Technology course
- SAPTHAGIRI COLLEGE OF HOTEL MANAGEMENT, Airport Road, Kavoor, Mangalore 575015 (Ph 0824-2481672 Fax 0824-2481686 Email somaiyaji@saptagiri.com Website www.saptagiri.com) (Affiliated to Mangalore University) offers 4-year Bachelor's degree in Hotel Management (BHM).

Eligibility: Pre-University/Class XII (10+2) in any discipline. The candidates who are appearing in the qualifying examination in the year of admission may also apply.

Selection: Interview conducted at Bangalore/ Kolkata/ Kochi/ Lucknow/ Mangalore/ Mumbai and New Delhi during June.

- SAROSH INSTITUTE OF HOTEL ADMINISTRATION, Pentagon Complex, Kankanady Pumpwell, Mangalore 575002 (Ph 0824-2245140 Fax 0824-2246700 Email sihainst@hotmail.com Website www.sihainst.com) (NITTE Education Trust) (affiliated to Mangalore University) offers 4-year Bachelor of Hotel Management (BHM).

Eligibility: PUC/10+2 or equivalent examination in any discipline with 45% aggregate marks. Those appearing in the qualifying examination may also apply. Further details and application form can be had from the Principal of the Institute.

Also offers 2-year (4 semester) Diploma in Hospitality Management.

Eligibility: Pass in class XII (10+2) or its equivalent examination.

Hostel facility available for Boys and Girsl separately. There is provision for earn while you learn scheme. Facilities are provided for students to learn in Australia & U.K.

- SHREE DEVI COLLEGE OF HOTEL MANAGEMENT (Shree Devi Education Trust), Punjab Building Lal Bagh, Maina Towers,

Ballalbagh, Mangalore 575003 (Ph 0824-2456501, 2456511, 2457937, Mob 09844045622 Fax 0824-2451108 Website www.sdc.ac.in) (Affiliated to Mangalore University) offers 3-year Bachelor of Hospitality Sc. (B.H.S).

Eligibiltiy: Pass in 10+2 exam. in any discipline.

- SRINIVAS COLLEGE OF HOTEL MANAGEMENT, Srinivas Building Ganapathi High School Road, Mangalore 575001 (Ph 0824-2425966, 2421566, 2444891, 2440838 Fax 0824-423302 Email asrao@sancharnet.in Website www.srinivasgroup.com) (affiliated to Mangalore University) offers
  - 4-year Bachelor's degree in Hotel Management (BHM). Eligibility: PUC/Class XII (of 10+2) or its equivalent with 45% of the aggregate marks.
  - 3-year Diploma in Hotel Operation Catering & Applied Nurtition. Eligibility: Pass in XII Std./PUC.
  - 3-year Diploma in Hotel Management & Catering Technology. Eligibility: 10+2 Std./PUC.
  - 1-year Diploma in Crafts course (Bakery, Cookery, Front office, Housekeeping) Eligibility: 10th std.
  - one and half year Diploma in Crafts Courses (Bakery, Cookery, Front Office, Housekeeping) Eligibility: 10th class.
- ST. JOHN COLLEGE OF HOTEL MANAGEMENT, Vijya Nagar, IInd Stage, Bangalore offers Hotel Management and Catering Technology Course.
- T. JOHN COLLEGE, SG-4, Manipal Centre, # 47, Dickenson Road, Bangalore 560042 (Ph 080-25597817, 25092057 Fax 25285338 Email drthomas@blr.vsnl.net.in Website www.tjohncollege.com) (Affiliated to Bangalore University) offers Bachelor of Hotel Management (BHM).

Eligibility: PUC/Class XII (10+2) or Graduates.

- TAHA COLLEGE OF MANAGEMENT, Armstrong Road, Shivajinagar, Bangalore 560051 (Ph 080-5541047, 2215324, 2238748) (Affiliated to Bangalore University) offers Bachelor of Hotel Management (BHM).

Eligibility: Passed/ appeared in II PUC/10+2/Equivalent.
Hostel facilities are available.

- THE OXFORD COLLEGE OF HOTEL MANAGEMENT, (Recognised by the Govt. of Karnataka, Affiliated to Bangalore University & Approved by AICTE) C.A. Site No. 40, 1st Phase, J.P. Nagar, Bangalore 560078 (kar) (Ph 080 25737285/6/7/8, Fax 26548658, EPABX 26552500-04 (5-lines) Email info@theoxford.edu. Website www.theoxford.edu) offers 4-year Bachelor of Hotel Management

Eligibility: 10+2/ P.U.C.

Selection: Merit and Interview.

- VIDYA VIKAS INTITUTE OF HOTEL MANAGEMENT & CATERING TEHNOLOGY, 345 Mansara Road, Indira Nagar, Mysore 570010 (Ph 0821-2431818, 2449779)

  (Affiliated to Mysore University) offers Bachelor of Hotel Management.

Eligibility: XII standard/equivalent (10+2) exam.

- VIGNAN EDUACTIONAL FOUNDATION, 5/3, Hosur Road (Near Lakkasandra) Bangalore 560029 (Affiliated to Bangalore University) offers Bachelor's Degree in Hotel Management.

Eligibility: Pass in 10+2 in anydiscipline with a minimum of 45% marks in aggregate

- WELCOMGROUP GRADUATE SCHOOL OF HOTEL ADMINISTRATION. Valley View, Manipal 576119 (Ph 08252-571101 www.manipal.edu/wgsha) offers 4-year Bachelor's Degree in Hotel Management

Eligibility: PUC/Class XII in any discipline with a minimum 50% of the aggregate marks.

HOTEL MANAGEMENT COLLEGES KERALA

INSTITUTE OF HOTEL MANAGEMENT AND CATERING TECHNOLOGY, G.V. Raja Road,Kovalam PO, Thiruvananthapuram 695527 (Kerala) offers 3-year Diploma in Hotel Management and Catering Technology.

Eligibility: 10+2 with a minimum of 50% marks in aggregate with English as a compulsory subject in academics streams of Science, Arts, Commerce or in vocational stream with Hotel Management only.

Age: Not more than 22 years as on July 1st of the year of admission. (25 years for candidates belonging to SC/ST).

Seats and Reservation: Total seats 30 only.

Selection: Marks obtained in the qualifying examination, personal interview. Weightage is given for participation in sports at National level and successful completion of Craft course(s) from any one of the recognized Institute of Hotel Management/ Food Craft Institute.

The admission is subject to medical fitness. Further details can be had from the Institute of Hotel Management, C/ o director, Department of Tourism, Park View, Trivandrum.

- ORIENTAL SCHOOL OF HOTEL MANAGEMENT, Lakkidi, Vythiri, Wyanad Dist., Kerala 673576, (Ph 04936-255355, 255716-19 Fax 04936 2557520 Email koz_oshm@sancharnet.in): Admn. Office: 29/924, Almaz Building, Kotooli, Calicut 673016 (Ph 0495-2740778,

2741028, 2740217 Fax 0495-2740004 E-mail Koz_oshm@sancharnet.in Website www.orientalschool.com) (Approved by AICTE) offers the following courses:

- 3-year Bachelor in Hotel Management & Catering Technology (approved by AICTE, affiliated to Calicut University). (Also opportunity to receive International Diploma in Hospitality Management awarded by E.I of AH & LA, USA) Students enrolled for diploma programs also have the unique opportunity to acquire Bachelor of Science in Hotel & Tourism Management awarded by Hotel and Tourism Institute, Switzerland or Bachelor of Business Administration in Hospitality Management awarded by CHN University, Leeuwarden, Netherlands.Eligibility: 10+2 pass or equivalent in any discipline. Candidates appearing for final year of +2 may also apply.
- 3-year Bachelor in Hotel Management & Culinary Arts (Awaiting Govt. Approval). Eligibility: 10+2 pass or equivalent in any discipline. Candidates appearing for final year of +2 may also apply.

Selection: for both the courses: Written test and interview held during May.

Last date: April.

HOTEL MANAGEMENT COLLEGES MADHYA PRADESH

- IPS ACADEMY OF HOTEL MANAGEMENT & CATERING TECHNOLOGY, Indore (Approved by AICTE) (PVT.) offers Diploma in Hotel Management & Catering Technology. Further details regarding eligibility criteria, course content etc.can be had from the institute.
- KOHINOOR-IMI SAYAJI SCHOOL OF HOSPITALITY MANAGEMENT, Indore, H/1, Scheme No. 54, Vijay Nagar, Indore 452010 (Ph 0731-5005454 Fax 0731-5003131 Mob. 9826033664) offers 3-year Higher Diploma in Hospitality Management (HDHM). Eligibility: 10+2 or equivalent from any stream. Selection: Through an Aptitude test, group discussion and interview.

HOTEL MANAGEMENT COLLEGES ORISSA

- INDIAN INSTITUTE OF HOTEL MANAGEMENT & CATERING, 435, Old Station Square, Bhubaneshwar 751006 (Ph 0674-2570484 Fax 2570606 Email iihmctbbsr@yahoo.co.in Website www.iihmc.alot.com) (Approved by Govt. of Orissa, Dept. of Tourism & Affiliated to Utkal University of Culture) offers 3-year Diploma in Hotel Management & Catering Technology. Eligibility: +2 passed or appeared in any discipline form a recognized Board/

Council. Age: Not more than 22 years (25 years for SC/ST). Selection: Marks, merit and personal interview. Last date: June. Placement/ hostel facilities available.

- INSTITUTE OF HOTEL CATERING & STUDIES, Jagda, P.O. Jhirpani, Rourkela, Sundargarh 769042 offers 3-year course in Hotel Management. Eligibility: Passed +2/Intermediate examination.
- NATIONAL INSTITUTE OF HOTEL MANAGEMENT & CATERING, 457, Bomikhal, Bhubaneswar 751010, offers 3-year Diploma in Hotel Management & Catering. Eligibility: 10+2 or equivalent in any discipline. Selection: Merit and marks secured in 10+2. Last date: August.
- RANJITA INSTITUTE OF HOTEL MANAGEMENT & CATERING TECHNOLOGY, Bindyanagar, At/Po Mahura-752054, P.O. Janla, Bhubaneswar Orissa)
- WOMEN'S POLYTECHNIC, Berhampur (Approved by AICTE) (Govt.) offers Diploma in Hotel Management & Catering Technology

HOTEL MANAGEMENT COLLEGES RAJASTHAN

- GYAN VIHAR SCHOOL OF HOTEL MANAGEMENT, Gyan Vihar Campus, Mahal Jagatpura, Rajasthan 302025 offers BHMCT.
- MAHARISHI ARVIND INSTITUTE OF SCIENCE AND MANAGEMENT, Bharati Path, Ambabari Circle, Ambabari, Jaipur (Ph 0141-3345487) offers the following Hotel Management Courses:
  - 3-year Diploma in Hotel Management & Catering Technology. Eligibility: Senior Secondary (10+2).
  - 2-year P.G. Diploma in Hotel Management & Tourism. Eligibility: Graduate.
  - 1-year P.G. Diploma in Hotel Management & Tourism. Eligibility: Graduate.
- SEEDLING ACADEMY OF DESIGN, TECHNOLOGY AND MANAGEMENT, (Proposed Deemed University) Khorebariyan. Jagatpura, Jaipur 302025 (Raj.) (Ph 0141-2754399, 9314088086 Email seedlingacademy@hotmail.com Website www.seedlingeducation.com) (Affiliated to Rajasthan University) offers 4-year Bachelor's degree in Hotel Management and Catering Technology.
- Eligibility: 10+2. Selection is made on the basis of score obtained at 10+2.
- Hotel Management Colleges Pondicherry
- PONDICHERRY INSTITUTE OF HOSPITALITY CRAFTS, Pondicherry 695527 (Ph 0413-26555245-248 Website www.pondiuni.org) offers Hotel Management and Catering Technology.

- Hotel Management Colleges Punjab
- DESH BHAGAT INSTITUTE OF HOTEL MANAGEMENT AND CATERING TECHNOLOGY, Amloh Road, Mandi Gobindgarh (Ph 01765-501999 Email dbinstitutes@rediffmail.com Website www.dbinstitutes.com) (Approved by AICTE and affiliated to Punjab technical University, Jalandhar) offers
  - Diploma in Hotel Management,
  - Diploma in hotel Management and Catering Technology,
  - B.Sc. in Hotel Management-Tourism.
- Hotel Management Colleges Sikkim
- INSTITUTE OF HOTEL MANAGEMENT, CATERING TECHNOLOGY & APPLIED NUTRITION, P.S. Road, Gangtok, Sikkim 737101 (Ph 03592-23502, 28239 Fax 03592-22707 Email ihmgangtok@rediffmail.com) (Govt. of Sikkim, Dept. of Tourism, Affiliated to National Council for Hotel Management& Catering Technology, New Delhi) offers 1 ½ year Diploma in:
- Cookery
- Food & Beverage Service
- Front Office Operation
- PG Diploma in Accommodation Operation
- Craftsmanship Course in Food Production
- Craftsmanship Course in Food & Beverage Service.
- Eligibility: Senior Secondary 10+2 or equivalent examination in any academic or vocational stream with English as a compulsory subject. Candidates who have appeared in the qualifying examination in the academic year are also eligible to apply provisionally subject to the condition that they should produce proof of having passed the qualifying examination at at the time of admission.
- Age: Not more than 22 yrs. As on 1st July of the year of admission. (Maximum age relaxable up to 3 yrs. For SC/ST Candidates).
- Reservation: 15% seats are reserved for SC and 7.5 % for ST candidates.
- Selection: Written test at the Institute at Gangtok and interview. The final selection is on the basis of the candidate's overall performance of both the tests.
- Last date/Written Test/Interview: June.
- Hotel Management Colleges Maharashtra
- Mahatma Gandhi Vidya Mandir Institute of Hotel Management and Catering Technology, Panchavati College campus, Panchavati, Nashik.

- AISSM'S INSTITUTE OF HOTEL MANAGEMENT AND CATERING TECHNOLOGY, 55/56, shivajinagar, Pune 411005 (020-5520488 Email aissms5@vsnl.net).
- ALL INDIA SHRI SHIVAJI MEMORIAL INSTITUTE OF HOTEL MANAGEMENT & CATERING TECHNOLOGY, 55/56 Shivaji Nagar, Pune (Approved by AICTE) (Pvt.) offers Bachelor of Hotel Management & Catering Technology.
- AMRO TOURISM ACADEMY (The College of Hotel Management, Nashik), C/o The Plaza, S. No. 910/2, Mumbai-Agra Highway, Nashik 422009 (Ph 0253-397501-09 Fax 0253-394225 Email rajan@sonihotels.com) offers 3-year Diploma in Hotel Management.
- Eligibility: Passed or appeared in class 12 level Board examination or higher.
- Selection: Admission Test & Personal Interview held at Nashik, Pune, Mumbai, New Delhi, Ahmedabad, Indore, Chandigarh, Jaipur, Bhopal during June. Course Commences in August.
- ANJUMAN I-ISLAM'S A.K.HAFIZKA INSITUTE OF HOTEL MANAGEMENT AND CATERING TECHNOLOGY, 92, D.N.Road, Next to Times of India Building Mumbai 400001, Maharashtra (022-22652272/2263, 2817 Email: principal@anjumanitmct.org) offers Diploma in Hotel Management & Catering Technology.
- B.V. INSTITUTE OF HOTEL MANAGEMENT & CATERING TECHNOLOGY, Sector 8 CBD, Navi Mumbai 400614 (Approved by AICTE) (Pvt.) offers Diploma in Hotel Management & Catering Technology.
- B.V. INSTITUTE OF HOTEL MANAGEMENT & CATERING TECHNOLOGY, Pune (Approved by AICTE) (Pvt.) offers Diploma in Hotel Management & Catering Technology. Further details regarding eligibility criteria, course content etc. can be had from the institute.
- DINA INSTITUTE OF HOTEL & BUSINESS MANAGEMENT (DIHBM), No. 3, Timanna Niwas, 940/2, Model Colony, Pune 411016 (Telefax 020-25677666, 25663108 E-mail dina@pn3.vsnl.net.in, dihs@eth.net Website www.dinainstitute.com) offers 2 ½ year Diploma in International hotel Management (Affiliated to the EI-AH & LA, USA and Accredited by Middlesex University, Landon, UK).
- DR. D.Y. PATIL EDUCATIONAL ACADEMY'S DR. D.Y PATIL INSTITUTE OF HOTEL MANAGEMENT & CATERING TECHNOLOGY, Dr D.Y. Patil Vidyanagar,Sector 7,Nerul,New Mumbai 400706 offers 3-Year Diploma in Hotel Management and Catering Technology.

- Eligibility:Pass in 12th std. of Maharashtra Board of Higher secondary Education or its equivalent with minimum of 50% marks(45% marks in case of Backward Classes).
- Last date: June.
- Hostel facilities are available for Girls only.
- DR. D.Y PATIL INSTITUTE OF HOTEL MANAGEMENT & CATERING TECHNOLOGY, Opp. H.A. Factory, Sant Tukaram Nagar, Pimpri, Pune 411018 (Ph 020-27420188) offers 4-year full time Bachelor of Hotel Management & Catering Technology (BHMCT).
- Eligibility: 10+2 of Maharashtra Board of Higher Secondary Education or its equivalent with minimum 50% marks (45% marks for Backward Class candidates).
- Last date: June.
- GARDEN ANGEL INSTITUTE OF HOTEL MANAGEMENT & CATERING TECHNOLOGY, Goa (Approved by AICTE) (Pvt.) offers Diploma in Hotel Management & Catering Technology. Further details regarding eligibility criteria, course content etc. can be had from the institute.
- GLOBAL COLLEGE OF HOTEL MANAGEMENT, Prestige Complex-1, Shri Anand Rishi Marg, Telco Road Road, Above Mahesh Bank, OPP. MIDC Office, Chinchwad Station, Pune 411019 (Ph 27450400 Email globalsai@ip.eth.net) offers Diploma in Hotel Management (DHM).
- GLOBAL INSTITUTE OF HOTEL MANAGEMENT, 265, Navipeth above Janjira Hotel, Pune 411030 (Ph 020-4001863). Futher details can be had from the Institute.
- HUTATMA KARVEER CHHATRAPATI CHUTHE SHIVALI MAHARAJ INSTITUTE OF MANAGEMENT RESEARCH & RURAL DEVELOPMENT, Ahmednagar (Approved by AICTE) (Pvt.) offers Bachelor of Hotel Management & Catering Technology. Further details regarding eligibility criteria, course content etc. can be had from the institute.
- IHM-A (INSTITUTE OF HOTEL MANAGEMENT), Aurangabad Dr. Rafiq Jakaria Campus, Rauza Bagh, Aurangabad 431001 (Maha) (Ph 0240-2381127/ 2381113 Fax 0240-2381104 Email: ihm.aurangabad@tajhotels.com Website: www.ihma.ac.in, www.ihmaurangabad.ac.in) in Collaboration with Taj Hotels Resorts and Places offers
- 4-year BA (Hons.) in Hotel Management (Degree is awarded by the University of Huddersfield, U.K and is recognized by the All India

Council of Technical Education. It has also been granted equivalence to a Bachelor's Degree in Hotel Management by the Association of Indian Universities (AIU). Students are also prepared for specialization in Tourism and Event Management as part of the BA (Hons.) Hotel Management Degree in the second year).

- 4-year B.A. (Hons.) in Cullinary Arts (Degree is awarded by the University of Huddersfield, UK and is designed to prepare students for Careers in restaurants, hotels and commercial kitchens as chefs or entreprenures.
- Eligibility Criteria: Passed Std. XII (10+2) or equivalent examination in any stream with English as medium of instruction. Students appearing for their board exams in the current year are also eligible.
- Maximum Age: 22 years on the 30th August in the year of Admission. Students IHM-A can avail of the facility to take the Bachelor of Business Administration Degree from Dr. Babasaheb Ambedkar, Marathwada University.

Application form can be obtained on the payment of requisite charges from Taj Hotels accross the country or at select HDFC branches in Major Locations.

- Last date: May.
- INSTITUTE OF HOTEL MANAGEMENT AND CATERING TECHNOLOGY, (Affiliated to Bharati Vidyapeeth, Pune), Katraj-Dhankawadi, Pune-Satara Road, Pune 411043 offers Bachelor of Hotel Management and Catering Technology. Also offers Diploma in Hotel Management and Catering Technology.
- INSTITUTE OF HOTEL MANAGEMENT AND CATERING TECHNOLOGY, Sector no. 8, CBD, Belapur, Navi Mumbai 400614 (Affiliated to Bharati Vidyapeeth, Pune) offers Diploma in Hotel Management and Catering Technology
- INSTITUTE OF HOTEL MANAGEMENT & CATERING TECHNOLOGY, Atey Lay-out, Nagpur 440022 (Approved by AICTE) (Pvt.) offers Diploma in Hotel Management & Catering Technology.
- KOHINOOR-IMI, School of Hospitality Management, 51, Hill Top, Khandala, Dist. Pune 410301 (Ph 02114-72631, 77715/16 Telefax 02114-277714 Email kimi@kohinoor-group.com) offers 4-year B.A. degree in International Hotel and Tourism Management.
- Eligibility: Passed or appeared in 12th Std. exam. Details can be had from the institute.
- LAD COLLEGE OF WOMEN OF ARTS. SC. & SMT. R.P. COLLEGE

OF HOME SC. & TECH, Shankar Nagar, Nagpur 440001 (Approved by AICTE) (Govt.) offers Bachelor of hotel Management & Catering Technology. Further details regarding eligibility criteria, course content etc. can be had from the institute.

- M.G. INSTITUTE OF HOTEL MANAGEMENT & CATERING TECHNOLOGY, Panchavati, Nasik 422003 (Approved by AICTE) (Pvt.) offers Diploma in Hotel Management & Catering Technology.
- MAHARASHTRA STATE INSTITUTE OF HOTEL MANAGEMENT & CATERING TECH., 412, KM Munshi Marg, Shivajinagar, Pune 411016 (Ph 020-5676640/5677189, Fax 020-5676640 Email msismct@pn3.vsnl.net.in). Further details can be had from the Institute.
- MAHARASHTRA STATE INSTT. OF HMCT, 412/C, Bhambudra, K.M. Munshi road, Shivaji Nagar, Pune 411016 offers BHMCT.
- MAHATMA GANDHI VIDYA MANDIR'S INSTITUTE OF HMCT, Panchavati College Compus, Panchavati, Nashik 422003 offers BHMCT.
- NIBR'S COLLEGE OF HOTEL MANAGEMENT, Sant Tukaram Sankul, Pradhikaran, Nigdi, Pune 4110044 (Ph 020-27640182, 30963811, 9822254678) offers (i) 1-year Diploma in Hotel Management, (ii) 2-year Diploma in Hotel Management and Catering Technology, (iii) 18-month certificate in Travel and Tourism.
- Eligibility: SSC passed and HSC passed/appeared.
- P.A.B. INSTITUTE OF HOTEL MANAGEMENT & CATERING TECHNOLOGY, Bageshree, Dr. Deodhar Compound, Chiplum 415605 (Approved by AICTE) (Pvt.) offers Diploma in Hotel Management & Catering Technology. Further details regarding eligibility criteria, course content etc. can be had from the institute.
- RAZVI COLLEGE OF HOTEL MANAGEMENT & CATERING TECHNOLOGY, Off. Cater Road, Bandra (W) Mumbai 400050 (Approved by AICTE) (Pvt.) offers Diploma in Hotel Management & Catering Technology. Further details regarding eligibility criteria, course content etc. can be had from the institute
- SAI SHIVAJI EDUCATION TRUST'S INSTITUTE IN TRAVEL & TOURISM, Thane (Approved by AICTE) (Pvt.) offers Bachelor of Hotel Management & Catering Technology. Further details regarding eligibility criteria, course content etc. can be had from the institute.
- SHRI B.T. COLLEGE OF HOTEL MANAGEMENT, Nagpur 440001 (Approved by AICTE) (Pvt.) offers Bachelor of Hotel Management & Catering Technology. Further details regarding eligibility criteria, course content etc. can be had from the institute.

- SINHGAD INSTITUTE OF HOTEL MANAGEMENT & CATERING TECHNOLOGY (SIHMCT), Gate No. 309,310 &314, Kusgaon BK (Lonavala) Pune-Bombay Express Highway, Tal. Maval, Dist. Pune-410 401, offers BHMCT.
- SMI-HOTEL MANAGEMENT AND CATERING TECHNOLOGY, Indraprastha, Near Akashwani, Manjri Phata, Hadapsar, Pune 411028 (Ph 9520-26993588, 26998586 Email edo@vsnl.net Website www.metrustindia.org) (Affiliated to Alagappa University) offers Bachelor's degree in Hospitality and Tourism, 3-year Twin Diploma in International Hospitality Management and Catering Operations, 1 ½ year PG Diploma in

  Hospitality Management (MBA equivalent), 1-year Diploma in Hotel Management and Catering Technology.
- Eligibility: Graduates, HSC & SSC.
- Last date: June.
- TULI INSTITUTE OF HOTEL MANAGEMENT & CATERING TECHNOLOGY, (Affiliated to Directorate of Technical Education, Govt. of Maharashtra, recognized by All India Council for Technical Education, Govt. of India. Delhi), Near Koradi Octroi Post, Bokhara Road, Nagpur 440011 (Ph 0712-2669154, 2669176 Fax 2534473 Email tuli_c_hm@rediffmail.com Website: www.tuli eduservices.com) offers Diploma in Hotel Management & Catering Technology.
- Eligibility: HSSC (12th std.) in any stream with 50% marks.
- Hostel facilities are available for boys.
- YOUGANTAR EDUCATION SOCIETY'S SHRI BALASAHEB TIRPUDE COLLEGE OF HOTEL MANAGEMENT AND CATERING TECHNOLOGY, Near sadar Police Station, Civil Lines, Sadar, Nagpur 440001 (Ph 0712-522948, 526886) (Affiliated to the Nagpur University) offers 4-year Bachelor's degree in Hotel Management and Catering Technology.
- Eligibility: XII (H.S.C.) with minimum of 50% marks (45% marks for reserved category).
- ZAHMEDNAGAR JILHA MARATHA, Vidya Prasarak samaj's Institute of Hotel Management & Catering technology, Lal Taki Road, Ahmednagar 414001 Dist. Pune.
- Hotel Management Colleges Tamil Nadu
- ARSAN INSTITUTE OF HOTEL MANAGEMENT, Thillai Nagar, 1st Street, Trichy 620018 (Ph 0431-2763202/201 Email arasansistrichy@yahoo.co.in) Diploma in Hotel Management.

- ASAN MEMORIAL INSTITUTE OF HOTEL MANAGEMENT & CATERING TECHNOLOGY (approved by AICTE, New Delhi & D.T.E.., Govt. of Tamil nadu Chennai 601302, Co-educational)Tambaram-Velachery Road,Jaladampet,Chennai 601302 (Malayalam Minority Institution) (Ph 28235857, 28275858, 22461418/ 0032 Email asanedn@md3.vsnl.net.in Website asaneducation.com) offers 3-yearDiploma in Hotel Management & Catering Technology
- Eligibility: 10+2 or equivalent.
- Also offers 1-year Short Term courses in Cookery, Bakery, Front Office, Food & Beverage Service.
- Eligibility: 10th pass or equivalent.
- Hostel facilities are available for boys and girls separately. Hostel facility available. Placement assistance also available.
- Further Details can be had from Asan Memorial Educational Institutions, "Cochin House" No 1, Anderson Road, Chennai 600006.
- BHAKTAVATSALAM MEMORIAL COLLEGE FOR WOMEN, Korattur, Chennai 600080 (Affiliated to University of Madras) offers 3-year Hotel Management& Catering Technology Course.
- BHARAT COLLEGE OF SCIENCE AND MANAGEMENT, Near New Bus Stand, Trichy Road, Thanjavur 613005 (Ph 04362-227937, 228081 Fax 232567 Email bharathcollege@hotmail.com Website www.bharathcollege.com) offers B.Sc. in hotel Management and Catering Technology.
- BISHOP APPASWAMY ARTS & SCIENCE COLLEGE, Coimbatore 641018 (Ph 215798/218401) (Affiliated to Bharathiyar University) offers B.Sc Catering and Hotel Management.
- CMS COLLEGE OF SCIENCE AND COMMERCE, Chinnavedampatty, Coimbatore 641006 (Ph 0422-2866465/2867496 (Affiliated to Bharathiyar University) offers B.Sc in Catering Technology & Hotel Management.
- CSI BISHOP APPASWAMY COLLEGE OF ARTS & SCIENCE, 129 Race Course, Coimbatore 641018 (Ph 0422-2211840/221801 Website www.qubee.net/coimbatore) offers B.Sc in Catering Technology.
- CANAN SCHOOL OF CATERING & HOTEL MANAGEMENT. 1/ 75, Poonamallee High Raod, Nerkundram, Chennai 600107 (Ph 24872689, 24873189 Fax 24770104 Email canan@md4.vsnl.net.in) Website www.cananschool.org) offers 3-year Bachelor of Hotel Management.
- CHENNAI INSTITUTE OF HOTEL MANAGEMENT, Catering Technology & Applied Nutrition, CIT Campus, Tharamani, PO

Chennai 600113 (Ph 044-2352029/2351615 Fax: 044-22541615) offers Diploma in Hotel Management & Catering Technology.

- CHENNAI NATIONAL COLLEGE OF ARTS & SCIENCE, Sriperambathur Parthipattu, Kancheepuram, Chennai 602105 offers B.Sc in Catering Technology & Hotel Management.
- CHERAN ARTS & SCIENCE COLLEGE, Cheran Nagar, Thittupurai, Periyar, Kangayam 638701 (Ph 04257-243316/43711 (Affiliated to Bharathiyar University). Offers B.Sc in Catering Technology. Further details regarding admission criterion etc, may be had form the university.
- EMPEE INSTITUTE OF HOTEL MANAGEMENT & CATERING TECHNOLOGY, (Empee Educational and Charitable Trust), D-103, Aruna Complex, Anna Nagar East, Chennai 600102 (Ph 26631843, 26630179 Fax 044-26631843 Email empeeihmct@vsnl.net Website www.empeeihmct.com) offers Diploma in Hotel Management & Catering Technology & Certificate courses.
- Eligibility: SSLC/+2 or equivalent.
- FIVE STAR INSTITUTE OF HOTEL MANAGEMENT & CATERING TECHNOLOGY, The Hotel Academy No. 14, Pondy Bazar, Chennai 6000017 (Ph 044-28152391/92, Fax 044-28152394 Email mail@hotelacademyonline.com Website: www.hotelacademyonline.com) offers Bachelor's Degree in Hotel Management (BHM)
- FOOD CRAFT INSTITUTE, Thuvakudi, Tiruchirapalli 620015 (Approved by AICTE) offers 3-year Diploma in Hotel Management & Catering Technology.
- Eligibility: HSc. (10+2).
- Selection: Entrance Exam. And Interview.
- Age: Not more than 22 years as on 1st July. (Relaxable upto 3 years for SC/ST).
- HAJIRATNAM COLLEGE OF HOTEL MANAGEMENT, No. 29 A, Hotel Anand Campus, Spencer Nagar, Dindigul 624003 (Ph 0452-2427772/510 Email hrchmctdgl@rediffmail.com) offers Hotel Management & Catering Technology Course.
- HOLY CRESCENT SCHOOL OF CATERING, 50, Trunk Road, Poonamallee, Chennai 600056, offers 3-year Diploma in Hotel Management and Catering Technology.
- Eligibility: Passed or appeared in 10+2 or equivalent exam with a minimum of 45% marks.
- Selection: Written examination and personal interview.

- IDEAL INSTITUTE OF HOTEL MANAGEMENT & CATERING TECHNOLOGY-PAVENDER, Bharathidasan College of Arts & Science, 15 Brindavan Gardens, Nataraj Nagar, Puddukotai Road, Trichy 320020 (Phone 04339-250357/250358 Fax 04339-250730) offers Bachelor of Hotel Management.
- INDIAN INSTITUTE OF CATERING TECHNOLOGY & HOTEL MANAGEMENT, No. 22, Shivaji Nagar, Near Membalam, Thanjavur 613001 (Ph 04362-232567/278776 Fax 04362-232567 Email iicthm@hotmail.com) offers following courses:
- Combined 3-year course in Hotel Management & Catering Technology. Eligibility: 10 Std./S.S.I.C/ Matriculation (H.S.C./ 10+2 Std Preferable).
- 3-year B.Sc in Hotel Management and Catering
- 3-year Diploma in Hotel Management & Catering Technology
- 1-year Diploma in Hotel Management
- 1-year Diploma in Catering Management
- 1-year Craft courses in:
- Food and Beverage Production
- Food and Beverage service
- House Keeping
- Bakery & Confectionery
- Eligibility: HSC/+2.
- Hostel facilities are available.
- JAYA COLLEGE OF ARTS & SCIENCE, Thiruninravur offers B.Sc. in Hotel & Catering Management. Further details can be had from Jaya Education Institutions, Thiruninravur Near Avadi, Chennai 602024 (Ph 23690808/ 26340953 Fax 044 26390982 Website www.Jayagc.org.) offers B.SC in Catering Technology.
- JENEYS ACADEMY OF TOURISM & HOTEL MANAGEMENT, Manikandam Road, Ramjinagar, Trichy 620018 (Ph 0431-2650294/ 394 Website www.jennysacademy.com) offers 3-year Diploma in hotel Management & Catering Technology.
- KARPAGAM ARTS AND SCIENCE COLLEGE, Pollachi Main Road, Eachanari Post, Coimbatore 641021 (Ph: 0422-2873146/2874082 Fax 0422-2611043 Website www.karpagameducation.com) offers B.Sc in Hotel Management & Catering Technology.
- KODAIKANAL CHRISTIAN COLLEGE, Prakasapuram (P.O.), Paradise Hill, Kodaikanal 624104 (Ph 04542-242216 Fax 04542-242216/

242217, 241024, Email: kcc@kodaichristain.ac.in Website www.kodaichristian.ac.in) offers B.Sc. in Hotel Management and Catering Science.

- Eligibility: 10+2 or Equivalent.
- LEAGUE INSTITUTE OF CATERING AND HOTEL MAMAGEMENT, No. 105, Vinayagapuram, IInd Street (100 feet Road), Arumbakam, Chennai 600106 (Ph 044-24752570, 24755185 Email league@eth.net) offers 1-year craft course in the following fields: (i) Food production & Pastissrie (ii) Front Office Management (iii)Food & Beverage Service (iv) Accommodation Operation Management.
- Eligibility: 10th Std./12th Std./degree
- KARPAGAM ARTS AND SCIENCE COLLEGE, Pollachi Main Road, Eachanari Post, Coimbatore 641021 (Ph: 0422-2873146/2874082 Fax 0422-2611043 Website www.karpagameducation.com) offers B.Sc in Hotel Management & Catering Technology.
- KODAIKANAL CHRISTIAN COLLEGE, Prakasapuram (P.O.), Paradise Hill, Kodaikanal 624104 (Ph 04542-242216 Fax 04542-242216/ 242217, 241024, Email: kcc@kodaichristain.ac.in Website www.kodaichristian.ac.in) offers B.Sc. in Hotel Management and Catering Science.
- Eligibility: 10+2 or Equivalent.
- LEAGUE INSTITUTE OF CATERING AND HOTEL MAMAGEMENT, No. 105, Vinayagapuram, IInd Street (100 feet Road), Arumbakam, Chennai 600106 (Ph 044-24752570, 24755185 Email league@eth.net) offers 1-year craft course in the following fields: (i) Food production & Pastissrie (ii) Front Office Management (iii)Food & Beverage Service (iv) Accommodation Operation Management.
- Eligibility: 10th Std./12th Std./degree
- MGR INSTITUTE OF HOTEL MANAGEMENT & CATERING TECHNOLOGY, Lakshmi Nagar, 1st Main Road, Sri Devi Garden, Vallasaravakkam, Chennai 600087 (Ph 044-24869006-07, Fax 044-28152394) offers Bachelor's Degree in hotel Management.

Also offers following courses":

- 1-year course in Food Production. Eligibility: A pass in HSC or its Equivalent.
- 1-year course in Front Office and Book Keeping. Eligibility: A pass in HSC or its equivalent.
- 1-year Craft Certificate course in Food & Beverage Service. Eligibility: A pass in HSC or its equivalent.

- 1-year Certificate course in Bakery and Confectionery. Eligibility: a pass in HSC or its equivalent.
- 1-year Craft Certificate course in Bakery and Confectionery. Eligibility: A Pass in HSC or its equivalent.
- M.M. A. COLLEGE OF CATERING OF CATERING TECHNOLOGY & HOTEL MANAGEMENT, No. 12, Santhome High Road, Mylapore, Madras 600004, offers 3-year Diploma in Hotel Management & Catering Technology.
- Eligibility: 10+2/P.D.C./ Intermediate examination..
- MADRAS INSTITUTE OF HOTEL MANAGEMENT & CATERING TECHNOLOGY, Budhar Coloney, Porur, Cennai 600016 (Ph 044-247616162/9621 Email Chennai@mihmct.com Website mihmct.com)offers Bachelor of Hotel Management.
- MADURAI KAMARAJ UNIVERSITY, Madurai 625021 (T.N.), (Ph 0452-2782718, 2458471, Fax: 0452-2459181, Email: vcmku@rediffmail.com Website mkuniversity.org) Madurai Kamaraj University College, Madurai 625002 (Affiliated to Madurai Kamaraj University).
- MAHARAJA WOMEN'S COLLEGE, Perunthurai, Erode 638052 (Ph 04294-220129/220659) (Affiliated to Bharathiyar University). Offers B.Sc in Catering Technology & Hotel Management.
- MEASI INSTITUTE OF HOTEL MANAGEMENT & CATERING TECHNOLOGY, 87, Peters Road, Royapettah, Chennai (Ph 044-28259982/28261050) Diploma in Hotel Management & Catering Technology.
- Eligibility: 10+2/P.D.C./Intermediate examination
- MERIT SWISS ASIAN SCHOOL OFHOTEL MANAGEMENT, 22, Havelock Road, Ooty 643001 (Ph 0423-2443601-6, 2442486 Fax 0423-2440198 Email mief@mertiworldwide.com, mailmerit@yahoo.com

  Website www.meritworldwide.com) offers
  - 3-year Merit Swiss & American (AH & LA) Diploma.Eligibility: Passed 10th or its equivalent.
  - 3-year Optional Swiss Degree course in Hotel Management Eligibility: Passed 10+2 or its equivalent.
  - 1-year PG Diploma in Advanced Cullinary Arts and Management. Last date: July.
  - MBA in Hotel Management. Eligibility: Degree. Further details regarding admission criterion etc. may be had from the University. Placement assistance is also available.
- MOHAMED SATHAK COLLEGE OF ARTS AND SCIENCE,

Sholinganallur, Chennai 600096 (Ph 24501578, 24502577, 24502576 Fax 24501114 Website: www.mscas.in) (Affiliated to University of Madras) offers B.Sc. in Hotel & Catering Management & B.Sc. in Nutrition, Food Service Management and Dietetics.

- Eligibility: 10+2/P.D.C./Intermediate examination.
- ORIENTAL INSTITUTE OF CATERING TECHNOLOGY & HOTEL MANAGEMENT, 22-A, Chinnakanmal Street, Near Post & Telegraph office, Tallakulam, Madurai 625002 (Ph 0452-2522005 Fax 0452-2524898 Email oicthm@hotmail.com Website www.orientalcatering institute.com) offers 3-year course in Hotel Management & Catering Technology.
- Eligibility: H.Sc/ +2/10th Std. Matriculation or Equivalent.
- Age: Not below 22 years.
- Last date: June.

Further details can be had from the Institute:

- P.C.ARTS & SCIENCE COLLEGE, Periyampalli, Dharmapuri 636701 (Affiliated to Periyar University) offers Hotel Management course. Futher details can be had from the College.
- P.G.P. COLLEGE OF ARTS & SCIENCE, Vettambai, Namakkal Dist. 637207 (Affiliated to Periyar University) (Ph 04286-267591, 267592 Website: pgpedu.ac.in) offers 3-year B.Sc. Hotel Management & Catering Science course in association with 5-star Deluxe Hotel Le Royal Merdian, Chennai. Placement Assistance available. Further details can be had form the College.
- P R INSTITUTE OF CATERING & HOTEL MANAGEMENT, Thanjavur, Trichy 613403 (Phone 04362-266960 Email prich@prcolleges.com Website www.prcolleges.com) offers Bachelor in Hotel Management & Catering Technology.
- P.S.G.S. ARTS & SCIENCE COLLEGE, Coimbatore 641014 (Affiliated to Bharathiyar University) offers Hotel Management course. Further details can be had from the College.
- PARADISE ACADEMY OF CATERING & HOTEL MANAGEMENT, Prakasapuram, Kodaikanal 624104, offers 3-year Diploma in Catering & Hotel Management. Offers Hotel Management & Catering Technology course. (Ph 04542-242216, 242217) Further details can be had from the Institute/Academy.
- PAVENDAR BHARATHIDASAN COLLEGE OF ARTS & SCIENCE, Mathur, Pudukottai 622515 (Approved by Govt. of Tamil Nadu and affiliated to Bharathidasan University, Trichy) offers 3-year Bachelor of Hotel Management.

- PIONEER INTERNATIONAL SCHOOL OF HOTEL MANAGEMENT, 18, Chikkana Chettair Street, Tirupur 641604 (Ph 0421-2743091 Fax 0421-2741284 Email info@pioneerschool.net Website www.pioneerschool.com) offers Hotel Management course
- POONGA COLLEGE OF ARTS & SCIENCE, Babu Rajendra Prasad Road, West Mambalam, Chennai 600033 (Affiliated to University of Madras) offers B.Sc in Hotel Management course. Further details can be had from the College.
- R N SHETTY COLLEGE OF HOTEL MANAGEMENT & CATERING TECHNOLOGY, No. $ Kaviraja Marg, Ballappanavar, Nagar, Hubli 580029 offers Bachelor in Hotel Management
- R.V.S. (RATNAVEL SUBHRAMANIAM) COLLEGE OF ARTS & SCIENCE, 242, Trichy Road, Sulur, Coimbatore 641402 Ph 0422-2687421/2687603 Fax 0422-2687604 Website www.rvsfroups.com/education) offers B.Sc in Catering Science & Hotel Management.
- RATNAVEL SUBRAMANIAM COLLEGE OF ARTS & SCIENCE, Coimbatore 641402 (affiliated to Bharathiyar University) offers Hotel Management Course. Further details can be had form the College
- ROYAL INSTITUTE OF HOTEL MANAGEMENT & CATERING TECHNOLOGY, No. 30B, Melur Road, KK Nagar, Next to ICICI Bank, Madurai 625020 (Phone 0452-2584441 Website richmct@rediffmail.com) offers Bachelor in Hotel Management.
- SCS KOTHARI ACADEMY FOR WOMEN, SBK House No.17, Venkatapathi Street, Kilpauk, Chennai 600033 (Ph 044- 26460558/0820) offers Bachelor in Hotel Management & Catering Technology course.
- SNR SONS COLLEGE, SNR College Road, Coimbatore 641006 (Ph 0422 2562788) offers Hotel Management & catering Technology Course (Website: snrsonscollege.org) offers Hotel Management & Catering Technology.
- S.R.M. ARTS & SCIENCE COLLEGE, Ramapuram 603205 (Affiliated to University of Madras). Offers Hotel Management course. Further details can be had from the College
- S.R.M. INSTITUTE OF HOTEL MANAGEMENT, C/o Valliammai Society, 2 Veerasamy Street, West Mamblam, Chennai 600033 (Ph 24747231, 24742836, 24893688, 24892621 Fax 24748925 Email srmadm_2@yahoo.com Website www.srmec.org, www.srmgroup.ac.in) (Affiliated to University of Madras) offers 3-year B.Sc. in Hotel Management & Catering Technology.
- Eligibility: Passed 10+2 or equivalent examination.

- SANKARA COLLEGE OF SCIENCE & COMMERCE, West Periyaswamy Road, Saravanampatty, Coimbatore 641035 (Ph 0422-2666491/2665934 Fax 0422-2395539 Email Sankara@md5.vsnl.net.in.) B.Sc. in Catering Technology & Management.
- SAPTAGIRI COLLEGE OF ENGINEERING, Chinna Swamy Street, Dharmapuri 636701 offers Hotel Management course.
- SATHYABAMA INSTITUTE OF HOTEL MANAGEMENT AND CATERING TECHNOLOGY, Jeppiaar Education Trust, Jeppiaar Nagar, Old Mamallapuram Road, Chennai 600119, offers 3-year Diploma in Hotel Management and Catering Technology.
- Eligibility: 10+2 or equivalent.
- SHEVAROYS INSTITUTE OF CATERING TECHNOLOGY AND HOTEL MANAGEMENT, Hotel Shervaroy complex, Yercaud Hills 636601, Salem Dist (Ph 04281-222383) offers 3-year Diploma in Hotel Management and Catering Technology.
- Eligibility: 10+2 (12th Standard) or equivalent and students appearing for 10+2 can also be apply.
- Age: Not more than 22 years as on July (25 years for SC/ST).
- Selection: Entrance Test, Merit and Personal Interview.
- SIDDHARTHA COLLEGE OF CATERING AND HOTEL MANAGEMENT, Chittadavu, Manjalumoodu, (Via) Kuzhithurai, Mannargudi Taluk, Kanyakumari 629 151 Kanyakumari Dist. Tamilnadu.
- SMALL INDUSTRIES SERVICE INSTITUTE, 65/1, G.S.T. Road, Guindy, Chennai 6000 32 (GOI, Ministry of Industry) (044-22341011/12/13 Fax 044-22341014 Email sisichennai@eth.net Website www.sisi-chennai.com) offers the following Diploma/Certificate course:
- Diploma courses:
- 6-months Diploma in Catering Technology (Age: 18 years and above).
- 4-months Diploma in Office Management & House Keeping (Age: 16 years and above)
- Eligibility: 10th completed and above.
- Selection: Personal Interview.
- 2-month Certificate courses: 1. Bakery & Confectionery, 2. Cookery

Note: Govt. of India certificate is issued to the successful candidates.

Fee concession available for SC/St and Physically handicapped candidates.

- Last date: January.
- SHRI AMMAN ARTS AND SCIENCE COLLEGE, V. Thayarpalayam Post, Chithode Via, Erode 638102 (Ph 0424-2533987/ 2535172 Fax 0424-2535171 (Affiliated to Bharathiyar University) offers B. Sc in Catering Technology & Hotel Management. Further details regarding admission criterion etc. may be had from the university.
- STAR INTERNATIONAL ACADEMY OF HOTEL MANAGEMENT, Greems Road, Madras, Tamil Nadu. Offers Hotel Management Course
- STATE INSTITUTE OF HOTEL MANAGEMENT, Thuvakudi, Trichy 620015 (Phone 0431-2500660/2501383 Fax 0431-2500960 Email sihmct@sify.com Website www.sihmct.com) offers 3-year Diploma in Hotel Management & Catering Technology.
- SUBBALAKSHMI LAKSHMIPATHY COLLEGE OF SCIENCE, T.V.R. Nagar, Madurai 625022 (Affiliated to Madurai Kamaraj University) offers the following courses:
  - 3-year B.Sc. in Hotel Management & Catering Sciences. Eligibility: Pass in 10+2 of any group. B Age: Not more than 21 years as on 1st July of the year of admission
  - 1 ½ year Craft Course in Food Production (CCFP) (Inclusive of six months Industrial Training). Eligibility: Pass in 10th Std. Age: No age limit.
  - 1-year Craft Course in Bakery & Confectionery (CCBC) (Inclusive of six months Industrial Training). Eligibility: Pass in 10th Std. Age: No age limit.
  - 1-year Craft Course in House Keeping (CCHK) (Inclusive of six months Industrial Training). Eligibility: Pass in 10th Std. Age: No age limit
  - 6-month Craft Course in Food Service (CCFS). Eligibility: Pass in 10th Std. Age: No age limit.
  - Notification:March
  - Last date:March
- SWISS HOTEL MANAGEMENT SCHOOL, offers 3 internationally recognized qualification in only 3 years. (i) Swiss Higher Diploma in Hotel Management & Tourism. (ii) American AH & LA Diploma in Hotel Management. (iii) British BA Degree in Hospitality/Tourism/ Events/ Spa Management. Further Details can be had from Flat 6, Vasanth Apartments, 9, Montieth Lane, Egmore, Chennai 600008 (Ph 28554339, 28555190. Fax 28554604 E mail -mancomp@satyam.net.in.)
- SWISS MANAGEMENT ACADEMY, R.S.B. Towers, 1274 MTP Road,

Near Saibaba Temple, Coimbatore 641043 (Ph 0422-5533389, 5382563, 9894193209 Website www.agieducation.com) offers Bachelor's course in Hotel Management.

- THE HOTEL ACADEMY, No. 114, Pondy Bazaar, Bazaar, Chennai 600017 (Ph 044-28152391/92, 52124431 Fax 044-28152394 Email mail@hotelacademyonline.com Website hotelacademyonline.com) offers 3-year Diploma in Hotel Management & Catering Technology.
- Eligibility: 10th and 10+2 pass.
- THE MONARCH INTERNATIONAL COLLEGE OF HOTEL MANAGEMENT, Off. Hovelock Road, Ooty 643001 (Ph 0423-2444408/18/20, Mob 9843010087, 9811078634 Fax 0423-2442455, 2443827 Email themonarch@vsnl.com Website www.themonarchcollege.com, www.themonarchschool.com) offers the following courses:
- 3-year Bachelor of Hotel Management and
- 2-year Advanced Diploma in Hotel Management & 1-year Bachelor degree in Australia.
- Eligibility: Passed 12th or Graduation.
- V.G.P. COLLEGE OF CATERING TECHNOLOGY & HOTEL MANAGEMENT, Parijatham Salai, Uthandi, Sholinganalore PO Chennai 600119 (Ph 044-4490486, 8587298 Fax 8557298 Email vgphma@hotmail.com) (Affiliated to the American Hotel & Motel Association) offers 3-year Diploma in Hotel Management.
- Eligibility: 12th Standard pass with fluency in English.
- Age: Not more than 24 years.
- Commencement of course: July.
- V.J.P. COLLEGE OF CATERING HOTEL MANAGEMENT, 89/1, Devar Colony, 1st Cross, Thillai Nagar, Trichy 620018 (Ph 7600094) (Approved by AICTE, New Delhi) offers 3-year Diploma in Hotel Management & Catering Technology. Eligibility: Candidates who have passed +2/P.D.C./Intermediate examination.
- Also offers 1-year Craft Courses in: 1. Front Office Operations 2. House-Keeping 3. Fod Production 4. Food & Beverage Service.
- Eligibility: 10th Std. pass.
- V.L.B. JANAKI AMMAL COLLEGE OF ARTS AND SCIENCE,Kovaipudur, Coimbatore 641042 (Ph 0422-2607779/7288 Fax 0422-2607359 email vlbjcasug@vsnl.net (Affiliated to Bharathiar University) offers B.Sc. Hotel Management & Catering Technology.
- VEL'S INSTITUTE OF HOTEL MANAGEMENT, Velan Nagar, P.V.

Vaithiyalingam Road, Pallavaram, Chennai 600117 (Ph 044-22362712, 22413471, 22415862 Fax 22385593 Email velscolleged@vsnl.net Website www.velcollege.com) City Centre: 521/2, Anna Salai, Nandanam, Chennai 600035 (Ph 044-24315541/42) (Affiliated to University of Madras and American Hotel and Lodging Association) offers B.Sc. in Hotel & Catering Management.

- Eligibility: 12th Std.
- Hostel facilities are available for boys and girls separately.
- VELANKANNI MALATHY PANICKER COLLEGE OF ARTS & SCIENCE, Kovur, Chennai 603205 (Affiliated to University of Madras). Further details regarding admission criterion etc. may be had from the University
- VINAYAGAM MISSION ARTS & SCIENCE COLLEGE, Salem 636001 (Affiliated to Bharathiyar University) offers course in Hotel Management. Further details regarding admission criterion etc. may be had from the University.
- Hotel Management Colleges Uttar Pradesh
- UTTAR PRADESH STATE ENTRANCE EXAMINATION (SEEUPTU) is conducted by the U.P. Technical University, Lucknow for admission to 4-year Bachelor of Hotel Management & Catering Technology (BHMCT) at various Private Colleges/Institutions in U.P. during the month of April.
- Eligibility: Passed in the Intermediate/ (10+2) Exam or equivalent in any discipline. The Aptitude Test, Paper 7, for Hotel Management is of 300 marks consisting 75 objective type questions.
- Last date: February. Entrance Exam: April.
- ALLAHABAD AGRICULTURAL INSTITUTE, Allahabad 211007 (Ph 0532-2684281, 2684284 Fax 0532-2684394 Email registrar@aaidu.org Website www.aaidu.org) offers Bachelor of Hotel & Tourism Management (BHTM).
- Last date: May. Further details can be had from the institute.
- BABU BANARASI DAS NATIONAL INSTITUTE OF TECHNOLOGY & MANAGEMENT, Sector -1, Akhilesh Dass Nagar, Faizabad Road, Lucknow (Ph 0522-2815182-187, 2815204, 3911001102 Fax 0522-2815294 E-mail bbdnitm@msn.com Website www.bbdnitm.edu Mobile 9415019775) (Affiliated to UP Technical University) offers B.H.M.C.T.
- BUNDELKHAND UNIVERSITY, Institute of Tourism & Hotel Management, Kanpur road, Jhansi 284128 (Ph 0517-2320496, 2321214 Website www.bundelkhanduniversity.org/bundelkhand.univ.org) offers 4-year Bachelor's Degree in Hotel Management.

- Eligibility: 10+2 with 50% marks.
- Selection: Entrance test. Test: June. Last date: June.
- CH. CHARAN SINGH UNIVERSITY, Meerut 250005 (Ph 2763539, 2765353 Website www.hau.nic.in) offers admission to 1st year of 4-year Bachelor's Degree programme in Hotel Management. Further details can be had from the University.
- GRADUATE SCHOOL OF BUSINESS & ADMINISTRATION (GSBA), HS-02, Block F, AlphaGreater Noida 201306 (Ph 0120-2320521/3/4/5 Fax 0120-2320522 Email netgsba@nda.vsnl.net.in Website www.gsbaindia.com) offers 3-year Hotel Management Programme.
- Eligibility: 10+2 or equivalent examination.
- Selection: Entrance Test followed by GD and personal interview. NRIs seats are reserved.
- Last Date: November.
- IIMT HOTEL MANAGEMENT COLLEGE, IIMT Nagar,"O" Pocket, Ganga Nagar, Mawana Road, Meerut (UP) 250001) (Ph 0121-2621006, 2620284, Fax 2450925 Mobile 9897702695 E-mail iimtcollege@rediffmail.com Website www. iimtinida.com) offers BHMCT.
- INSTITUTE OF HOTEL MANAGEMENT, CATERING TECHNOLOGY & APPLIED NUTRITION, 11, R.A. Lines, Dogra Mandir Lane, The Mall, Meerut Cantt. 250001 (Ph 0121-2643590, 2656096 Mob: 09837078296 Fax 0121-2643724 Email info@ihmmeerut.com Website www.ihmmeerut.com) (Approved by AICTE, affiliated to UP Technical University, Lucknow, Affiliated to Board of Technical Education, Govt. of UP) offers the following courses:
- Bachelor's degree in Hotel Management (BHM)
- Diploma course in Hotel Management.
- Eligibility: 10+2 or equivalent. Students appearing in the final year exam may also apply.
- Selection: Admission is made in accordance with BTE and UPTU, Lucknow through written test of UPTU written test at different centers.
- Hostels facilities are available for boys and girls separately.
- Last date: April.
- INSTITUTE OF HOTEL & TOURISM MANAGEMENT, Hotel Gopal Plaza, Railway Road, Opp. Clock Tower, Ghaziabad (Ph 0120-

2835043, 2625531, 9810329941 Email ihtm@eth.net Website www.ihtm2000.com) (Affiliated to Punjab Technical University, Jalandhar) offers following courses:

- 3-year B.Sc. in Hotel & Tourism Management. Eligibility: 10+2.
- 2-year M.Sc. in Hotel & Tourism Management
- 1-year P.G. Diploma in Cookery & Catering. Eligibility: Graduate or equivalent.
- J.P. INSTITUTE OF HOTEL MANAGEMENT & CATERING TECHNOLOGY, P.O. Rajpura, Mawana Road, Meerut 250001 (U.P.) (Ph 0121-2621515, 3292113, 2623005, 2620767 Mob. 9837013785 Fax 0121-664101 Email jpihm@rediffmail.com Webiste www.jpihm.com) (Affiliated to U.P. Technical University and approved by AICTE) offers the following courses (i) 4-year Bachelor's Degree in Hotel Management and (ii) 3-year Diploma in Hotel Management.
- Eligibility: 10+2 or equivalent in any academic or vocational stream with English as compulsory subject with minimum 50% marks. Candidates appearing in 10+2 exam can also apply.
- Age: Not more than 22 yeas.
- Selection: is made on the basis of written test followed by counselling. Application from and Prospectus can be obtained from the institute's office on the payment of requisite charges.
- Hostel facilities are available for boys and girls separately.
- Last date: April
- M.J.P ROHILKHAND UNIVERSITY, Facilities of Management and Engineering, Bareilly (Ph 0581-2527263, 2528108 Website www.mjpru.ac.in) offers 4-year Bachelor's Degree in Hotel Management and Catering Technology.
- Eligibility: 10+2 or equivalent examination from any recognized Board/University with a minimum of 45% marks in aggregate (40 % for SC/ST.OBC candidates).
- Selection: Group discussion and Interview.
- Reservation of seats for SC/ST/OBC etc. as per U.P. govt. rules.
- Notification/Last date: July/August. Test: August.
- SHIVGARH METROPOLITAN INSTITUTE OF HOTEL MANAGEMENT & CATERING TECHNOLOGY, Campus: Village Kankaha, Tehsil-Mohanlal Ganj, Dist. Lucknow (Ph 0522-2821067Email smccl@indiatimes.com) offers 1-year Diploma in hotel Management & Catering Technology.
- Hotel Management Colleges Uttaranchal

- ALPINE INSTITUTE OF PARAMEDICAL SCIENCE, Nanda Ki Chowki, Prem Nagar, Dehradun (Ph 0135-2773869, 2771628 Mob. 09412054604 Fax 2774430 Website www.aipsddn.com) offers 3-year Bachelor of Hotel Management.
- Eligibility: 10+2 any steam.
- AMRAPALI INSTITUTE OF HOTEL MANAGEMENT, Civil Lines, Nainital Road, Haldwani (Affiliated to Kumaun University, Nainital & Approved by AICTE) offers 4-year degree in Hotel Management & Catering Technology.
- LAST DATE: May
- CENTRE FOR MOUNTAIN TOURISM & HOSPITALITY SUTDIES, Srinagar Garhwal 246 174 offers B.H.M.C.T.
- GOVT. INSTITUTE OF HOTEL MANAGEMENT & CATERING, Dehradun offers hotel Management curse.
- GOVT. INSTITUTE OF HOTEL MANAGEMENT CATERING, Almora offers Hotel Management course.
- GHRAPHIC ERA INSTITUTE OF TECHNOLOGY, 566/6, Bell Road, clement Town, Dehradun (Uttaranchal) (Ph: 0135-2643420, 3291534). Resource Centre: B 6/11, Safdarjung Enclave, New Delhi (011-41354520, 41354521, 41354522) (Approved by AICTE and affiliated to Uttaranchal Technical University and HNB Garhwal University) offers 4-year BHMCT.
- Eligibility: 10+2 in any stream. For Management quota seats preference is given to UTUEE rank holders.
- HIMALAYAN INSTITUTE OF TECHNOLOGY, 13, Subhash Road, Opp. Back Gate of ST. Joseph's Academy, Dehradun (Uttaranchal) (Ph 0135-2671934, 2650859, 2710809) offers 3-year full-time regular B.Sc.in Hotel Management (Degree is awarded by the HNBG Univeristy, Uttaranchal.)
- Eligibility: 10+2 passed/appeared in any stream (Arts. Commerce/ Science).
- Selection is made on the basis of written test & interview at Delhi, Chandigarh, Dehradun, Jalandhar, shimla, Dharamshala, Lucknow, Jammu, Ludhiana and Patna. Application Form and Prospectus can be obtained on payment of requisite charges.
- Last date: May.
- IIAS SCHOOL OF TOURISM AND HOTEL MANAGEMENT, D.S. Thapa (PVC) Marg, Garhi Cantt., Cantonment Road, Dehradun (Ph 0135-2751252/3200303, 9412225330, 9411341014 Email: iiasdehradun@gmail.com) offers the following courses

  - Degree/Diploma in Hospitality & Tourism Management Eligibility: Pass/10+2 in any steam
  - Diploma in Hotel Operation. Eligibility: Pass in 10+2 in any stream.
  - Diploma in Food Production & Bakery. Eligibility: Pass in 10 (SSC).

- INSTITUTE OF HOTEL MANAGEMENT AND CATERING TECHNOLOGY, Dehradun (Managed by Independent Society registered under Society Registration Act.) offers Bachelor of Hotel Management.
- Eligibility: 10+2.
- INSTITUTE OF MEDIA, MANAGEMENT AND TECHNOLOGY, 113/1-2, Rajpur Road, Dehradun 248001 (Utt.) (Ph 0135-2741979, 2747159 email info@immtddn.com Website www.immtddn.com) (Affiliated to Bhartiya Vidya Bhawan, Mumbai and H.N. Bahuguna University, Srinagar, Garhwal) offers 3-year B.Sc. in Hotel Management & Catering.
- Eligibility: 10+2 or equivalent examination. Professional bachelor's degree is awarded by HN Bahuguna University, Srinagar.
- Last date/Test: November.
- Also offers Autonomous Diploma and 6-month Industrial Training courses in: Hotel Management, Hospitality Mgmt., house Keeping, Front Office, Cookery & Production.
- Eligibility: 10th/10+2/ Graduation.
- Last date: June. Professional Bachelor's degree is awarded by HN Bahuguna University, Srinagar.
- NATIONAL INSTITUTE OF HOTEL MANAGEMENT, 29, Dilaram Bazar, Rajpur Road, Dehradun 248001 (Ph 0135-2745196, 2742183) offers 3-year Bachelor of Hotel Management. Also offers 3-year Diploma in Hospitality Management and Advanced Programme in International Hotel Business and 3-year B.Sc. Hotel Management & Tourism (the degree awarded by the university by the recognized/ approved by UGC/Ministry of HRD Govt. of India).
- Admission Procedure: Students should have passed or appeared in the class 10+2 (any stream). Students have to appear for a written test.
- RAM INSTITUTE OF HOTEL MANAGEMENT & CATERING TECHNOLOGY, Niranjanpur, Saharanpur Road Dehradun (Ph 0135-2749500, 3125950 Fax 2743959) (Approved by AICTE and affiliated to HNB Garhwal University) offers 4-year Degree in Hotel Management and Catering Technology.

- Eligibility: Passed/appearing 10+2 level of Senior Secondary or equivalent.
- Hotel Management Colleges West Bengal
- ADVANCED INFORMATION & MANAGEMENT STUDIES, A-5, Abanindra Bithi, City Centre, Durgapur 16 (Ph 0343 -2547328, 254830 Fax 2546266 Website www.aimshmi.com) offers 3-year Diploma course in Hotel Management.
- Eligibility: 10+2 appeared/passed.
- DURGAPUR EDUCATIONAL SOCIETY'S INSTITUTE OF HOTEL MANAGEMENT, Fujihore, Durgapur 713216(W.B) (Ph 0343-2502481 Email des_ihm@sancharnet.in) (Approved by AICTE & recognized by WBSCTE, Govt. of W.B.) offers 3-year Diploma in Hotel Management, Catering & Food Science.
- Eligibility: 10+2 passed/appeared. Age: Maximum 22 years. Selection Procedure: Written Examination is held for common admission test at different Centres.
- Hostel facilities are available for girls and boys separately. Placement facilities available..
- DURGAPUR INSTITUTE OF MANAGEMENT SCIENCE, Dr. Zakhir Hussain Avenue, Bidhannagar, Durgapur 712206 (West Bengal) offers Bachelor's degree course in Hotel Management
- IAM- THE HOTEL SCHOOL, AE-486, Salt Lake City, Kolkata 700064 (Ph 033-23377726, 23588232, 23596065 email: iamcal@vsnl.net Website www.iam-cal.net) (Approved by AICTE and affiliated to the Council for The Indian School Certificate Examination) offers 3-year Integrated Degree courses in Hotel and Hospitality Management. (Degree is awarded by Queen Margaret University, UK).
- The curriculum ensures that the students undergo a 22 weeks supervised workplace experience at 5-star Hotels in India, UK, Dubai, Singapore and other exciting destinations.
- Eligibility: 10+2 passed or appeared. Selection is made on the basis of Admission Test, Group Discussion and Interview held at all major cities in India and online Admission Test (CHAT) Age: Age of the candidate should be below 22 years

Application Form and Prospectus can be had from specified branches of UTI Bank or can be downloaded from the website of the institute given above. Further Details can also be had form AE 486, Salt Lake City, Kolkata 700064.

- I.I.A.S., ICMARD Building, 14/2 CIT Scheme VIII (M), Ultadanga, Kolkata 700067 (Ph 033- 30948039, 23562038/39 Website www.iiasindia.com) (Approved by AICTE.) offers the following courses:

- Degree/Diploma in Hospitality & Tourism Management. Eligibility: Passed 10+2 in any stream.
- Diploma in Hotel Operation For Course (1) Selection is made on the basis of written test and Personal Interview. For Course (2): Selection is made on the basis of Personal Interview only.

- Hostel facilities are available for girls and boys separately.
- Placement facilities available. Further details can be had from: CD-24, Sector 1, Salt Lake, Kolkata (Ph 033-23212570)
- INSTITUTE OF HOTEL & RESTAURANT MANAGEMENT, 131, Kanungo Park, Garia, Kolkata 700064 (Ph 033-24305612/24309105 M: 9830529846/ 9331007995 Fax: 033-24346885 Website: www.ihrmacal.com) offers the following Courses: (i) B.Sc in Hotel Management & Tourism.
- (ii) Diploma in Hotel management & Catering Technology
- Eligibility: Passed or appeared in 10+2 in any discipline from a recognized board. Selection is made through written test & Interview. Further details can be had from: Sonargaon Park, P.O Ramakrishnapally, Tegharia, Sonarpur, Kolkatta 700150 (Ph: 033-24346885/24347138 M: 9830529846/9331007995 Fax: 033-24346885
- INTERNATIONAL INSTITUTE OF HOTEL MANAGEMENT, International Tower, X-1, 8/3, Block EP, Sector V, Salt Lake, Kolkata 700091 (Ph 033-23577663-64, 23577550-59 Fax 23577550 Email admin@iihm.ac.in Website www.iihm.ac.in) offers
- 3-year Full-time Diploma in Hotel & Catering Management (In collaboration with the Queen Margaret Univ. College, Edinburgh, UK)
- BA Degree course in International Hospitality Mgmt. (of QMUC).
- The course include 22-week of compulsory Industrial Training in reputed 5-star Hotels in India, Singapore, Dubai or at United Kingdom. The students have the option of doing the year 3 of the course at QMUC, Edinburgh, UK or at any of the IIHM campuses in India. The Student can also choose to study the final year of the course at the Napier University or at the sprawling Mega Campus of the Thames Valley University, London.
- Eligibility: Candidate must have passed or appeared in Class 12 level Board examination from a recognized Board and should possess good communication skills.

- Age: 22 years. Selection: The Selection is made through online admission test-common Hospitality Admission Test (CHAT). Selected candidates are required to appear for Group Discussion and Interview to be held at all major cities in India.
- Application form and Prospectus can be obtained from the specified branches of UTI Bank/Reliance Web World or may also be downloaded from IIHM Website.
- NATIONAL SCHOOL OF MANAGEMENT STUDIES DURGAPUR CHAPTER, P-46, Recol Par, City Centre, Durgapur 713216 (Ph 0343-2549378 Fax 0343-2546267 email nsmsdc@inidatimes.com) offers Bachelor's Degree in Hotel Management and Diploma in Hotel Management.
- Eligibility: 10+2 (approved/passed).
- NIGHTINGALE INSTITUTE OF MANAGEMENT STUDIES, BD-97, Salt lake City, Kolkata 700064 (Ph 033-32210466/8612 Email nims_web@vsnl.net.) offers Hotel Management course.
- NIPS SCHOOL OF HOTEL MANAGEMENT, EC 98, Salt Lake, Kolkata 700064 (Ph 23586476, 23343079 Fax 23343067 Email nipscal@vsnl.com, admissions@nipsindia.com. Website www.nipsindia.com) (Approved by AICTE, An ISO9001:2000 Institution) offers
- 3-year Diploma in Hotel Management, Catering Technology and Tourism
- B.Sc in Hotel Management form Annamalai Univeristy (PCP Centre of Annamalai University)
- Bachelor in Hospitality Management from West Bengal University of Technology.
- Eligibility: Candidates must have passed or appeared in class 12 level Examination from a recognized Board. Age: Maximum 22 years Selection is made on the basis of written examination, group discussion & Personal Interview held at Kolkata, New Delhi, Mumbai, Bhopal, Lucknow, Patna, Ranchi Bhuwneshwar & Guwahati.
- NSHM ACADEMY, Arrah, Shibtala, Via-Muchipara, Durgapur 12 (Ph 0343-2533813/15 email info@nshm.com) (Affiliated to West Bengal University of Technology) offers 4-year Bachelor of Hotel Management & Catering Technology. Also offers 3-year Diploma in hotel Management & Catering Technology.
- SUBHAS BOSE INSTITUTE OF HOTEL MANAGEMENT, CF-132, Salt Lake City, Sector-1, Kolkata 700064 (Ph 23589673/23598508/

55344800 Website www.sbihm.com) offers the following Courses: (i) 3-year Diploma in Hotel Management Catering Technology & Applied (ii) 3-year B.Sc. In Hotel Management (iii) 2-year M.Sc. in Hotel Management

- Eligibility: Passed or appeared in 10+2 in any discipline
- For M.S.C: Graduation. Age: 17 to 24 years.

Index